D1715814

Atomic Testing in Mississippi

Louisiana State University Press)|(Baton Rouge

ATOMIC TESTING
IN MISSISSIPPI

PROJECT DRIBBLE AND
THE QUEST FOR NUCLEAR
WEAPONS TREATY VERIFICATION
IN THE COLD WAR ERA

DAVID ALLEN BURKE

Published by Louisiana State University Press
Copyright © 2012 by Louisiana State University Press
All rights reserved
Manufactured in the United States of America
First printing

DESIGNER: Michelle A. Neustrom
TYPEFACE: Chaparral Pro
PRINTER: McNaughton & Gunn, Inc.
BINDER: Dekker Bookbinding

LIBRARY OF CONGRESS CATALOGING-IN-PUBLICATION DATA

Burke, David Allen, 1967–
    Atomic testing in Mississippi : Project Dribble and the quest for nuclear weapons treaty
verification in the Cold War era / David Allen Burke.
        p. cm.
    Includes bibliographical references and index.
    ISBN 978-0-8071-4583-8 (cloth : alk. paper) — ISBN 978-0-8071-4584-5 (pdf) — ISBN 978-
0-8071-4585-2 (epub) — ISBN 978-0-8071-4586-9 (mobi)
        1. Nuclear arms control—Verification—History. 2. Nuclear weapons—Testing—Detec-
tion—Research—History. 3. Underground nuclear explosions—Detection—Research—History. 4. Underground nuclear explosions—Mississippi—History. 5. Lamar County, Mississippi—History—20th century. I. Title. II. Title: Project Dribble and the quest for nuclear
weapons treaty verification in the Cold War era.
    UA12.5.B87 2012
    623.4'51190287—dc23

                                                                        2012006530

CONTENTS

Illustrations follow page 86.

ACKNOWLEDGMENTS AND DEDICATION

THIS BOOK IS THE RESULT OF NEARLY A DECADE OF HARD WORK and research. I could not have done it on my own. Throughout the process I have had the benefit of collegial feedback and the support of family and friends. It has made this process bearable and even enjoyable at times.

I want to thank my parents: my father, John Burke; my mother, Diane Thompson; and my stepmother, Betsy Burke. Without them I wouldn't be who I am; they supplied unflagging support in more ways than I can mention. The same could be said for my extended family, which has always been there for me.

This work resulted from my doctoral dissertation at Auburn University. I do not have enough space to thank everyone who helped mold me into a historian. I want to especially thank William F. Trimble, my dissertation chair, whose tireless editing shaped this manuscript into a solid work. I also thank James R. Hansen, Jennifer Brooks, and David King for their most capable contributions as members of my committee. Their suggestions and direction compelled me to examine avenues in this story that I would have otherwise overlooked.

I also thank several colleagues who provided critical feedback and acted as a sounding board during the dissertation and book process: James Hoogerwerf, Gary Frost, and Daniel Winer. They are some of my best friends, and I am grateful to them for their opinions and input. Jim Hoogerwerf and I entered the doctoral program at the same time, and throughout the process his friendship was invaluable.

I am grateful for the generous assistance of the staff at the McCain Archives at the University of Southern Mississippi; the Purvis, Mississippi, Regional Library; and to all those to whom I spoke in the area. Joe Tatum, nephew of Frank Tatum, kindly took the time to speak to me on the telephone, and our conversation influenced the trajectory of my story. I would also like to mention the Mississippi Department of Archives and History, whose staff members were professional and helpful during my trips to Jackson. The Congressional and Political Research Center at the Mitchell Memorial Library at Mississippi State University holds the John C. Stennis Collection; this was a crucial source of material for my work. The genial archival staff there was a pleasure to work with. I hope to have reason to return for future research. Richard Weaver was generous in arranging my research visits to the Marnie and John Burke Memorial Library Archives and Special Collections department at Spring Hill College.

I am grateful to Dr. Robert Frosch, who was kind enough to speak to me about his time as the director of the ARPA program at the test site. I would especially like to thank Dr. Charles Bates, whose e-mail correspondence was and is enlightening. I count him among those friends whom I have not yet had the pleasure to meet personally. I express my appreciation to the Department of Energy's Nuclear Testing Archives, which was a surprisingly open and accessible information source. I would also like to thank Rand Dotson and the staff at LSU Press for their feedback and support. For a writer of history there is no greater ego boost than learning that someone is interested in your project and willing to work with you. I appreciate the time they devote to their authors and the books they produce.

I dedicate this work to several people who played an important role in my life. David George Pushcar was a close friend—a Marine, an aviation enthusiast, and fellow scale modeler. He instilled the spark of research in me and was part of the reason I returned to graduate school for an advanced degree. Dave, who died in 2004, will never be forgotten.

Walter David Lewis was my first adviser. He knew more details about more subjects than anyone I have ever known. Friendly, grandfatherly, and always open to conversation, he looked out for me while I was a graduate student. I could not have had a better friend on my side during those challenging times. He was a highly regarded author and historian and a notable professor in Auburn's history department. I have the bittersweet honor of being his last graduate student; he died in 2007 just weeks after seeing me through to ABD status. I think he would have been proud of this work.

On the morning of June 16, 2009, while I was writing chapter six, I received the most terrible telephone call of my life. My brother, Robert Calvert Wimsatt, had been murdered in New Orleans. This project helped keep me sane and let me channel my grief while coming to grips with that tragedy. Rob was the big brother I never had as a kid; in adolescence and in later life, we developed a strong bond and a lasting friendship. I, my family, and his friends miss him tremendously.

Rob, this book is for you.

Atomic Testing in Mississippi

Introduction: I Had No Idea

> At ground-zero, some wag left a Confederate flag and a sign, "The South will rise again!" This it did by about 10 cm amidst a cloud of dust. Observers five km away heard a "whoomph" and felt a shock comparable to jumping off a street curb. However, the surface ground roll did not die down as quickly as expected, and later homeowners as far away as Hattiesburg asked to be reimbursed for cracked plaster.
>
> —Bates, Gaskell, and Rice, *Geophysics in the Affairs of Man*, 204

ON SEPTEMBER 22, 1964, AFTER YEARS OF CAREFUL PLANNING AND frustration, a nuclear device was detonated below the wooded country-side in south-central Mississippi. Unleashing a force roughly one-third that of the bomb that destroyed the Japanese city of Hiroshima in 1945, the explosion produced seismic waves that traveled outward from the subterranean shot point. Nearby stations and those from around the world monitored these disturbances. A little more than two years later a second, much smaller, device test followed the first; it hardly registered at all and, unlike its predecessor, caused no damage to structures in the vicinity of the test site.

Even today, an outside researcher must approach this topic delicately. As I experienced firsthand, people in the region are friendly and open to conversation, but when the atomic tests are mentioned, the air feels a little chillier. It is something that residents have strong feelings about, and many do not want to discuss it with outsiders.

This book began as a research paper for a seminar conducted by Dr. Wayne Flynt on the history of the New South at Auburn University. It then became the subject of my doctoral dissertation, itself a product of several years of research and numerous trips to Hattiesburg and Purvis, the closest cities to the test site. During this time, I had the opportu-

nity to talk casually to a wide range of individuals. Most notably, there
was a general sense of misunderstanding about what really had happened. Some thought that the explosions in the massive subterranean
salt plug—known as a "salt dome"—were weapons tests. To be sure,
the program had a military component, but it was not intended to test
weaponry. Indeed, the reason for the two atomic tests (and later gas
explosions) was quite the opposite. They were part of a growing effort
to control the worldwide development of nuclear weapons. They helped
devise the systems used today to detect nuclear tests conducted by nations that conceal their destructive aspirations from public scrutiny.
But in researching the background of the atomic tests, I found that this
story quickly became far more complex than I had originally expected. It
changed from a study confined to nuclear-test and test-detection technology to one of geology, southern industry, and aspirations to bring
high technology to the region. The original title of this book was "Southern Devices: Geology, Industry, and Atomic Testing in Mississippi's Piney
Woods," indicating the multilayered intersection of three seemingly disparate entities that converged in the Piney Woods region in the 1960s.

There are two groups of people regarding the history of these tests:
those who have heard about them or remember reading about them,
and those who have no knowledge of them at all. Most of those familiar
with the tests either live in the area near the test site, have relatives who
live near the site, or were part of the test operations. Those unfamiliar
with the tests generally fall into one of three subgroups upon learning
of them: those who feel that the tests might somehow explain what
was wrong with Mississippi in the 1960s; those who think that it was
a good idea; and those who respond, "I had no idea." Among several of
the scientists and personnel, who came from places other than Mississippi, there was a joke concerning the tests that if there was a civil rights
riot, the plan was to nuke Hattiesburg. Obviously, most southerners do
not find this humorous. But to others around the country during the
1960s, it was a common reaction when it was announced that atomic
testing would take place in that embattled state. After all, Mississippi
had become a symbol for all the evils that the Civil War and Reconstruction had failed to fix. Its governor, Ross Barnett, was an unrepentant
segregationist who stood alongside Orval Faubus of Arkansas, George

Wallace of Alabama, and Lester Maddox of Georgia as bulwarks of anti-federal resistance to forced integration. Racial violence dominated the front pages of national newspapers, leading many to conclude that if there was going to be nuclear testing, why not set off the bombs where they might actually do some good? After all, you could not nuke many Klansmen by keeping the testing in Nevada.

What really happened at the test site? This was my initial question when I began my research about 2003 after viewing Peter Kuran's documentary *Atomic Journeys: Welcome to Ground Zero*. Kuran's earlier *Trinity and Beyond: The Atomic Bomb Movie* is a well-worn item in my videotape collection, and it led to my acquisition of *Atomic Journeys*. This production includes a few minutes devoted to the Mississippi tests, and I was immediately intrigued: why had Mississippi been chosen for atomic tests, especially when it was widely condemned for its social and economic backwardness during the 1960s? What led to these tests being conducted? What was gained from them, and why was there so little public knowledge of an atomic-test program in the heart of the Deep South? Finally, what were the results of these tests on those living around the site, and what had they gained or lost because of them?[1]

The two tests conducted at the Tatum Salt Dome site, code-named Dribble, were unique because of their location: they were the only atomic tests conducted in the continental United States east of the Mississippi River. Few books mention them; Charles Bates's *Geophysics in the Affairs of Man* describes the events at the site in a page and a half. It is one of the longest treatments of these two tests to be found in any work. The most likely reason for this is that there was no fallout from the Mississippi tests—no serious, widespread damage. Despite localized contamination, there were no incidents of civilian contamination, as noted in Howard Ball's *Justice Downwind* and numerous other works about those living near the nuclear-test site in Nevada. This in itself is remarkable, for maps clearly show that the Dribble site was within 150 miles of several cities and large towns; no other American nuclear-test site sits in such a highly populated area. Near the site is the Lamar County seat, Purvis, and within 35 miles is Hattiesburg. The state capital, Jackson, is within a 150-mile radius, as are the coastal cities of Biloxi, Gulfport, and Pascagoula; Slidell, Baton Rouge, and New Orleans, Louisiana; and

Mobile, Alabama. By comparison, the only densely populated area within 150 miles of the Nevada Test Site is Las Vegas.[2]

So why did the government choose Mississippi as a test site? The answer lies in its geology. W. David Lewis used to describe certain histories as "Michenerian"—that is, in the style of the author James Michener, who established the formation of the very ground where his stories took place, making it another character in the tale. I have chosen to do the same in telling the story of the Tatum Salt Dome test site, because special geological factors shaped the events that unfolded. This is a story of geological determinism. Had the geology been different, had there been no salt domes in Mississippi, there would have been no atomic tests there. Without the salt domes, the land in south-central Mississippi would have been different, perhaps lending itself to other agriculture and industries. Without the salt domes there would have been no oil in the region.

People initially came to the pine belt of southern Mississippi, the "Piney Woods," not for petroleum but for trees. Longleaf pines dominated the region, and their long, straight trunks made excellent lumber; the resin also had several uses. The hard life of the woodsman had its benefits not only in the potential for profit but in its isolation as well. Although slavery existed in the Piney Woods, it was nowhere near as widespread as in the central and northern parts of the state, where cotton was the primary cultivated crop. (Timber harvesting did not lend itself readily to the plantation system.) These areas remained predominantly white, and though it could never be successfully argued that blacks were treated as equals—they were certainly not—this may explain the relative lack of racial violence in the region, as suggested by the lower number of lynchings as compared to the rest of the state.

The post–Civil War period drew timber speculators and entrepreneurs to the area. Northern speculators snapped up enormous tracts of land and leased them to those who were willing to literally hew timber operations out of the Piney Woods. The Tatum family, who played a leading role in the story of the atomic tests, was drawn from Tennessee to Mississippi. The paterfamilias, William Sion Franklin Tatum, carved out a growing timber empire near the small town of Hattiesburg, served as its mayor for a time, and established his family's influence in the region.

As he moved from leasing tracts of land to buying them, he acquired a piece of land near the towns of Purvis and Baxterville that had excellent stands of trees. Unknown to him, deep below the ground lurked a massive salt dome that would later be named for him.

Timber led to oil prospecting. In the late nineteenth and early twentieth centuries, Mississippi's timber industry fluctuated. The discovery of oil at Spindletop Dome in Texas in 1901 suggested a new set of financial opportunities. Small lumber companies delinquent in paying their taxes often sold their harvested property cheaply to larger companies, or they simply allowed the land to be seized by the state. Apparently worthless due to its denuded condition, the land held potential wealth in the form of mineral rights; it was snapped up by larger timber companies. The Gulf Coast oil boom resulted in widespread prospecting, with timber companies becoming the primary beneficiaries of any finds. Thus the timber industry was directly involved in bringing the petroleum industry into the South.[3]

Spindletop was important not only as a major oil field but because it underscored the geologic relationship between salt domes and oil. The oil prospector learned to look for salt domes to find petroleum. Not all salt domes contained petroleum or gas deposits; some were "dry." Yet some dry domes were shallow enough to be mined for minerals, or for the salt itself. Other dry domes were too deep beneath the surface to bother with. They were for all intents and purposes worthless. A massive salt plug under Tatum's land was discovered, assayed, and found to be dry. The Tatum Salt Dome was considered worthless.

One of the dynamics in post–Civil War southern history is the conflict between "insiders" and "outsiders." The Tatum family represented both: they came from the Upper South—Tennessee—but technically they were still southerners. They acclimated to the Deep South readily. They leased and later bought their timber tracts from outsiders, northern timber speculators, thus returning local control and ownership to these lands and resources. Oil prospecting brought outsiders in the form of geologists, but it also spurred southern universities to educate a new generation of trained geologists to look for the valuable substances hidden below the ground in reservoir formations and salt domes. "Outsider" knowledge thus progressively became internalized, while the drilling operations themselves were familiar to anyone who had drilled a well to tap the region's abundant aquifers.[4]

Mississippi sought to attract outsiders in other industries. In 1935 Governor Hugh White's Balance Agriculture with Industry (BAWI) program lured outside manufacturers to the state by offering special deals to companies that located operations there. In this case, outsiders offered jobs to insiders—local workers. But the ultimate outsider was the federal government, which was both welcomed and resented. Military installations were greatly desired owing to their economic benefit. But following World War II, federal programs designed to introduce desegregation were seen as the imposition of outside influence unfairly brought to bear on Mississippi. Many civil rights workers who risked their lives throughout the state were outsiders, and too often they paid a high price for their perceived intrusion.

Government outsiders came to the Piney Woods in the form of the Atomic Energy Commission (AEC). In 1960, the AEC's need for a contained underground test site wherein it could analyze the physical and seismic effects of a nuclear blast in a salt dome led it to the Deep South, where numerous dry salt domes were located. Governor Barnett's segregationist rhetoric did not prevent Mississippi's selection as the state where the tests would be conducted; two salt domes there were deemed most acceptable for the proposed program.

Why was the AEC interested in Mississippi's salt domes in particular? The answer is technical and lies in the trajectory of atomic testing. Despite the radiological hazards presented by atmospheric nuclear testing, the fallout from Soviet testing was the primary source of weapons-development data; even before the first Soviet atomic test in 1949, the United States had developed aircraft capable of gathering samples of fallout. Radiochemical analysis of this fallout, which contained bomb debris, could give detailed information as to the originating device's explosive yield and construction. But the international outcry over fallout forced the nuclear superpowers to consider moving their testing activities underground. Project Dribble, which was planned for Mississippi, was part of a larger atomic test series, Vela Uniform (VU), which was in turn part of an overarching program called Project Vela. Vela addressed the detection of covert Soviet atomic tests, deemed necessary as negotiations toward the Limited Test Ban Treaty progressed in the late 1950s and early 1960s, while distrust of the Soviet Union grew. This treaty, which the United States, Great Britain, and the Soviet Union entered into in 1963, forbade nuclear testing in the atmosphere, in space, or under water. It was also a means to de-escalate further from the 1962 Cuban Missile Crisis, while eliminating the health threat from global radioactive fallout created by atmospheric testing.[5]

Vela had three primary components, each to address covert testing in different media. Vela Hotel would use orbiting satellites to spot illicit detonations at high altitude and in space. Vela Sierra sought high-altitude nuclear detonations but used ground-based stations. Vela Uniform investigated seismic means to detect and monitor underground nuclear testing, and whether such methods could be employed to fool detection systems. Conceived during the voluntary Atomic Test Moratorium of 1958 to 1961, it was initially hampered by the inability to conduct nuclear explosions and instead relied on chemical explosive programs, although these could not provide the full range of data desired by the Department of Defense and the AEC. The high-explosive test series known as Cowboy suggested that deception through detonating a test device in a cavity, a process known as decoupling, could pose problems for a seismic-detection system and begged the use of atomic-device-test verification.

The Tatum Salt Dome was judged to possess the desired qualities for an underground test site. It was large, more than two miles in diameter at its top; it was too deep underground for practical commercial mining; and it had no attendant oil or gas. As will be discussed later, the properties of salt offered the possibility to create an ideal site to test the decoupling theory with a nuclear device. These features brought the AEC to the Tatum Salt Dome and began a saga of changing test programs, technical problems, seemingly interminable delays, and ultimately alienation from local residents. Initially, there was much popular excitement over the location of the test site in Mississippi. It meant jobs, money, and the presence of the atom, America's most guarded military technology and high-tech industry. It would be located in a state where a reputation for backwardness, poverty, and violence prevailed.

Frank Tatum, owner of most of the land leased by the AEC for the test program, was a shrewd businessman, locally powerful as president of the

Tatum Lumber Company, which his father had begun. The Tatum family was politically connected and heavily involved in the local natural-gas industry, which had originated from petroleum deposits created by salt domes. Tatum pleaded his case as a victim in correspondence with Sen. John Stennis and other political representatives; his main complaint centered on the mineral rights in the salt dome.

Was this then a case of "atomic carpetbagging"? Carpetbaggers were northern opportunists who went to the South after the Civil War to exploit the devastated economy for their own benefit. The federal government brought the Dribble program to the Piney Woods; it is a matter of debate whether anyone was actually exploited by it. Local residents were inconvenienced through repeated evacuations, but they were compensated. Their property, when damaged, was generally paid for, although perhaps not as much as they would have liked. In addition, the federal government brought many other projects and benefits to the South. The space program, for instance, was hailed as a means to develop the South's technical and technological potential. Politicians "envisioned NASA as the Moses that would lead the South to a High-tech promised land." Yet much of the technical know-how in rocketry depended on true outsiders—imported German scientists. Still, regional universities benefited from the technical influx from the space program. Federal defense contracts supplied an ever-increasing economic resource, and formed part of a "carrot-and-stick" relationship between the national and state governments. The AEC program was fully committed to the Tatum Salt Dome site by 1962, the year of the riots at Ole Miss over the admission of the university's first African American student, James Meredith. In the case of Huntsville, Alabama, white residents turned against the segregationist governor George Wallace, fearing the loss of the Marshall Space Flight Center and the NASA presence if their schools did not integrate. In Mississippi, Ross Barnett eventually attempted to negotiate with Atty. Gen. Robert Kennedy a dramatic armed showdown between Barnett and federal marshals. The answer to whether this was related to pressure from AEC officials as to the suitability of Mississippi as an atomic-test location may be somewhere in Barnett's personal papers, which have yet to be located.[6]

With the introduction of numerous contracts and projects after World War II, the federal government gained cultural leverage in areas it had never previously held, especially in the move toward desegregation. This relationship was simple: once a state accepted and budgeted federal money from a contract, it was bound to obey federal mandates lest the contract be jeopardized and the funding canceled or reallocated. In this relationship, the federal government's wishes held sway. Thus it was less an issue of carpetbagging than a paternalistic relationship.[7]

The presence of the Dribble test site led residents and government leaders in the region to continue their association with the atom. After the first test, Hattiesburg strove to attract a particle accelerator as part of its attempt to attract high-tech industry to the Piney Woods. The city made it through the selection process to the final list of candidate locations, but it lost. This may be interpreted as a snub, although indications are that it was the result of political agreements made beforehand. Mississippi would see nuclear tests, but it would not have a nuclear-research facility. The outsider knowledge chose to locate itself elsewhere.

The Dribble program experienced numerous technical delays in conducting its first atomic test, Salmon, at the salt dome in 1964. The Salmon test set an unenviable record: it was the most delayed atomic test America ever conducted. The capricious nature of southeastern weather manifested itself beyond the expectations of anyone at the test site. Weather delays and engineering problems unique to the location delayed and reconfigured the program. In the end, only a change in test procedures could allow the test to proceed. Two years later, the second and last test, Sterling, was conducted at the location, followed several years later by methane/oxygen explosive tests.

Once the tests were finished, the site was closed. The AEC undertook remediation of the land before returning it to the Tatum family. But once Mississippi's salt domes had shown their value for nuclear tests, they were considered nuclear-waste repositories. That led to a curious affair concerning biological monitoring, possible environmentalist manipulation, and fears that the atomic tests at the Tatum site had left a dangerous legacy that threatened the health and well-being of those living around it.

This last point is the most important, according to people who live near the Tatum Salt Dome. People still claim that a higher-than-average number of cancers and chronic illnesses exists around the test site. I am not a medical specialist; I am a historian. I offer my interpretation of the available data. I do not question that people are ill, but I think that is probably due to other sources, which I discuss near the end of this book. There will likely be some who disagree strongly with my assessment, and I welcome the disagreement. I do not, nor could I, excuse any party for injuring the general population through intent, negligence, or dismissive carelessness. Still, the Dribble site activities cannot be conflated with the open atmospheric tests conducted at the Nevada Test Site, which resulted in civilian contamination. Except for incidents noted later, Tatum's contaminants appear to have been contained deep underground, permanently entombed.

Although the tests are interesting in themselves, several other threads run through this book: the rise of local industry and its change, as exemplified by the Tatum family; the trajectory of international events leading to the Tatum Dome; the effort to bring nuclear technology fully into the Hattiesburg area, much as NASA brought space technology to Huntsville; and the public sentiment of those living near the test site—they began their experience with the AEC with high hopes and some trepidation, which later turned to resentment and fear that their very lives were threatened by activities at the Dribble site. Finally, there is the land itself, which is currently being allowed to revert to its prehuman condition. It deserves its rest.

1. Humble Origins

ON OCTOBER 22, 1964, THE EARTH SHOOK NEAR THE SMALL TOWN of Baxterville, a hamlet of about 150 people in rural Lamar County in south-central Mississippi. The ground motion, though stronger than expected, was not a surprise. It had been caused by the long-planned and well-publicized detonation of a nuclear-test device. There was no brilliant flash, nor was there a mushroom cloud rising dramatically over the rolling countryside and thick pine groves. The only thing out of the ordinary was the ground motion, which radiated out from the deep underground detonation point and caused dust to rise over the test site, throwing one man's refrigerator contents onto his kitchen floor, cracking numerous foundations, and rattling windows as far away as Hattiesburg, some thirty miles distant.

The atomic detonation in the verdant pine belt of Mississippi was no random act designed to subdue the violent passions of a state embroiled in the civil rights movement, nor was it the result of the seemingly ubiquitous southern male's tendency to blow something up just for the hell of it. The nuclear test, codenamed Salmon, was precisely planned and metered, conducted under unique surroundings and circumstances. The Salmon device yielded 5.3 kilotons of explosive force, roughly one-third that released by the bomb dropped on Hiroshima near the end of World War II. The test, conducted at a depth of about twenty-seven hundred feet below the surrounding countryside, was fully contained and monitored. Essentially, Salmon was an unusually large outdoor laboratory experiment.

Salmon, and a subsequent atomic detonation codenamed Sterling, were the only two nuclear tests to be conducted in the continental United States east of the Mississippi River. Their purpose was to ascertain whether the United States and its allies could enter into subsequent treaties placing controls on nuclear tests following the 1963 Limited Test Ban Treaty, which forbade atmospheric, undersea, and space tests with nuclear devices. With the growing desire to limit the size of nuclear weapons, it became clear that restricting test yields would be an important step—but underground testing presented unique limitations to verifying these yields. Seismology, a field rapidly gaining importance in disarmament efforts, would play a major role in test monitoring, yet its incorporation into a system of monitoring and observation raised questions. How did one distinguish an atomic test from an earthquake? What about the explosive eruption of volcanoes or other natural phenomena? How small a test could be detected? Even more to the point, could tests be intentionally hidden in an effort to evade treaty stipulations?

These questions were the focus of the Vela Uniform program, a series of seven nuclear detonations spread across several test series. They were conducted in various locations: the Mississippi test site, known as Dribble; the Fallon, Nevada, test site; and Amchitka, Alaska, where the largest of the seven, an eighty-kiloton underground shot, was fired. Vela was also intended to answer the question of the effects of different soil and rock types on seismic signals. The varied locations allowed tests to be conducted in several different environments.

Geologically, Mississippi had a unique role in this program. The choice of test site in that state was not accidental. In fact, the location was many millions of years in the making. It was a remarkable geological structure that allowed not only for a fully enclosed and sealed shot location, but also presented an opportunity for assessing theories relating to the concealment of nuclear tests. This geological structure is a mammoth column of solid rock salt, seven to eight miles in height and well over a mile in circumference at its top, poised fifteen hundred feet below the earth's surface. Because of this enormous salt pillar, Mississippi was chosen as a site for underground nuclear tests. The pillar, or salt dome, that was host to the atomic tests was large but not uniquely so. These enormous salt domes along and under the Gulf Coast, and extending inland for several hundred miles, were extruded upward from a thick subterranean salt formation known as the Louann Salt. Formed during the Jurassic Period, it was up to ten thousand feet thick in some places. The Louann Salt, one of the basal formations within the northern Gulf

Basin, ran (or "trended") in a large arc, starting in eastern Texas, with its northwestern maximum extent located just southeast of Shreveport, Louisiana. Then it extended due east and north into Arkansas, where it joined another large salt formation located along the eastern half of the border between Louisiana and Arkansas. The Louann then spread into central Mississippi and curved southeast toward Mobile Bay in Alabama. Interestingly, there was a salt-free zone between the Louann and another salt-bearing basin to its south, known as the Coastal Basin, which ran along the coast westward from southeastern Louisiana to Galveston, Texas, where it then stretched north almost to the Oklahoma border.[1]

The origin of this bed likely lay within the formation of the Gulf of Mexico—itself created when the supercontinent of Pangaea fragmented and the North American, South American, and African tectonic plates split apart. What ultimately became the Gulf started as a shallow body of salt water. Repeated evaporative cycles allowed thick layers of salt to be deposited at its bottom. As the Gulf expanded through tectonic motion, the bulk of this deposited salt slid northward with the North American plate, as the Pacific plate pressed eastward. The Gulf basin enlarged and became a trap for alluvial and marine sedimentary deposits formed during the Cenozoic Era. These Cenozoic sediments buried the salt. Fluctuating global sea levels contributed to further salt deposits as rising and subsiding sea levels formed large shallow inland bodies of salt water that evaporated over time and allowed layers of salt to be laid down.[2]

Rock salt is a remarkable material. At the surface, at room temperature, it is a hard, crystalline substance like table salt. When it is subjected to intense pressure and heat, about 300 degrees C as it is several miles below the surface, it behaves as a plastic material. Lighter in density than the surrounding and overlying sedimentary deposits, rock salt tends to rise under pressure, following fractures in the overlying strata. As long as the salt remains connected to the hot mother bed, it will continue to force its way upward hydraulically owing to the geostatic pressure caused by the overlying burden. This process of deep subterranean plastic material rising through overlying material to shallower levels is known as diapirism; although similar to volcanism, it refers to low-temperature piercing of strata by sedimentary materials. Most diapiric structures tend to remain buried, although in some instances they reach and exceed the surface level. The Darbast salt plug in Iran, for example, rises some two thousand feet above the surrounding valley floor. Some of the salt mountains in Iran are enormous, up to one and one-half miles wide and two to three miles long; they survive owing to the dry climate.

The origin of the Louann salt deposits and associated organic sediments was sea water. As is the case today, the seas of the Jurassic were full of life. Dead sea creatures, primarily microscopic organisms, fell to the bottom of shallow waterways and were buried in prodigious quantities. The deep briny sea bottom provided an anoxic environment that partially preserved this organic material from decay. Specialized bacteria survived the alkaline and anoxic conditions and slowly digested these enormous masses of biological material. This digesting mass was then buried with the salt to great depths. With the diapiric movement of the salt came the remnants of this ancient oceanic life.

In cross section, salt diapirs generally have a mushroom shape. This is because of a process that occurred while the salt progressed towards the surface, whereby the salt column generated an important feature known as a caprock. The caprock generally isolated the salt from the overlying strata and was at the same time pressed upward against the overburden with immense force. If one imagines a salt diapir as an active fluid convective column, with most of the convective activity occurring near the center, then it is easier to understand the process of caprock formation. The caprock was formed from the detritus left over from bacterial digestive processes and the insoluble residue from rock-salt dissolution. Caprock comprises a calciferous material known as anhydrite, as well as gypsum, sulfur, and some metallic deposits. Salt continually moved from great depths to the top of the salt column, where the caprock occurs, forming an ever thickening layer.[3]

Caprock was important, as it increased the area over which the upthrusting salt diapir pressed against the upper layers of earth. Ground layers were faulted and displaced by the growth of the caprock and the upward progress of the diapir. If an aquifer was encountered that eroded the diapir and undercut the caprock, the resulting subsidence could leave visible surface effects. In short, the salt dome and its caprock affected the topography of a region, even when the caprock checked the progress of the salt diapir far below the surface. Rolling hills, valleys, and other features that occurred along the north and northwestern Gulf of Mexico were sure signs of the presence of recent or active salt diapirism.

Caprock was not the only material transported or created by salt diapirs. The bacterial digestion of organic matter in an anoxic environment produced a material called kerogen. The hydrogen content in the kerogen determined whether it became oil or gas; hydrogen-rich marine kerogen was more likely to become crude oil, whereas kerogen from nonmarine sources tended to become gas.[4] These light materials were transported from the depths to pockets or reservoirs caused by upthrust or downthrust faulting; the disjointed strata acted as traps to hold the material. Salt domes played a crucial role in the development of oil and gas, for not only did they create faults that trapped and accumulated hydrocarbons, they also provided a crucial element for petrochemical formation: heat. As the hydrocarbons rose near a salt diapir, they were exposed to a "radiator effect" from the heat that was effectively conveyed from the mother salt bed up through the diapir. This heat helped to "cook" the petroleum and preserved it from further bacterial action and decay.[5] This effect would later make salt domes highly sought after for their petroleum reserves.

Periodically, a salt dome encountered an aquifer where the water quickly eroded the salt, and occasionally the brine reached the surface as a spring. Salt is critically important to animal life; salt springs attracted game animals and other wildlife. The salt and the ready availability of game in turn attracted humans to these hidden salt formations. Native Americans were more than aware of these precious brine springs in the inner Gulf Coast region, and they certainly knew that the salt attracted animal life.[6] Europeans were slower to realize the bounty of these resources as they first explored inland from the Gulf. One biographer of Spanish explorer Hernando de Soto noted that as he and his party trekked northwestward from the Alabama settlement of Mauvilia toward Tuscaloosa, and then westward to the Mississippi River, they suffered not only from starvation but also from salt deficiency.[7] De Soto's path roughly paralleled the outer reaches of the Louann bed; had his path been fifty to a hundred miles south, at least one of his shortages might have been avoided.

What De Soto missed was a region that has been known for some time as the Piney Woods or the Pine Belt of Mississippi. Underlain by numerous salt domes and the massive Louann Salt, this region today features a thin layer of soil that covers layer upon layer of clay and sand. The area is generally wet, with occasional swamps and streams. The major watercourse in the region, the Pearl River, flows south to the Gulf of Mexico, and numerous smaller tributaries feed it as it gently runs to where Louisiana and Mississippi meet. The watershed, which covers southern Mississippi, is heavily forested today; when the first humans reached the area it was densely covered with tall, longleaf yellow pine trees and various deciduous species. The proximity to the Gulf provided ample annual rainfall despite the occasional drought, and a mild climate, with the occasional hurricane cutting through the area. Winters were mild, with the occasional freeze, but the cold never lasted for an extended period of time. Summers were hot and humid, but as any visitor to the region knows, in the forest or the surrounding swamps, the shade of the trees and mysterious breezes that seem to come from nowhere cool the air and make it far more comfortable than areas closer to the coast. When the daytime heat and humidity reached a certain level, thunderstorms appeared from the thickened air, providing torrential downpours and vivid lightning. These storms also pushed inland with the sea breeze; a daily exhalation of cooler humid air from the Gulf moved northward over the rapidly heating land, resulting in towering storms that regularly soaked the area.

As it happened, De Soto did not travel through southeastern Mississippi, although some of his escaped swine and cattle apparently did. He entered the state west of present-day Cuba, Alabama,. His swine and cattle added to the game Native Americans hunted in the fire-cleared forests. These peoples lived throughout the Piney Woods, subsisting on the land and its wildlife until the incursion of European settlers and traders in the eighteenth century. The newcomers, primarily French and Spanish colonists venturing from the larger settlements of Mobile and New Orleans, came northward to investigate the possibilities of rich lands farther inland. Southern *coureurs de bois* engaged the local Native Americans in the lucrative deerskin trade. The subsequent rapid decline of the native deer population and the extinction of the eastern bison were coupled with ever-growing numbers of herd animals—primarily horses and cattle. Settlers also brought hogs into the area. These animals, allowed to roam the woodlands, were periodically rounded up and sold.[8]

The southernmost extent of the Piney Woods experienced the quick succession of national ownership that began in 1763, when the British claimed the territory from the French and named it West Florida; it was ceded to the Spanish at the end of the American Revolution, and it was finally made part of the United States after the War of 1812. In 1820, the Treaty of Doak's Stand surrendered five and a half million acres of Choctaw land in central and western Mississippi and effectively cleared the inland regions for settlement by Americans. Although the bottomlands, watered and nourished by alluvial deposits from the Pearl River, were highly valued for their fertility and ability to support cotton, many people remained within the Piney Woods, preferring a pastoral lifestyle within this pocket of frontier. This decision was likely due to the lower prevalence of diseases endemic to the lower regions, such as yellow fever and malaria. It was common in other locations, primarily on the Atlantic coast in places like Georgia and the Carolinas, for the wealthy to migrate annually to higher elevations to avoid these poorly understood maladies.[9]

In 1862, *Harper's New Monthly Magazine* published an account by J. F. H. Claiborne of his recent travels through the Pearl River watershed and into the Piney Woods. His priceless account of the land and its people provides one of the few descriptive passages from the period:

> Along the Gulf of Mexico, or what the United States Coast Survey styles the Mississippi Sound, extending across the State of Mississippi, with a depth in the interior of about one hundred miles, there lies a region of country usually denominated the Pine Woods. The soil is sandy and thin. . . . But it sustains a magnificent pine forest, capable of supplying for centuries to come the navies of the world. The people are of primitive habits, and are chiefly lumbermen or herdsmen. Exempt from swamps and inundation, from the vegetable decomposition incidental to large agricultural districts, fanned by the sea-breeze and perfumed by the balsamic exhalations of the pine, it is one of the healthiest regions in the world. . . . I have never seen so happy a people. Not afflicted with sickness or harassed by litigation; not demoralized by vice or tormented with the California fever; living in a state of equality, where none are rich and none in want; where

the soil is too thin to accumulate wealth, and yet sufficiently productive to reward industry; manufacturing all that they wear; producing all they consume; and preserving, with primitive simplicity of manners, the domestic virtues of their sires. [10]

Claiborne described a Jeffersonian yeomanry, with minimal production of the crops commonly associated with large-scale slave agriculture —sugar cane, indigo, and cotton. That which was locally grown was intended for domestic use. The thin, sandy soil was much different from the rich alluvium that attracted cotton planters to the Mississippi and Yazoo River Delta region in the northwestern part of the state, as it differed from the Pearl River floodplain to its south. The terrain and the soil were inappropriate for the cultivation of plantation crops, as Claiborne asserted: "the country through which I am journeying is sparsely settled, and is only adapted to grazing."[11] Slavery, though not unknown, was not as prolific as it was in other areas of the state. The soil did allow the growth of trees, and slaves did work in the timber industry, cutting trees and toiling in sawmills, though not in the numbers one might imagine. Slaves never outnumbered whites in the Piney Woods counties; beginning with the rise of timber operations in the 1840s, they were primarily used to fell, transport, and raft logs downstream to waiting lumber mills. They were also used in the mills for heavy manual tasks, although at least one operation employed its slaves in the manufacture of circular saws and steam engines. The 1850 and 1860 censuses show that the majority of slaves in the region worked in "forest industries" and brickmaking. The forest industry employed two hundred slaves in 1850 and four hundred in 1860.[12]

Along with slaves, lower-class and landless whites provided manual labor. Despite the limited number of historical works directly addressing the Piney Woods region, there are studies of poor whites in northeastern Mississippi, including examples of illicit interactions and trade between slaves and poor whites. The "triracial trade" among poor whites, Native Americans, and African slaves existed for a substantial period of time; the removal of Native Americans from the state did little to stop this interaction. After all, the black and white races commonly worked together performing manual labor and other unsavory tasks. Their existence in close proximity would have interesting consequences later, once the nation's question of the future of slavery was solved.[13]

The Piney Woods saw no great battles during the Civil War, nor did large armies march across the region despoiling all in their path. It was practically forgotten, save for a number of volunteers who enlisted in the Confederate cause. One wonders why these people of the lingering frontier went to fight. There are two plausible answers: first, the white yeomen and poor whites feared economic competition from, and loss of social status to, emancipated slaves. Second, the Yankees represented modernity and outside change—something the locals were happy to do without. People of the Piney Woods preferred to determine their own course of existence and to be left alone.[14]

Black and white workers commonly toiled together in the Piney Woods during and after Reconstruction. The southern timber industry grew quickly with the demand for lumber to repair the ravages of the war and to supply the requirements of the great migration westward to the Pacific Coast. Members of Rankin Hickman's log-rafting crews "ate out of the same pots, slept in close proximity around campfires, and joined in singing at night. Wages were equal and skin color was of little significance to those of both races, who were often neighbors and longtime friends."[15] Later though, in the 1880s, trouble arose as union organizers came to the Gulf Coast and its lumber mills to gather support among the work force. The Noble Knights of Labor (KoL) arrived to address working conditions in and around the sawmills along the Gulf Coast and won concessions on issues such as twelve-hour workdays and higher wages. But by 1900 the KoL's presence disappeared along the Mississippi Gulf Coast as its role was progressively overtaken by the American Federation of Labor. Unionization attempts occasionally occurred, and owners of forest industries within the Piney Woods became adept at using race as a means to discourage them. Although the timber industry remained highly lucrative until the early twentieth century, competition for menial labor in the forest forced the races apart.[16]

In 1954, William Faulkner wrote an article for *Holiday* magazine, describing the changes Mississippi had experienced over time. Regarding the woodlands, he lamented that some time after the 1870s railroad lines had opened the interior of the state, allowing sinister forces entry:

[A]ll the way from Chicago and the Northern cities where the cash, the money was. . . . the rich Northerners could come down in comfort and open the land indeed: setting up with their Yankee dollars the vast lumbering plants and mills in the southern pine section, the little towns which had been hamlets without change or alteration for fifty years, booming and soaring into cities overnight above the stump-pocked barrens which should remain until in simple economic desperation people taught themselves to farm pine trees as in other sections they had already learned to farm corn and cotton.[17]

Faulkner's outrage at this influx of "Yankee dollars" and wasteful forestry practices overlooks an important point: before the intrusion of northern business into the Piney Woods, there was a surge of Upper South capital and entrepreneurs who had established themselves by the 1890s. One wealthy and ambitious Tennessean, Willie Sion Franklin Tatum, made his lasting mark on the Piney Woods. Born three years before the outbreak of the Civil War, Tatum entered the family mercantile business in Bethel Springs, Tennessee, when he was fifteen years old. By 1881, despite his long mustache and beard (which his fiancée barely tolerated, but which would later become his trademark), he had married and was operating the family business as W. S. F. Tatum & Company. He developed a reputation for business acumen. He was reputed to be quite intelligent, and he combined this quality with his determination to expand his business in Bethel. He was also known for his strict adherence to his Baptist faith, which later influenced his business practices. In 1882, his brother-in-law entered into partnership with him, and the business became known as Tatum-O'Neal & Company. Among the machinery and goods he dealt in was pine lumber.[18]

The lure of moving southward to investigate the potential of the longleaf-pine timber industry drove him to travel to the Piney Woods of Mississippi in 1891. Finding a promising tract in Forrest County, located near Hattiesburg and bordering a railway line, he bought the timber rights for 2,200 acres from a Michigan timber speculator for $27,125.00. A $9,000.00 down payment, with a contract to satisfy the balance in two years, was agreed upon, and in 1893, the Tatum family permanently moved to the small town of Hattiesburg, which had but seven hundred residents. Before the Tatums had reached their new home, temporary milling equipment had been shipped to begin production of lumber for the new 160-acre lumber mill, to be sited at a location known as Bon Homme, three miles south of Hattiesburg. Bon Homme was also on the New Orleans and Northeastern Railroad, which was critical for transporting the lumber.[19]

Tatum's dreams were tied to the dense forests of longleaf yellow pine. He had no idea that his enterprise had been built over the Louann salt bed, nor had he any notion that the rolling terrain was a direct consequence of salt domes welling up from deep below his feet. His primary concern was reaching the stands of old-growth forest, cutting trees, and moving them to the mill at Bon Homme. He became notable for his energy and creativity in putting together one of the longest-lived timber operations in the Piney Woods. He could never have envisioned the role that his land would play in local, state, national, and international politics, becoming a critical laboratory of Cold War science. Beneath his feet, the product of millions of years of geologic change awaited discovery.

2. Timber, Oil, and Atoms

INDUSTRY DROVE THE PINEY WOODS UNLIKE ANY OTHER REGION of Mississippi. Aided by the area's geology, several industries developed in succession. Timber, transportation, and later oil and gas all developed in the region, unlike in the rest of the state. Despite overwhelming segregationist sentiments elsewhere, the Piney Woods appears to have suffered less from violence, which may attest to the nature of those who lived there and the industries that developed. The land yielded its trees; to the spirited, industrious, and wise, their gift was prolonged through extended harvesting. Later, hidden salt domes offered the promise of vast wealth.

Following Reconstruction, the timber industry in the Piney Woods began to increase in size. Northern investors and timber speculators bought large woodland tracts and looked forward to leasing logging rights to lumber companies. The family of William Sion Franklin Tatum took advantage of this opportunity to carve a business empire out of the pine forests of Lamar and Forrest Counties; at the same time, they played an increasing role in the development of the town (later city) of Hattiesburg.

When the Tatum family stepped off the train from Bethel Springs, Tennessee, at 4:00 a.m. on January 5, 1893, they knew there were trying times ahead. Hattiesburg was a small town, nurtured by the railroads and the growing demand for timber. Family and friends were far away. W. S. F. (Willie) Tatum, his wife Rebecca, and their son West, who was less than a year old, moved into a hotel on Main Street. Willie Tatum's planning had been thorough; before he and his family had moved to Hattiesburg, the machinery for his Bon Homme mill site had been delivered. Less than a week after the Tatums felt the predawn chill of that winter morning, workers finished the first house for mill employees. They would construct twenty-two in all. They also built more commodious homes for Tatum's brother-in-law and partner M. Frank O'Neal, and for George W. Haynes, who supervised the operation of the temporary mills that manufactured the lumber to build the permanent mill. Willie Tatum's younger brother Barca L. Tatum also moved down from Tennessee to work at the new mill. By the middle of January, they had begun grading the roadbed for a spur line from the New Orleans and Northeastern Railroad; two weeks later, they broke ground for the mill itself. By the end of June, the first load of rough timber had left the mill.[1]

Tatum designed his milling operation from the outset to utilize steam-powered machinery as much as possible. Several things made the Tatum-O'Neal lumber operation noteworthy. He understood the importance of railroads in getting his lumber to market and to access and extract timber from his forests. In its early form, logging in the Piney Woods relied on human and animal power to cut and move logs to streams and rivers to be rafted to mills. Loggers left substantial stands of trees uncut because they were too difficult to remove or were not close enough to waterways. Rails could be laid in areas where no water was available, allowing men and animals, or steam winches and cranes, to lift the freshly cut trees onto logging cars for the trip to the mill. Tatum was determined to avoid the waste of careless logging; he was not the forest-industry operator of whom Faulkner wrote in 1954. Tatum knew that his wealth lay in trees and that only a fool would rip them out faster than they could be replenished.[2]

Bon Homme's name was changed to Bonhomie later in 1893. Perhaps the new name was a gesture of regard from transient workers who were happy for the employment Tatum provided; a biographical sketch of Tatum implies that the site was already so titled. Despite an economic downturn, Tatum's operation seems to have been designed to attend to the well-being of his workers. Indicative of the nineteenth-century-industrialist's paternalistic sentiments, a one-room schoolhouse was built near the mill in 1896 to save the children of mill workers from having to travel to Hattiesburg. The mill also featured a company store, stables, and a post office.[3]

Two years after Tatum's railroad operation began in November 1894, the mill boasted two miles of standard-gauge rail. At about the same time, he constructed a planing mill on the site for the production of fin-

ished boards rather than rough-cut timbers; a large drying kiln was begun in January 1895. In mid-February, the first three logging cars arrived
at the mill; by the end of September 1896, the mill's first locomotive—a
small four-wheel saddle-tank engine later named Old Puss—made its
debut and began a working career that lasted more than a generation.
Despite the young entrepreneur's eagerness to branch out into finished
lumber, and his use of powered machinery to manufacture it, financially
the operation ran on a shoestring. The company quickly cleared out the
land allotted in its initial contract with J. Henry Moores, a renowned
timber speculator from Lansing, Michigan, from whom the timber rights
were leased. As Tatum paid off percentages of the lease, additional tracts
opened to logging, presumably to make sure the lumber would not be
cleared from the entire 2,200 acres before he paid Moores. The problem
was an issue of increasing debt and diminishing timber. Despite a deal
with Moores that kept the operation going, Tatum and O'Neal continued
to struggle. In 1895, they borrowed five thousand dollars from a Hattiesburg merchant to secure turpentine rights on some of Moores's land.
Not until the end of 1897 did both the economy and the timber industry
begin to improve; Tatum then pursued as many extra logging rights as
he could secure on the lands around his mill complex.[4]

Tired of Mississippi and yearning to move to Arkansas, O'Neal left
the firm in 1898. Unable to buy out his interest in cash, Tatum promised
him payment in three installments of $5,500.00, as well as the store
in Bethel Springs. Renamed the Tatum Lumber Company, the business
surged on the upturn of the market, allowing Tatum a luxury he had
not had before: he began buying timberland rather than logging rights.
He bought 3,848 acres of land between 1897 and 1901, adding to his
logging rights on the Moores tract. Interestingly, he bought the last
block of 1,924 acres from a lumber speculator named McPherson who,
like Moores, lived in Michigan. The increased size of Tatum's holdings,
together with a flourishing economy, meant that timber shortages were
a worry of the past. Tatum Lumber products enjoyed wide distribution
throughout the major cities of the Midwest during the 1890s. At the turn
of the twentieth century, the Tatum family, which had added twin boys
Will Sion and Frank Murry in 1895, was doing well.[5]

Following a three-month family trip to Europe in 1904, during which
time the mill was closed, Tatum acquired more timber rights and land

and continued to expand the amount of standard-gauge track running through the Piney Woods. Named for the former senator, secretary of the interior, and Supreme Court justice Lucius Quintus Cincinnatus Lamar, Lamar County was created that same year by the annexation of portions of Marion and Pearl River Counties.[6] The shutdown of the Bonhomie mill, and the thorough logging of the mature trees on the lands that Tatum had acquired before the turn of the century, meant he held too little available timber to restart his operation economically. He had determined earlier that simple clear-cutting was a waste of future profitable lumber; he decided that only trees with a trunk diameter of more than ten inches should be taken. In 1901, he conducted an experiment, ordering his crews to take only the younger pine trees whose trunks were less than ten inches in diameter, and to harvest enough to supply the mill with enough volume for thirty days. His experiment left him with a five-hundred-dollar deficit after that period. Larger trees contained more wood, and were therefore more cost-effective. He also forbade the use of log skidders on his property because of their destructive effect on the thin layer of topsoil on the timber tracts. With a partner, he bought nearly fourteen thousand acres of timberland, known as the Okahola tract, for three hundred twenty-five thousand dollars. He also bought another tract that allowed him access to two important rail lines, the Gulf and Ship Island Railroad and the Mobile, Jackson, and Kansas City Railroad.[7]

By 1907, Tatum was again fully immersed in the timber business, with a new mill incorporating a doubled boiler capacity in the power plant for new machinery; he extended his logging railroads into his new holdings. In 1910, he even incorporated one of his lines—the Bonhomie and Southwestern—to connect the towns of Columbia and Hattiesburg. A religious man, Tatum was adamant that the line would never operate passenger or freight service on Sundays, except in extreme situations or for "the promotion of the Christian religion." This railroad never became a full reality; it stopped several miles short of Columbia. The Okahola tract and other timberlands bought and worked by the Tatum company kept the mill in continuous operation until 1914, when work again ceased. Tatum's explanation was that the timber close to his rail lines had already been taken and that it would not be feasible to continue laying track toward the remaining stands of trees. The real reason was likely due to a discovery that had been made in Texas just before he and his family moved to the Piney Woods. Willie Tatum's attention to his property had been confined to above-ground searches for profitable stands of trees. Now he wanted to look beneath the surface, where he hoped to find oil.[8]

The Texas oil industry had begun in the early 1890s with accidental discoveries, such as the one in Corsicana, where drillers seeking life-sustaining water instead found oil in their wells. Petroleum was a resource that was quickly put to new uses, from lighting and lubrication to powering newly developed internal-combustion engines. Beaumont mechanic Patillo Higgins felt certain that a hill on a flat plain near the town would yield oil and gas because of the presence of flammable gases he had encountered nearby on Sunday-school outings. Higgins called it The Big Hill, while residents knew it as Spindletop. Ridiculed for his beliefs by townspeople and geologists, he eventually received the attention and aid of Capt. Anthony Lucas. Lucas and Higgins began exploratory drilling in 1899. Their first efforts failed, driving the ridiculed prospectors to the wildcatter firm of Guffey and Galey in Pittsburgh.

Returning to Beaumont and Spindletop with Higgins, John Galey marked the spot of the next exploratory well near the gas springs that had first stirred Higgins's excitement. In late 1900, drilling began and slowly proceeded until it struck a modest amount of oil at 880 feet. Resuming drilling on January 1, 1901, the crews working the rig were shocked nine days later when the first Texas gusher blasted sand, drill pipe, oil, and rocks hundreds of feet into the air. Higgins, the self-educated prospector, had been right after all, and he had been fortunate to ally himself with Lucas, a successful mineral prospector who understood the properties of salt domes. Spindletop was a classic example of a Gulf Coast salt diapir that had reached close enough to the surface that its caprock had thrust a domelike hill into the midst of flat terrain.[9]

Even more important than the initial discovery of petroleum at Spindletop was the birth of understanding the connection between salt diapirs and petroleum. Not all salt domes yielded oil, but oil was commonly found in the presence of salt. Therefore it made sense to locate exploratory wells at salt domes. Even with the oil glut produced by the Texas fields, there was sufficient financial incentive to continue prospecting along the Texas Gulf Coast and farther east toward Louisiana. In September 1901, Louisiana's oil industry began with a well drilled near a salt dome near the town of Jennings. In the spring of 1903, the first exploratory oil well in Mississippi was drilled at Enterprise. As the timber industry began to decline in the early part of the twentieth century, the increasing importance of gas and oil to industry and transportation helped make up for up the financial shortfall. Natural gas proved abundant in the region, although oil initially was elusive. Mississippi's first well to produce significant quantities of oil was completed in 1932; it was rapidly followed by others. The discovery of the first salt dome in Mississippi four years later, by Sun Oil Company geologists, was a major disappointment; it yielded little if any gas and no oil.[10]

Mississippi's salt domes initially proved difficult to locate through seismic technologies. The sedimentary layers over the domes had the effect of damping seismic waves emanating from emplaced explosive charges as they radiated toward and reflected back from deep subterranean structures. There was little else to do but select likely sites, drill exploratory wells, and retrieve drill-core samples to locate salt domes and likely sedimentary beds where petroleum was concentrated.[11]

Willie Tatum's pursuit of this new industry was expensive and time-consuming. Yet, with characteristic determination, not only did he allow outside oil-exploration teams on his land, but he actively urged his sons to enter the oil-and-gas business. In 1922, locals petitioned Tatum to assume the unfilled term of Hattiesburg mayor Thomas E. Batson, who had died on July 1.[12] With this mandate, he assumed the office and remained mayor for sixteen years, leaving office in 1938. While serving, he entered the natural-gas-supply business by fronting nearly half a million dollars to a natural-gas enterprise, the Public Service Corporation of Hattiesburg, which sought to undercut the existing manufactured-gas system that already supplied Hattiesburg. Through questionable dealings, including resolutions designed to thwart outside companies from providing the city with natural gas, Tatum secured a favorable deal for the Public Service Corporation. In doing so, he faced a lawsuit charging him with conflict of interest—the judge later exonerated him, handing down an opinion that Tatum had performed a public service, because natural gas cost much less than manufactured gas. Following this decision in 1932, Tatum bought the assets of his manufactured-gas rival, who quickly went bankrupt. Tatum also bought the property of the Public Service Corporation, which had also fallen on hard times and declared bankruptcy in 1934. Shortly thereafter, he and his sons Frank and Will founded the Willmut Gas and Oil Company, which took its name from the first four letters of Tatum's first name and the last three letters of his last name in reverse. In addition to his tree business, Tatum was now in the oil business.[13]

Northern and central Mississippi remained primarily agricultural regions while industry developed in southern portions of the state and along its Gulf Coast. Depression-era economic hardships led Mississippi's government in 1935 to propose and endorse a larger program of industrialization, known as the Balance Agriculture with Industry, or BAWI, program. Credited to Democratic governor Hugh L. White, a former lumberman, the program subsidized twelve new industrial operations to shore up civic economies solely dependent on agriculture and timber production. Hattiesburg attracted a plant for the manufacture of silk hosiery, which switched to shirt manufacturing during World War II. BAWI's other major effect in the region was the development of Ingalls Shipbuilding in Pascagoula, which is still one of the largest shipbuilders in the country. Smarter lumbering practices forestalled the collapse of the timber industry, and it remained a staple of the local economy for some time after the war. BAWI was important to the state at the time, but it also presaged later developments. Mississippi was eager to attract as much industry as it could, as later programs ably demonstrated. BAWI was primarily intended for less industrialized areas than the Piney Woods, where timber and oil production provided most of the economic impetus. But BAWI was not the last program to bring industry to Mississippi. That would come later, from an unlikely source.[14]

Despite the Great Depression, Willmut not only expanded its natural-gas operation—with the purchase of the Public Service Corporation's assets, it also assumed a respectable gas-pipeline network—but also began prospecting on Tatum's extensive landholdings. Exploratory wells proved disappointing, although Willmut did make a name for itself in Illinois oil production. In 1940, following a visit by a Sun Oil Company magnetometer crew, the Tatums drilled an exploratory well at a promising location on one of their Lamar County properties. The magnetic signal registered the signature of a substantial accumulation of iron, which usually indicated a salt-dome caprock. Hoping for a geyser of oil, or at least the whoosh of a lucrative natural-gas well, the survey team struck nothing more remarkable than calcite and salt. Willmut leased the sulfur rights to the Freeport Sulphur Company and drilled deeper, to no avail. There was neither oil nor natural gas at the dome, now named for the Tatum family.[15]

But there was plenty of salt. Although the depth of the base of the dome had yet to be determined, it was obvious that it was an enormous mushroom-shaped diapir that measured more than a mile in diameter and whose uppermost surface was still more than twelve hundred feet below ground level. The Tatum Dome was born of the Louann Salt, yet it had no petroleum. This was an irony that would not be lost on Willie Tatum or his sons. In 1943, with World War II dominating the nation's fuel demands, Gulf Oil began prospecting just a few miles west of Tatum's dry hole, near the small town of Baxterville, also located in Lamar County not far from Lumberton. This field eventually became the state's most productive, yielding nearly a quarter-billion barrels of oil and more than four hundred billion cubic feet of gas between 1944 and 1990. Through a twist of geological fate, the vast wealth of the Baxterville field had eluded Tatum. Yet it further focused the oil industry's attention on the Piney Woods and fueled dreams of more hidden-oil bonanzas in the region.[16]

Geological and petroleum journals reported the Tatum Dome's existence, and it was noted on surveyors' maps. The salt was deep, but it was technically recoverable should the world salt market's prices rise high enough to make it economically practicable. Much the same could be said for the sulfur that could be recovered from the gypsum-rich caprock, but sinking a shaft to mine the deep deposits at the Tatum Dome made no economic sense, because much more easily accessed sources of sulfur existed. So the salt and sulfur on Tatum's land remained buried and nearly forgotten. The land over the Tatum Dome was left to trees and wildlife, with occasional visits from hunters and picnickers.

In 1948, Willie Tatum died. The Hattiesburg he left behind was a thriving city of nearly thirty thousand residents, transformed from the small town of little more than a thousand persons it had been when he first arrived. His sons, steeped in the timber and oil industries, inherited a business empire that encompassed much of the Piney Woods. Other industries had come to the region, due in part to the wartime needs of the shipyards of Biloxi, Pascagoula, and Mobile to the south and southeast, and also to the availability of road and rail transportation. Nearly seven hundred persons labored in the chemical industry—a new category not listed in previous census reports. Wood-based industries for Forrest County and Hattiesburg had decreased from nearly a thousand in the 1930 census to about a third of that twenty years later. Census and occupational data show that industry continued to thrive in the Piney Woods despite the employment decline.[17]

The postwar and Cold War periods fostered an increased atmosphere of social and racial tension in the South. African Americans who had fought for their country and earned the respect of white comrades in combat returned to an atmosphere of racial inequality. Throughout Mississippi, racist groups, including the Ku Klux Klan, continued terror campaigns designed to intimidate blacks and preserve the segregated status quo and white supremacy. But the most violent terrorist act, lynching, was much more prevalent in the state as a whole than in Forrest and Lamar Counties. According to Julius E. Thompson's *Lynchings in Mississippi,* 617 people were lynched in the state between 1890 and 2002, and of those, fourteen were murdered in Forrest County and only one was lynched in Lamar County. Bearing in mind that Lamar County has been and is primarily rural, with Purvis as its county seat, while Forrest County has the much larger Hattiesburg as its seat, this violence likely came as a result of cosmopolitan contact rather than the agrarian subordination and subjugation seen in Mississippi's Delta region. Part of the explanation for the relatively low numbers also comes from the racial makeup of the two counties: census data shows both to be primarily white. This agrees with the industrial history of the region, which was neither plantation-based nor primarily slave-driven.

But even in the most urban settings in the Piney Woods segregation was observed; it was as much a social mechanism of oppression there as anywhere else, but it does not seem to have been as violently enforced. Newspapers such as the *Hattiesburg American* and the *Laurel Leader-Post* regularly ran news stories with headlines referring to "Negroes"; obituaries were segregated into "white" and "colored"; and there was an occasional advertisement for a Klan rally, but most of the violence was happening elsewhere. Whether this was because de facto segregation was not as threatened, or self-deception resulted from the lower level of violence, remains in question.[18]

Mississippi remained a bastion of hard-line segregation. Pres. Harry Truman's 1947 decision to desegregate the military and incorporate changes that threatened the South's "peculiar institution" caused a reaction in Mississippi, where "segregation forever" became the battle cry among many whites. In the 1954 election, firebrand segregationist Ross Barnett won his first term as Mississippi's governor and represented a blatant rejection of federal power in his state. Ironically, he did not object to the intrusion of the atom into Mississippi; he likely saw nuclear technology as a ready injection of cash into his state's economy.

Politically, Mississippi was in flux. The year Willie Tatum died was the same year many southern Democratic politicians, enraged by Truman's integrationist policies, left the party in protest to field their own presidential candidate. Mississippi's delegation to the Democratic convention of 1947 was the first to defect, leading to the formation of the States' Rights Party, commonly referred to as the Dixiecrats. In many ways this was a return to the Redemptionist mindset following Reconstruction. The titular head of the party that had originally been the political base of the segregationist system now threatened the social institutions that had become commonplace and accepted in the South. Refusing this new course, many southern Democrats instead defected to the Dixiecrats and began the trajectory that eventually made the South a conservative Republican stronghold, returning to the mantra of states' rights superseding national policies. At the 1948 Democratic National Convention, Mississippi's delegates led the secession from the Democrats to the States' Rights Party that later nominated South Carolina's Strom Thurmond for president and their own Fielding Wright for vice president.[19]

People of the Piney Woods certainly noticed this schism. Although the years between 1948 and 1960 saw significant growth in terms of economy and population, they were marred by racist rhetoric and an avowed determination to keep Mississippi segregated. According to historian Erle Johnston, every major election during this period became a referendum on segregation, and in every one the Piney Woods had a candidate running for governor or lieutenant governor. In the 1955 gubernatorial election, Hattiesburg native Paul B. Johnson Jr. lost to attorney general James P. Coleman. Johnson ran during the next election as Ross Barnett's lieutenant governor; he finally reached the governor's office in 1964. Before assuming the governorship, Johnson was an ardent segregationist, suggesting in the 1955 election that police power be used to maintain the state's "separate but equal" policies.[20]

Ross Barnett was an icon of segregationist political power. From his election in 1955 to his departure from politics in 1964, he was always at the forefront of racial division, actively denying James Meredith access to the University of Mississippi in 1962, and defending white attacks on African American bathers on Biloxi beaches. A model "states' rights" governor, Barnett never wasted an opportunity to stand against the rising national tide of desegregation. The election of John F. Kennedy signaled an important change in federal pressure on the South to alter its social institutions. Barnett and the Kennedy administration seemed to be natural antagonists, yet they found ways to work together. Barnett was a bigot, but he, Johnson, and John Stennis, who entered the United States Senate in 1947, were canny politicians who differed greatly from stereotypical "good old boys." Historians Stephan Shaffer and Dale Krane note that Barnett went so far as to discuss with Robert Kennedy a plan to enact a "symbolic surrender" at Ole Miss during the James Meredith crisis. Forced to accede to federal marshals at gunpoint, Barnett would save face in the eyes of his constituency while allowing Meredith into the university. The plan was cancelled for fear that state authorities might in turn draw their weapons on the federal marshals. Although publicly defying the Kennedy brothers on the Meredith issue, and capitulating in the face of force, Barnett also recognized the change in national attitudes. When Cleve McDowell, another African American, applied to enter Ole Miss's law school several months after the riots caused by Meredith's admission, Barnett overrode actions to close the school. He understood that there was little point in fighting the same battle to the detriment of the school, its students, and the state.[21]

Nevertheless, Barnett was publicly committed to preserving the outdated social mores of Mississippi in the face of federal plans to dismember and destroy them. He was not committed to excluding all federal influence, and correspondence indicates that he and his successor, Johnson, were more than amenable to allowing atomic testing in the state. This was due to two things: prestige and money. Atomic testing represented America's highest technology. As Mississippi was a poor, primarily agricultural state, atomic testing could prove to be the ultimate pinnacle in the BAWI concept: the state had the potential to serve as a base for the highest of high-tech defense industries. This was not as unreasonable as it may seem: neighboring Alabama was primarily agricultural before industry began to flow into the state as a result of outside economic sources after the Civil War. Over time, Alabama had become home to high-tech defense industries with the development of military aviation at Maxwell Air Force base and the concentration of German rocket and missile engineers at Redstone Arsenal and the Marshall Space Flight Center in Huntsville. Mississippi was already home to a large army base at Camp Shelby, in the heart of the Piney Woods. An influx of scientists and technicians could rehabilitate Mississippi's image. But unlike the original BAWI program, Mississippi did not have to sell itself to outside industry and lure it with publicly funded facilities. All it had to do was open the door to the federal government.

The most likely reason Barnett was happy to welcome the Atomic Energy Commission's interest in his state was that with scientists, technicians, well-drillers, and various support personnel would also come a substantial amount of money. Initially, Hattiesburg's economy anticipated that an atomic program would bring in fifteen to twenty million dollars, in stark contrast to Faulkner's dour impression of outside intrusion into the Piney Woods. The city would certainly be the center of operations, as it was the largest transportation node in the area. The structures necessary for the control, monitoring, and safety systems of the test site would have to be built, as well as infrastructure improvements to local runways and roads—all paid for by the federal government. The influx of federal capital was certainly welcome, and along with the millions to be spent on the test site and operations, there was a windfall when the salt dome was prepared for testing. As a byproduct of excavation and test-site preparation deep into the salt dome, at least two million tons of salt, worth at least sixteen million dollars, would be brought to the surface.[22]

There may be another explanation for Barnett's puzzling attitude toward bringing the AEC into Mississippi. The atomic program was a carrot, and social change was a stick. A common tactic of the federal government in relations with recalcitrant southern states was to fund highway and airport development. Local leaders received increased economic benefits and prestige in exchange for accepting growing federal influence. By the 1960s, the Department of Defense had assumed a primary role in this process, and the South emerged as a crucial region for military-related activities. Mississippi was no exception; between 1951 and 1976, the state saw a twenty-five-fold increase in the number of defense contracts awarded. To a great extent, these were rewards for acceptable behavior, with the unspoken threat that what the federal government granted, it could take away. To Barnett's credit, he was adept at playing both sides: negotiating with the Kennedy administration while continuing to appeal to his white power base.[23]

There were potentially serious drawbacks to any decision to carry out atomic testing in south Mississippi. Unlike the Nevada Test Site (NTS), there was no large reservation at the candidate salt domes to act as a buffer zone in case of an accidental radiation release. In case of containment failure, radioactive materials would be in immediate contact with pasture and farmland. The Tatum site was located roughly 130 miles north of New Orleans, 100 miles northwest of Mobile, 80 miles north of Biloxi and Gulfport, 25 miles southwest of Hattiesburg, and 12 miles west of Purvis, Mississippi. Winds had to be light, steady, and coming from the right direction, ideally from the south to the north. Such winds are common in the Piney Woods; they occur almost daily. As the ground heats up more quickly than the Gulf of Mexico to the south, air over the ground rises more quickly than air over water. Air tends to flow inland from the Gulf—commonly called a "sea breeze." Along the Gulf Coast, much of the thunderstorm activity occurs when a strong moisture-laden sea breeze pushes inland as a "sea breeze front" and is then lifted by the warming effect of the ground. Preferably, there would be a high-pressure region over the eastern Gulf or western Atlantic, pushing the air steadily over the Piney Woods from the south. This pattern is aided during the summer months as the Bermuda High pressure system builds up.

This weather pattern also explains why the Gulf Coast is subject to some of the most destructive weather on earth. The Bermuda High acts as an enormous steering system for tropical storms and hurricanes. It tends to push storms in the Atlantic south toward Florida and the Keys, and once past the most powerful influence of the high, these weather patterns commonly travel north toward the coastlines of Florida, Alabama, Mississippi, Louisiana, and Texas. The threat of tropical storms and hurricanes had to be taken seriously, even a hundred miles inland from the coast. Tropical weather aside, every day brought the potential for heavy thunderstorms to suddenly materialize and pelt the site with torrential rains, lightning, heavy winds, hail, and the occasional tornado.

The Piney Woods had been blessed with ample stands of tall longleaf-pine trees and was later found to have substantial deposits of natural gas and oil. The salt that had proved twenty years earlier to be uneconomical to extract would be recovered as a byproduct of a far more lucrative operation than a salt-and-sulfur mine. On October 29, 1960, Frank Tatum wrote to senators John Stennis and James Eastland and congressman James Colmer regarding an unusual visit by representatives of the United States Army Corps of Engineers concerning the Tatum Dome: "These gentlemen came first with the request that they be allowed to go on the land. When we inquired why, they said they simply wanted to look it over. After a number of conferences with them, it finally developed that the Atomic Energy Commission wanted to do some atomic shooting in the salt dome."[24]

3. The Road to Dribble

THE INTEREST IN THE TATUM SALT DOME WAS DUE TO MUCH MORE than a whim of the AEC. By 1960, despite a voluntary moratorium, it was clear that the days of atmospheric nuclear testing were numbered. This promised to lessen the global danger from increasing levels of highly toxic fallout from nuclear and thermonuclear blasts. But it also presented new technical challenges to those who monitored and assessed the results of atomic tests as part of intelligence gathering. The result was a scientific program intended to address these shortcomings once the voluntary moratorium ended. This program, Vela, was divided into three subprograms to investigate new means to detect, monitor, and assess foreign nuclear tests. The underground tests to be conducted near Hattiesburg were part of a program known as Vela Uniform (VU). The other two components, Vela Hotel and Vela Sierra, were created to detect space-based and high-altitude tests respectively.

To understand the importance of Vela, one must look at the trajectory of atomic testing and atomic-test monitoring in context. Atomic-test monitoring can be traced back to the first test of the atomic bomb. But monitoring is only part of the challenge; it is far easier to do when the planned time of a test is known. When it is not, the test must first be detected before it can be analyzed. From the first atomic test to the announcement of the Vela program, the United States tried and assessed several methods of remote nuclear-test detection and monitoring. The increased political momentum toward removing nuclear tests from the atmosphere caused some proven detection methods to be largely abandoned. They were replaced by others previously considered insignificant or impractical.

The first nuclear test took place in the predawn hours of July 12, 1945, in an isolated area of desert near Alamogordo, New Mexico. Along with scientific monitoring of the test, there was an unofficial experiment designed to rapidly evaluate the explosion and decide the winner of a betting pool set up among the new weapon's designers. Yield values ranging from zero (a dud) to forty-five kilotons (45kt),[1] were established before the test, code-named Trinity. Each bet cost a dollar. Edward Teller bought the highest yield, while Los Alamos laboratory director J. Robert Oppenheimer bet on a modest eight-hundred-ton yield. Knowing it would take some time to evaluate the test thoroughly using radiochemical methods after the experiment (should it succeed), Italian physicist Enrico Fermi devised a simpler means to settle the wager before the official yield was determined by examining the fission debris left by the test. He held scraps of paper in his hand and waited for the countdown to reach zero.[2]

One of the fathers of the atomic bomb, Fermi was responsible for crucial discoveries regarding nuclear-materials development and atomic reactors. He presided over the first sustained atomic chain reaction in December 1942, when he oversaw the withdrawal of the control rods of the first atomic pile in the squash court beneath Stagg Field at the University of Chicago, proving the feasibility of atomic fission as an energy source. But the experiment he now planned to conduct was far less technical; it was an elegantly simple measurement of the bomb's energy output, made by measuring the barometric fluctuation of the shock wave as it raced past. Ten thousand yards from Ground Zero, he waited for the test to commence. At 5:30 a.m., the area was instantly bathed in a blinding light as bright as the midday sun. Fermi later recalled that he opened his hand and dropped the scraps of paper as the blast wave visibly approached him some forty seconds after the detonation: "I tried to estimate its strength by dropping from about six feet small pieces of paper before, during and after the passage of the blast wave. Since, at the time, there was no wind, I could observe very distinctly and actually measure the displacement of the pieces of paper that were in the process of falling while the blast was passing. The shift was about 2½ meters, which, at the time, I estimated to correspond to the blast that would be produced by ten thousand tons of T.N.T." Fermi's measurement was significantly conservative, being some 8kt under the actual yield, determined by later radiochemical analyses as 18.6kt. The government had placed barometric and seismic monitoring equipment at distances of up to several miles from Ground Zero, but these were considered less important for monitoring the test; they were intended to limit claims of damage to personal property that might be caused by the blast. Through a simple method, Fermi demonstrated the possibility of analyzing weapon performance from a distance; this would become crucially important as events proceeded.[3]

The radiochemical analysis of the Trinity bomb was easy to accomplish —samples from the test were collected with relative ease. Yet it was a different story when it came to the atomic bomb dropped over Hiroshima. Physicist and engineer Luis Alvarez flew on the Hiroshima mission aboard one of the accompanying B-29s.[4] Alvarez supervised the dropping of several parachute-borne detector packages that gave initial data on the detonation of the Little Boy weapon over Hiroshima. Incorporating microphones to measure the positive and negative dynamic pressures created by the blast, the detectors were developed by Alvarez, in response to a request from Oppenheimer, as a means to assess the performance of the untested gun-type uranium bomb. The detectors then sent telemetry data back to the raiding aircraft via a radio transmitter and delivered information on the barometric effects of the blast. Alvarez had, in effect, found a way to replicate Fermi's experiment; in the process, he invented the ancestor to the dropsondes that meteorologists use today to study hurricanes.[5]

Scientists realized their most important means of test detection and monitoring when they turned their attention to a more natural source of massive explosions. Knowing that volcanically produced particulate matter rose high into the atmosphere, they suspected that the dust created by a nuclear bomb would also have quantifiable properties and could be collected as it floated in the stratosphere. Aircraft equipped with special filtration devices to sample the atmosphere flew carefully planned routes that intersected high-altitude air currents. After the airplane landed, the filters were analyzed with a special Geiger counter. Radioactive debris was readily detected in the upper atmosphere using this method. This became the primary means the United States used to detect weapons development by unfriendly nations.[6]

The next atomic devices to be detonated were targeted on a fleet of warships moored in the Bikini Atoll in the Pacific. The fleet consisted of vessels from the United States, Germany, and Japan and represented nearly every class of naval combat vessel, from the aircraft carrier USS *Saratoga* to battleships, cruisers, and submarines. The test program, code-named Crossroads, was initially to comprise three tests: the air-dropped shot, Able; a shallow underwater shot, Baker; and a deep underwater shot, Charlie. There was little concern that the bombs would not work. Shortly after the Able test bomb missed the target fleet, unmanned drone aircraft flew through the rising cloud; manned B-29s carrying special oil-coated paper filters were later flown through the debris cloud as it drifted away from the target area. Once the bombers landed, their filters were removed and placed against specially sensitized film. The radioactive particles produced spots on the film; after it was developed analysts used it as a map to find individual specks of debris in the filters. The specks were then collected and analyzed to indicate how well the weapons had performed.[7]

Acoustic monitoring and seismic detection were also investigated as ways to detect atomic blasts. These methods had been used during the Trinity test and again at Bikini in 1946. Pressure sensors and seismographs measured the intensity of shock waves on several islands of the lagoon, and sensors were also placed on the floor of the lagoon. With regard to the acoustic method, the possibilities of blast detection through the atmosphere came from a cataclysmic and unlikely source: the volcanic explosion of the island of Krakatoa in 1883, when sound waves from the blast reverberated back and forth numerous times across the globe. Although greater by orders of magnitude than the largest atomic bombs of the 1940s (it was estimated to have released some 500mt of energy), the blast's seven detectable atmospheric reverberations suggested that an anticipated Soviet test might be detected by ultra-sensitive barometers, or microbarographs. Barometers might be placed at likely antipodean locations on the opposite side of the globe from where a test was likely to take place. Scientists supposed that as the circular blast wave radiated away from the burst point, the shock front would expand radially outward, finally meeting on the opposite side of the globe. There it would be detected and analyzed for magnitude of yield. It was an intriguing idea; the only problem was that it did not work. Later experiments by the United States showed that numerous atmospheric factors occluded symmetrical shock-wave propagation. The signal that reached the antipode would be too disrupted to be useful.[8]

The same uncertainties that made barometric and acoustic monitoring not feasible made seismic monitoring inconceivable. Seismic equipment was unable to detect an atomic burst at any useful range; during the Yoke test, seismographs were unable to record the blast from five hundred miles away. Tectonic phenomena could be seismically detected at great distances, but there were numerous uncertainties as to how one might distinguish between an earthquake or a volcanic eruption and an atomic bomb. Seismology promised to be a more useful means of detecting atomic tests. But uncertainties as to what signal strength an above-ground detonation might create were an important concern in the creation of a practical test-detection method. As it turned out, seismic methods of detecting atmospheric explosions would not work unless the test device was detonated close to the ground. It appeared for the time being that the aerial sampling method—"sniffing" the atmosphere for fallout—was still the most fruitful means of detecting a Soviet test.[9]

Atmospheric sampling methods were simple and used equipment that had already been developed. They allowed timely detection of tests owing to the fairly consistent wind patterns at higher altitudes. Soviet tests could be detected within a day or two, depending on whether the sampling mission flown by an individual aircraft penetrated the debris cloud. Samples found in the oil-soaked paper filters were chemically analyzed, allowing precise information to be collected regarding bomb design and yield. Those samples indicating a high ratio of plutonium to other radionuclides might indicate an inefficient design, wherein the reaction was not sufficient to consume the fission material. A sample with a high level of plutonium's fission product americium could indicate that plutonium fission had taken place efficiently. The inclusion of other materials in fission debris could suggest design elements as well. A large amount of beryllium could suggest an added neutron reflector within the device, for example. The process of chemically analyzing bomb debris for data regarding bomb performance worked, but it depended solely on the collection of debris.

Operation Sandstone consisted of three "shots" in April and May

1948 on the Pacific island of Enewetak.[10] Sandstone was a test program designed to evaluate new designs for deployable weapons. It was also an excellent opportunity to test detection methods. Two of the three important avenues of detection, acoustic and seismic detection, yielded poor data. But the air-sampling method again worked well, and a serendipitous discovery further endorsed its use. Technicians at Tracerlab, a private Boston company that contracted with the government to analyze materials from atomic tests, analyzed the collection apparatus and noticed an interesting phenomenon—tiny spherules had mixed into the sampled dust and debris from the test. The lab quickly determined that these spherules were metallic residue from the device itself. They not only stood out from the sandy debris from Enewetak, they also strongly suggested that even in a high-altitude test, bomb residue could be collected.[11]

One obvious drawback to relying on aerial sampling was that it could not provide information as to the exact moment of the detonation. Acoustic and seismic methods had failed to provide conclusive data during Sandstone. The largest device tested during Sandstone was a 49kt weapons-development shot code-named Yoke, with well over twice the yield of the bomb dropped at Nagasaki. All of the tests were conducted on steel towers two hundred feet above the ground. Although the proximity to the ground was enough to generate large volumes of fallout, Yoke, the largest device the United States had tested to date, did not generate sufficient seismic energy to travel from Enewetak in the Pacific to seismic recording stations in the United States; indeed it was undetectable five hundred miles from the shot point. Instantaneous notification of Soviet tests, although they were not immediately expected, required technology and methods not yet developed.[12]

Aerial sampling proved its importance on September 3, 1949. Noting elevated radioactivity during a routine sampling mission, the pilot, technicians, and crew of an air force Boeing WB-29 brought home incontrovertible evidence that the nuclear monopoly of the United States had been lost. Despite the general attitude that the Soviet Union would not be able to test a bomb of its own for some time, the aerial-sampling missions had been flown in the knowledge that one would eventually occur. Known in the West as Joe-1, the device was comparable to the first

American test device. This was not surprising considering the aid provided to the Soviets by Klaus Fuchs and other agents operating within the nuclear-weapons-development complex. Still on a semiwartime footing under Joseph Stalin and his sadistic lieutenant Lavrenti Beria, the Soviet atomic program rapidly escalated; the air force and Tracerlab would be busy until the Limited Test Ban Treaty of 1963.[13]

Joe-1 was an eye-opener. Once it had been confirmed that the Soviets possessed a bomb, it was crucial to maintain vigilance over the development of their arsenal. It also became necessary to distinguish between American and Soviet material that had been collected. Espionage and high-altitude aerial sampling could ensure that most of the collected matter was of Soviet origin. Without advance notification, radiochemical analysis determined the date a particular test was conducted. Remarkably, the American aerial-monitoring system was even able to assess the amount of plutonium being produced in the Soviet Union by sampling the atmosphere in several locations and analyzing the percentage of krypton-85, which is a byproduct of plutonium production and separation.[14]

From the detection of Joe-1 until the detonation of America's largest test, the Castle Bravo hydrogen bomb in 1954 with a yield of 15mt, the United States tested thirty-seven devices; the Soviet Union tested seven. Despite the technological triumph and military significance of achieving increasingly larger fission, and later, fusion reactions, the residue from atmospheric testing quickly overshadowed any benefits these tests presented. The American nuclear arsenal promised to safeguard the country from communist aggression. But Americans themselves were not immune to the effects of fallout. In 1953, St. George, Utah, and surrounding areas were irradiated when unexpected device yields and wind patterns blew fallout from the nearby Nevada Test Site (NTS) over pastoral land. Mysterious illnesses and mass die-offs of sheep aroused fears about atomic testing in the continental United States, although most of this concern remained concealed from the general public.[15]

Nuclear tests quickly grew larger. Most of America's largest tests were conducted at remote locations in the Pacific Ocean. In just nine years, explosive yield had ballooned from Trinity's roughly 18kt to Bravo's 15mt; in essence the destructive power had increased by a factor of more than eight hundred twenty-five. Bravo's ash-like precipitation created an international furor when civilians, including the Japanese crew of the *Lucky Dragon* and Marshall Islanders, were accidentally irradiated. Like the irradiation of St. George, this was due to unpredictable wind patterns and the unexpected yield of the weapon. Radiation effects were also found in tuna caught in the area, raising fears for the safety of the Japanese crew, for whom it was a dietary staple. The victims of America's military use of atomic weapons were now victimized further by an American nuclear-weapons program.[16]

Ironically, the earlier 1952 Ivy Mike test pointed toward the future of nuclear test detection and limitation. Banned from the test site due to his predilection for constantly changing aspects of site operations, Edward Teller nervously awaited news of the test—whether it had succeeded or failed. Teller felt slighted, because with Stanley Ulam he had finally managed to solve the problems inherent in achieving thermonuclear fusion—the key to the "super" or hydrogen bomb. Using a seismic instrument at the University of California that recorded data on photographic paper, he watched a pinpoint of light from the machine in a darkened room. Fifteen minutes after the scheduled shot time, Teller thought he saw a faint motion of the light. A check of the paper records confirmed his observation.[17]

Ivy Mike's seismic signal was detected primarily due to two factors: first, the device detonated at ground level. Not a weapon but a physics experiment, Mike was enormous, comprising a large building-and-refrigeration plant designed to keep the deuterium (a type of hydrogen) liquefied. The explosive energy, 10.4mt, was transferred directly to the ground, with no air gap to attenuate the blast signal. Second, Mike's yield was at the time the largest explosion produced by humans. Teller had teleseismically monitored this nuclear test, although, oddly, he later became a vocal opponent of seismology as a primary means of test detection. Teller noted in his memoirs that Livermore director Herbert York supported the growing call for an atomic-testing moratorium and a ban on atmospheric testing and believed seismology would serve as well for detection purposes in underground tests as aerial sampling had for atmospheric tests.

Teller's opposition to relying on seismic detection methods lay more with his suspicion of Soviet intent than with his distrust of a relatively young science. The issue was not whether seismology could be made sensitive enough to detect underground tests, but whether a low-yield underground test could be effectively hidden among the background noises of earthquakes and volcanic eruptions. Underground testing in earthquake-prone areas might be simply misread, or it could be paired with an earthquake that could mask the test. As Teller later stated, as long as testing remained atmospheric, it was easily detectable. For him, a nuclear-armed Soviet Union was still the primary threat, despite "a few highly publicized liberal reforms in the period following Stalin's regime."[18] Underground testing presented difficulties in detection that Teller was certain were impossible to overcome. He thought that problems with detection might lead to Soviet superiority in weapons design, whereas open-air tests allowed for the continued radiochemical analysis that the United States knew it could rely upon. Such sampling revealed the Soviets' first attempt at a thermonuclear bomb, the RDS-6, detonated on August 12, 1953. Radiological analysis of the test debris allowed physicist Hans Bethe in effect to "recreate" the bomb—later it was shown that his analysis had been remarkably accurate. Underground testing would prevent releases of radioactive materials into the atmosphere, releases crucial to determining the level of Soviet nuclear-weapons development.[19]

America's atomic scientists believed that they should play a critical role in constraining nuclear-weapons development. They belonged to an arcane fraternity—an international brother- and sisterhood that had transcended international boundaries before World War II. Not only did many dream of restoring this supernational correspondence as a way of overcoming the damage wrought by the war, they were informed by the administration of Dwight D. Eisenhower that they would be the perfect persons for the Conference on the Peaceful Uses of Atomic Energy to be held in 1955.[20] Although they could not deter nations from fighting, they could limit nuclear arsenals and help prevent nations from using the weapons they had created. They would also become responsible for preparing the means to end the need for atmospheric testing, including developing new detection and monitoring methods. If the nuclear genie could not be forced back into his bottle, perhaps he could at least be forced underground, where he posed less of a threat.

The year 1955 was critical for atomic testing. The United States tested at least fourteen atomic devices, thirteen of which were in the atmosphere, detonated either on towers or on the ground; most of these tests were under 10kt, with many having a 1kt yield. The Soviet Union detonated seven with a wide range of yield, from a single ton as part of a torpedo warhead test, to a 1.6mt yield as part of its first true two-stage thermonuclear bomb.[21]

Soviet weapons technology had made a leap forward, and so had the Soviet Union's political leadership. Stalin's death in 1953 unleashed a spasm of uncertainty and chaos in the Soviet government. The most brutal totalitarian aspects of the government were controlled by Beria, the man who had overseen the crash program to build Joe-1. He rapidly assumed power, if only for a short time, before being deposed and executed. His replacement was Georgi Malenkov, whose tenure was also brief before he was forced out of power. In 1955, Nikita Khrushchev attained political supremacy. Although numerous differences existed between the two men, one was particularly important: Malenkov was convinced that the Soviet Union would be devastated in a nuclear war, while Khrushchev initially shared Stalin's sense of nuclear invulnerability.[22]

There was a temporary thaw in Cold War relations in 1955. The Soviet government offered a "major concession" in which it granted that inspection and on-site monitoring were necessary to advance general disarmament. Although the Soviets included unrealistic demands (such as eliminating all overseas United States military bases), they indicated that they would be willing after all to negotiate some form of nuclear-control treaty. The Soviets also called for the cessation of all nuclear testing. The meeting between Eisenhower and Khrushchev in Geneva reached no further conclusions on the issue. The Soviet leader concluded:

> We were encouraged, realizing now that our enemies probably feared us as much as we feared them. They rattled their sabers and tried to pressure us into agreements which were more profitable for them than for us because they were frightened of us. . . . They now knew that they had to respect our borders and our rights, and that they couldn't get what they wanted by force or by blackmail. They realized that they would have to build their relations with us in new assumptions and new expectations if they really wanted peace.[23]

One of the issues Eisenhower raised with the Soviet delegation in Geneva was his proposal of the Open Skies policy. Concerned less with detecting tests than spotting the impending signs of a surprise attack, the policy was a step on the road to more comprehensive nuclear-weapons control policies. The Soviets remembered German reconnaissance aircraft over their airfields in the days and weeks before Hitler launched Operation Barbarossa in 1941, and they rejected the proposal; the war was still fresh in the minds of Soviet policy-makers, and they were skeptical of American motives. In retrospect, it seems almost ludicrous that Eisenhower proposed it, despite the later success of space-based reconnaissance, because the technologies to make such activities possible had yet to be developed.[24]

The United States tested a 1.7kt device at the Nevada Test Site during Operation Plumbob in 1957. Code-named Rainier, it was the first American attempt at fully containing an atomic test underground. The radioactive contamination remained isolated under a mountain ridge in the cavity created by the detonation, and there was little or no surface disturbance. Aircraft or satellites might not be able to photograph underground tests below a certain size, or those detonated at a depth where surface effects were not apparent. Radiochemical analysis of atmospheric testing debris would be useless—there simply would be none released unless there was a catastrophic accident that caused the test chamber to vent to the atmosphere. Finally, the ground where Rainier was conducted consisted of a volcanic material called tuff, which dampened the seismic signal.[25]

The potential for cloaking future tests caused great concern in parts of the nuclear-weapons community. Teller, an ardent anticommunist, suspected the Soviet Union of malfeasance at every turn. Beginning in 1957, he led one side of a debate that divided members of the scientific community for years to come: should nuclear weapons continue to be tested out in the open where they were more easily monitored, or should they be conducted underground? Teller supported the former; as George Kistiakowsky noted, Teller and his lieutenants were particularly adept at devising numerous ways for the Soviets to circumvent a limited or comprehensive test ban. Kistiakowsky, a former Los Alamos scientist and member of the President's Science Advisory Committee (PSAC), later served as the Special Assistant for Science and Technology. He had worked on the implosion system for the Trinity bomb and consequently was well acquainted with most of the atomic scientists in the United States. He opposed the perpetually suspicious Teller, who believed that nuclear testing was an absolute necessity to the security of the West. Teller and several other scientists, notably Ernest O. Lawrence and Dr. Richard Latter from RAND,[26] were members of the "infinite containment" school of thought, which imposed a monochromatic conditional system upon international affairs: either the nations of the world would be totally open with their military and scientific secrets to guarantee free and open inspection, or they would be forced to develop armaments of increasing power and capability for self-preservation. The principal motivation behind Teller's work on the hydrogen bomb, this philosophy also justified his opposition to any treaty that would force atomic testing underground, thus limiting detectable efflux and ensuring increased secrecy. Those wishing to circumvent treaty stipulations would oppose developing any monitoring technology, ultimately rendering such detection systems obsolete.[27] "In the contest between the bootlegger and the police, the bootlegger has a great advantage," Teller wrote.[28]

Nevertheless, Teller knew from his own experience that there were ways to detect underground tests. Eventually, all innovative military systems are countered; the countermeasure then requires further innovation to the original system or the adoption of a new system altogether to fulfill the operational requirements of the battlefield. This philosophy also held true for a system of underground-test monitoring. If testing moved underground, it was more likely that the Soviets would cheat, and the fallout from their tests could no longer be used to assess the success of their weapons program. To counter this loss, a new method was required, and in actuality the method was not new at all. Teller recounted in his memoirs that he was impressed by the results of the Rainier test, observing that:

> Geologists, notified in advance of the test, gained many new insights by tracing the shock wave produced by the explosion through the mantle of the earth. The instrumentation designed to register the test information in a completely new manner worked well. Our questions were answered

in the Rainier test—muffling does occur, and underground testing can yield information about weapon design and about the composition of the earth. This line of testing made possible the evolution of safer nuclear testing procedures. More important, the Rainier test was crucial to the upcoming negotiations with the Soviets. But by the time it was possible to continue testing underground, the test ban was a well-established popular movement.[29]

The generosity of time ameliorates Teller's earlier skepticism regarding underground nuclear testing. The apparent contradiction between his experience with teleseismic monitoring (the Mike test), his comments on the Rainier test, and his beliefs about the effectiveness of newer monitoring methods are not mutually exclusive. Teller observed the Mike event because he knew when to look for it, and scientists were able to gather useful data from Rainier because they knew when it was going to be conducted. His argument was that seismology was not a useful system for observing unexpected events, or in discriminating between human-caused and geological phenomena. Teller, Latter, Doyle Northrup of the Department of Defense, and Harold Brown from the University of California Radiation Laboratory became concerned with the possibility that the Soviets would continue hiding their tests, primarily by muffling them through a process known as "decoupling." Decoupling became a significant issue that drove later tests to determine the extent of its effect on seismic signal attenuation.

Hans Bethe opposed the Teller-Latter position and argued that decoupling would not pose an obstruction to underground-test monitoring. Bethe believed that a future monitoring system could surmount any obstacles presented to it, given that it was carefully planned and extensively emplaced. A strong supporter of arms control, he consistently argued that the United States had tested its arsenal to the point that further experiments would yield little useful new data while generating further antagonism toward the United States as global opposition to atmospheric nuclear testing increased.[30]

Yet decoupling remained troubling because it was theoretically easy to accomplish. In a typical underground nuclear test, a shaft was bored to a predetermined depth and the test device inserted with various instruments designed to measure aspects of the detonation. If the device was close to the walls of the shaft, it was said to be "tamped." The shaft was then filled with material, commonly a sand-and-gravel mix, in a process called "stemming." This filler trapped the expanding gases in the hole, ensuring that all of the energy from the blast was transmitted directly into the surrounding ground; it also served as an ablative plug, wherein the fill material quickly melted due to the tremendous heat and sealed the mechanical holes used to lay instrument cables. With no leakage of gases from the chamber created by the blast, a seismic signal would be generated that could give important information about weapon design and strength.[31]

Teller argued that the Soviets wanted to avoid any sort of openness, and would attempt to attenuate the seismic signal. The easiest way to do this would be to decouple the test in a pre-excavated chamber. Once a large spherical chamber had been created, the test device could be suspended from the ceiling, or elevated on a scaffold sufficient to place it in the center of the chamber. At the moment of detonation, the spherical blast wave expanded and then dissipated to a degree dictated by the circumference of the chamber. A larger chamber would rationally, under most circumstances, have an increased attenuation effect. Theoretically, this diminished the seismic signal at its point of origin, because the air gap between the device and the wall of the chamber lessened the blast wave. Instead of a direct coupling between the blast wave and the ground, it was decoupled. The telltale motion detected by a seismograph was therefore markedly smaller. In addition, such a chamber could possibly have further unknown effects that could fool mechanical means of test monitoring. By 1958, no decoupling experiments had been conducted, and both sides of the argument were using theoretical calculations without the benefit of empirical data. Teller noted in his memoirs:

> Test-ban proponents claimed that underground tests could also be detected on seismographs because they cause effects similar to earthquakes. The tests could be distinguished from natural earthquakes by their sharply timed energy release and, of course, by their unusual location. Given the nature of muffling [decoupling], I thought those arguments incomplete.[32]

For those involved with nuclear-test detection, 1958 was an eventful year. In February and March, the United States conducted two tests designed to examine the safety of their nuclear devices at the Nevada Test Site. Less than a ton in yield, these tests, as well as two others detonated in December 1957 as part of Operation 58, were designed to verify the safety features of the devices to be detonated in the United States' largest nuclear test series to date, Operation Hardtack. The experiments would be divided into two subseries, Hardtack I and Hardtack II, and include seventy-two individual tests, ranging from "slight" yields, to a massive 8.9mt blast at Enewetak in June. Hardtack was to begin near the end of April 1958.[33]

A month before the first Hardtack thermonuclear burst rose above the Pacific, the Soviets dropped a bombshell of their own. They had tested fifteen devices between January 1 and the end of March 1958, ranging from subkiloton yields to 1.5mt. At the conclusion of these tests, the Soviets announced a unilateral test moratorium beginning on March 31. It was a canny political move, for it was timed precisely to coincide with the beginning of Hardtack, as Bethe noted. Added to this was the admonition that if the United States did not join in the moratorium, the Soviets would feel free to resume testing. With a multimillion-dollar test program in the offing, there was little the United States could do—it was unreasonable to cancel such a mass commitment of men and materiel. Hardtack proceeded as planned, and in the end the United States looked militarily aggressive. Eisenhower disregarded the Soviet moratorium, even though the world reacted to it with general approval; to him it was merely a publicity stunt, despite a letter from Khrushchev repeating his determination to end testing.[34]

If Khrushchev's offer had any effect, it was to underscore further that a test moratorium had global support, despite the nuclear powers' desire to continue testing. The Soviets won praise from the world community, and the Americans were left feeling outwitted. Teller felt a great deal of unease for, as he put it, "the Soviet Union had remained a tightly controlled, secretive, totalitarian state. The dangers of a treaty with such a nation were obvious to me, and I talked almost incessantly about the topic for many months." The Soviet Union was clearly setting the diplomatic agenda, and the West needed to regain the initiative; the solution was to engage scientists as allies in the negotiations. The Eisenhower administration had suggested in January a scientifically based conference on arms-control measures. The resulting 1958 Geneva Conference of Experts represented an unprecedented meeting of Eastern and Western scientists to discuss methods whereby their respective governments could reach political agreements on the immensely technical topic of arms control.[35]

Meanwhile, Bethe had reported to Eisenhower after the conclusion of the eponymous panel he had chaired to discuss the feasibility of joining the Soviet moratorium and the ability to detect violations of a test-ban treaty. Interestingly, no seismologists were included on Bethe's panel, nor was seismology as a field represented on the PSAC, although seismologists were certainly available. These seem unlikely omissions, although they may have been intentionally done as a political expedient, for there was no empirical data to confirm or discount the ability to identify nuclear tests through seismic means. In other words, it was easier to exclude seismologists from the panel than to risk a debate over unknown quantities that might stall discussions. Ultimately, the Bethe Panel suggested that the United States proceed with Hardtack and then work toward a moratorium agreement with the Soviet Union.[36]

The Conference of Experts began on July 1, 1958, as the Hardtack I tests continued at the Pacific Test Site. Dr. James B. Fisk, then a member of the PSAC and vice-president of Bell Laboratories, chaired the Western delegation, which also included Lawrence, substituting for Teller. Opposition to Teller stemmed from his outspoken nature and his work on hydrogen-bomb development.[37]

Their counterparts from the Eastern delegation included Soviet scientific luminaries. Unbeknownst to the American delegation, however, the Soviets had provided an expert diplomatic negotiator to support their scientists, while the Americans had neglected to do so. This disappointed scientists who had high hopes of reaching a momentous breakthrough independent of the tensions of the international diplomatic arena. Their efforts did yield some results, though, in the form of the proposed Geneva System, a land- and sea-based seismic-detection network designed to detect and monitor underground nuclear testing on a global scale and to discriminate among most artificial and natural signals.

The Geneva System was the logical outcome of the impetus to move testing underground, but it drew objections due to several inherent flaws. First, there was the problem of small earthquakes and small bombs. Seismology in the 1950s was a rapidly changing and growing field of research, lacking the complexity and sophistication it has today. The immediate detection, identification, and location of seismic signals was far more difficult then than now. It was known that numerous small earthquakes occurred every year, and nuclear devices could be, and had been, tested with yields at or less than one kiloton. It was distinctly possible that an unscrupulous nation could carry on a rewarding test program using small devices and still maintain secrecy from both automated and manned stations. A 1961 congressional hearing into the seismic problems posed to the Geneva Conference concluded that even if the West received full concessions to a system of 160 to 180 land- and sea-based stations spread some six hundred miles apart in seismically active areas, and eleven hundred miles apart in nonseismically active areas, they could certainly pick up the signal from a 1kt nuclear device or small earthquake, but they did not have the means to discriminate between the two. Added to this was the changing size and complexion of the Geneva System. Questions remained as to the amount of access granted to inspection teams, the degree to which remote monitoring stations might be tampered with, and the consequences of such chicanery.[38]

The Geneva System was not built. Despite its flaws, it showed that science and diplomacy were able to interact to propose solutions to the arms control and testing problem. The United States continued to increase its civilian seismic network through the United States Geologic Survey and geology departments in colleges and universities around the country. Heartened by efforts at the conference, the Eisenhower administration announced that the United States would call upon the Soviet Union to join in a one-year moratorium on all nuclear and thermonuclear testing, beginning October 31, 1958, and subject to extension should diplomatic efforts allow.[39]

Before the testing moratorium took effect there was a flurry of further atmospheric testing. The United States entered Phase II of the Hardtack series, which included tests of small-yield devices conducted almost exclusively at the Nevada Test Site. The Soviets also resumed testing, including megaton-yield thermonuclear weapons. Both sides wanted to get their last licks in before the moratorium. The Soviets even violated the test moratorium, testing two devices in November after the start of talks between the United States and Soviet Union. This prompted the United States and Britain to renounce the moratorium, but as a sign of good faith they retained their commitment not to conduct tests. The unofficial moratorium lasted until the Soviets resumed full-scale atmospheric testing in 1961.[40]

Perhaps it was the unofficial nature of the test ban that led the Eisenhower administration to conclude that it would eventually resume experiments. The political capital to be gained by moving tests underground was obvious, but the uncertainties concerning decoupling and other effects had to be addressed to quiet some of the most ardent critics, namely Teller and his allies. The effects of nuclear decoupling would not be investigated until the Project Vela series began in 1963.[41] Begun in 1959 at the behest of the 1958 President's Panel on Seismic Improvements, Vela was a comprehensive program to determine the accuracy and feasibility of new detection systems for underground and covert high-altitude and space tests.[42] In a sense, it was an extension of the International Geophysical Year's focus on the development of earth sciences, including seismology, which along with astrophysics stood to benefit the most from the large investment made by the Advanced Research Projects Agency (ARPA) into Vela. Eisenhower's press office announced the project on May 7, 1960.

> The President today announced approval of a major expansion of the present research and development directed toward an improved capability to detect and identify underground nuclear explosions. . . . Known as Project VELA, the program calls for increased basic research in seismology; procurement of instruments for a world-wide seismic research program; development of improved seismic instruments; construction and operation of prototype seismic detection stations; and an experimental program of underground detonations encompassing both high explosive and, where necessary, nuclear explosions. The planned program provides for investigation of all aspects of improvement that are considered to be feasible.
>
> Such nuclear explosions as are essential to a full understanding of both the capabilities of the presently proposed detection system and the potential for improvements in this system would be carried out under fully

contained conditions and would produce no radioactive fallout. In order to develop sufficient reliable data from the program, it is anticipated that it will be necessary to conduct a series of explosions of various sizes, in differing types of geologic formations.[43]

The announcement of this program, made during the middle of the voluntary test moratorium, might have made it possible to conduct the nuclear portion of the test program following special negotiations. The desire for positive global opinion forced the United States and the Soviet Union to reconsider their weapons-testing programs. While the test sites cooled off, the weapons laboratories continued to work feverishly to design the next generation of bombs. Each side waited for the other to end the moratorium so their arsenals could resume testing. Or so it appeared.

4. Cowboy and the Big Hole Theory

THE ADVANCED RESEARCH PROJECTS AGENCY AND THE ATOMIC
Energy Commission had not been idle between October 31, 1958, and
September 1, 1961, while the test moratorium was in effect. They were
busily planning future weapons-tests series while exploring technical
systems required for a detection and analytical capability to cope with
the technical requirements of underground nuclear testing. Several test
series utilizing high explosives determined the seismic characteristics of
various underground environments. Authorized early in September 1959,
Vela Uniform was publicly announced on May 7, 1960. ARPA was given
the task of designing and implementing a three-phase program designed
to detect and monitor subterranean, high altitude, and surface detonations. Decoupling gained enough credibility to warrant substantial field
research. Geologists were beginning to understand the differences in
seismic-energy transmission through different materials; a nuclear as-
say of underground structures needed to be made that approximated
zones where the Soviets would most likely conduct subterranean tests.
Two programs initially emerged, code-named Cowboy and Concerto.[1]

Cowboy directly addressed the question of decoupling and the potential magnitude of its effect on camouflaging a test signal. Begun in
December 1959 and lasting for three months, it was a non-nuclear test
series utilizing high explosives. The experiments provided useful data
while remaining faithful to the voluntary 1958 nuclear-test moratorium.
Begun at the end of 1958, the tests were both welcomed and resented
in the nuclear-weapons community, which preferred continuing atomic
tests. The work normally conducted at the Nevada and Pacific test sites
screeched to a halt once the two Hardtack test series were concluded.
While the threat of atmospheric fallout virtually disappeared, there was
concern about the possibility of small covert nuclear tests that could be

masked behind seismic background noise, providing the Soviet Union a tactical or strategic advantage in its arsenal development. There was another issue: the moratorium was voluntary and thus subject to being broken without the international accountability that would come from violating a brokered treaty. The nuclear establishment felt it crucial to remain in a position to resume testing when the moratorium eventually ended, as many felt it would. High explosives provided an alternative to no testing at all and at least kept the people at the NTS working on something while the Pacific test site sat practically abandoned.

Cowboy was the first program to give solid baseline data on the difference in seismic energy between coupled (or tamped) shots and decoupled shots fired in a test chamber in a salt dome. The tests were conducted below the working area of the Carey Salt Mine near Winnfield, Louisiana, utilizing thousand-pound high-explosive charges. Control readings taken from shaft detonations were compared with decoupled shots in excavated spherical chambers, one twelve feet in diameter and one thirty feet in diameter. The United States Coast and Geodetic Survey (USCGS) carefully measured the explosive energy at thirteen sites ranging from ground zero to sixty-one miles from the shot point. Seismic monitoring crews took multifrequency readings at specialized sites up to eight miles from ground zero.[2]

The paired tests produced good comparative data, proving that decoupling had a considerable effect on signal strength. Testifying before the Congressional Joint Committee on Atomic Energy (JCAE) in 1960, RAND Corporation's Dr. Albert Latter reported that the tamped shots fired during Cowboy yielded seismic signals that were one hundred twenty times stronger than the decoupled tests. His brother Richard, also employed by RAND, was another primary advocate of using decoupling to hide underground tests. The Latter brothers enjoyed the support of Edward Teller, who had long anticipated Soviet chicanery. Teller's suspicion of the Soviet nuclear-weapons complex, and its political and military leadership, led him to advocate the continuation of atmospheric testing. The Latter brothers' theories regarding decoupling suggested that atomic tests with a useful yield could be hidden. Albert Latter's testimony at the JCAE hearing led to his being credited with the "Latter big hole" theory. As he explained:

[I]f the explosion occurs in a small hole—as is the case for a tamped explosion
—the pressure which acts on the surrounding medium is very great, and
the medium is not strong enough to stand the pressure. As a result, the
hole must expand and this causes a large motion of the surrounding earth.
It is this large motion, in the immediate neighborhood of the explosion
which shows up at great distances as a tiny seismic signal. . . . On the
other hand, if the explosion is made in a big hole, the pressure which the
surrounding medium experiences is not very great and the medium can
stand the pressure. As a result, there is very little expansion of the hole
and essentially no motion of the surrounding earth.[3]

Latter also emphasized that it was not enough simply to excavate
randomly sized chambers to serve as covert test sites. There was an opti-
mal volume to any chamber in relation to the device yield. To go beyond
it could risk long-distance detection:

I want to mention a rather curious fact; namely that once a hole is big
enough, the signal will not be further reduced by making the hole any
bigger. . . . Once it reaches the critical size, this happens because of an
accidental cancellation of two opposing physical effects. One of these is
that as the hole gets bigger, less energy goes into the earth's motion. This,
of course, has a tendency to reduce the signal. On the other hand, it turns
out that the energy which does go into the seismic wave is of a longer
wavelength. As the hole gets bigger the wavelength increases. This longer
wavelength is just the kind of a signal which can be propagated to great
distances in the earth easily. The shorter wavelength signals tend to get
filtered out by the earth. The net effect of these two opposite phenomena
is that the seismic signal which occurs at a great distance from the scene
of the explosion is independent of the size of the hole—provided the hole
is big enough in the first place.

Latter believed that a decoupling factor of three hundred could be
achieved if the size of the test chamber was large enough. According to
his calculations, a spherical chamber excavated to the dimensions dictated by a factor of seventy thousand cubic meters per expected kiloton
of device yield could achieve this maximum decoupling effect.[4]

Although indicative of the possibilities of decoupling, the data from Cowboy was only practically applicable to high explosives; nuclear devices were another matter entirely. It is difficult to compare nuclear detonations and those caused by high explosives. Nuclear charges are measured in terms of tons of TNT (tri-nitro-toluene). Yet TNT comparatively "burns" much cooler and more slowly than a fissile mass. Furthermore, high explosives do not produce the flood of X-rays, gamma radiation, and other exotic progeny that stem from nuclear fission and fusion. These various forms of electromagnetic energy might have unknown effects on the walls of a test chamber; the uncertainties were numerous enough to suggest atomic testing in a salt environment as soon as possible, once the moratorium was broken. A major area of concern could have been the possibility of initial ablation of the cavity walls caused by the X-ray pulse from the detonation. Ionized plasma formed by X-rays striking the sodium-chloride walls would move rapidly inward toward the shot point just before the blast wave reached it. What effect, if any, this could have on the seismic signal was unknown. Until the moratorium ceased, this and other questions would remain unanswered.

Concerto's area of investigation was different. This test series was to discern the seismic signals created by the detonation of low-yield (1/4kt to 5kt) devices in tuff (a relatively loose volcanic soil) at varying depths, as well as one low-yield shot that was to be conducted off NTS property, and one medium-sized detonation of 50kt, again fired in tuff. Of the seven proposed tests to be fired during Concerto, six were to be nuclear tests, with one of the 1kt tests to be fired comparatively with a 1kt high-explosive shot to gauge seismic effects between the two. Unfortunately for the scientists at Livermore Radiation Laboratory (LRL), who were to oversee the project, the moratorium proved too politically tenuous for them to proceed with anything but the high-explosive shot. Looking ahead to the future possibility of resumed nuclear testing, they also conducted preparatory excavation for a tamped underground 5kt nuclear shot code-named Lollipop, which was planned to be fired in a granite formation at NTS.[5]

The moratorium was not the only thing that slowed the Concerto series. The atomic testing budget for Fiscal Year 1960 was four and one-half million dollars. Between the Cowboy tests and the single Lollipop shot preparations, more than half this amount had been committed. Because of budgetary limitations, Teller recommended to army general Alfred Starbird, director of the Division of Military Application (DMA), AEC, revision of a safety formula that dictated the minimum depth of test shafts. Starbird was amenable to reduced cost, but he warned Teller that radiation containment was of paramount importance to any test series. Whatever radioactive contamination was produced had to be contained underground.[6] Despite the important role of nuclear testing, it was still subject to a narrowing budget, and fiscal concerns continued to affect the configuration and process of atomic testing following the test moratorium's end. Any radiation release, even at the tightly controlled Nevada Test Site, would most certainly result in negative publicity.

Assurances from military and technical spokesmen following lapses of containment no longer had the credibility they had earlier in the atomic age. The 1951 irradiation of St. George, Utah, was handled through official information and radio bulletins; indeed, it appears that contamination in the town was light. The incident was considered so well handled that a short film produced afterward depicted the town's Rockwellian citizenry reacting promptly to alerts from official government sources and happily enduring the situation for the sake of a safer, more secure (and more radioactive) America. Yet fallout does not return to earth in a uniform pattern; it is sporadic. Some areas receive a light dusting while other spots nearby may be subjected to concentrations of material that are lethal to humans and animals. Radioactivity posed an important health hazard to the public, which became increasingly conscious of the threat of dangerous fallout in what many saw as the inevitable conflict between the Soviet Union and the United States. The decision to shave the safety margin later led to some of the large on-site releases at NTS, including the Baneberry event in 1970, wherein a subterranean 10kt shot in tuff released a large quantity of fallout through a previously unknown fault. Baneberry's fallout traveled as far north as Canada, and public furor caused all testing activities to be suspended for seven months.[7]

Outrage and protest were one thing; the accidental irradiation of heavily populated areas was another. Should continental testing be moved off site, it would be heavily constrained by population, possibly eliminating geological environments that were desirable for testing. Radiochemical containment had to be absolute, with no undue risk to those living near the test site. The overlying strata that were the primary shields against biological effects from testing had to maintain absolute integrity. Concerto would explore the capabilities of different types of geologic material and their relative abilities to absorb the immense and sudden strain caused by a nuclear test, as well as their readiness to transmit seismic energy.

While Concerto was in its planning stage, another important program was pursued with increased vigor. The Plowshare program was an ambitious idea designed to put a useful face on atomic explosives. Ultimately totaling twenty-seven tests compared to VU's seven shots, Plowshare was publicly touted as a program dedicated to investigating the use of atomic devices for peaceful purposes. These included the stimulation of underground gas deposits, the excavation of canals and harbors and other large-scale earth-moving projects, isotope manufacture, subterranean storage-chamber creation, and heat production. Plowshare, which took its name from a scriptural verse instructing people to turn their swords into plowshares, was always a sticking point in arms-control negotiations between the United States and the Soviet Union. The devices to be used were not bombs—that is, they were not weaponized or militarized and did not incorporate such elements as a ballistic case or fuzing. As they were intended to be the nuclear equivalent of high explosives, the AEC made every effort to limit the amount of radioactive contamination caused by their detonation. Small, low-yield thermonuclear devices looked to be especially useful as they produced little radioactivity, with most of this coming primarily from the small atomic device used to spark the thermonuclear reaction. In this area, Plowshare sparked no small concern, for cloaked within the guise of a peaceful atomic program lay the need to develop these smaller, "cleaner" devices—a capability that potentially tied it to weapons development. Plowshare and VU were both similar and different. Plowshare turned the military atom toward peaceful civilian purposes. Vela Uniform turned the military atom toward itself, ensuring continued peace through monitoring and detection methods. Nevertheless, they were commonly confused with each other.[8]

Enhancing this confusion, the first Plowshare test, Gnome, was conducted during the first American test series after the end of the 1958 test moratorium. Lasting more than thirty months, the moratorium had been a period of uneasy peace between the superpowers without the frightful nuclear saber-rattling. In 1961, the Soviet Union broke the moratorium and resumed atmospheric testing. The experiments included the largest explosion in human history, a roughly 60mt blast over their test site at Novaya Zemlya. While American politicians and the world community railed against the resumption of testing on grounds of opposing added radioactive fallout and military destabilization, America's nuclear community got the green light to proceed with its own testing.[9]

The 1957 Rainier blast had shown that tests could be conducted underground with little or no surface disturbance or release of radioactivity while still providing useful data on the effects of the explosion. Gnome marked the first time a nuclear device was tested in a subterranean salt bed—in this case near Carlsbad, New Mexico. The AEC sought to explore further the feasibility of constructing underground storage chambers, the production of useful heat energy for electrical generation, and the production of radioisotopes. Seismic monitoring stations included seismographs emplaced in Carlsbad Caverns and in a neighboring potash mine. The selection of the site was intended to allow the collection of data in a different medium from the volcanic tuff common at the NTS.[10]

The Gnome shot was fired on December 10, 1961. Apart from the failure of some equipment designed to prevent an accidental radiation release, little contamination was evident. The seismic damping that occurred due to the loose composition of tuff was absent in the salt bed. With little air space between it and the tunnel wall, the shot was tamped. The 3kt of force generated by the device traveled directly into the wall of the chamber. Monitoring personnel observed several interesting phenomena: first, the seismic travel times were not the same at stations located equidistant from the shot point, varying in delay times by as much as nine seconds. This indicated that previously unknown subterranean structures in the area had altered the travel time of the shock wave. Second, although no notable damage to nearby commercial or residential structures occurred, the shot had a substantially stronger signal than shot Logan, a 5kt device detonated three years earlier at NTS. This was directly attributed to the unique characteristics of the test in Nevada. Logan's seismic signal was comparable to a magnitude 4.5 earthquake while Gnome's signal was closer to a 4.6 to 5.0.[11]

Pointing the way to Vela, the report on Gnome's seismic program concluded: "[I]t is recommended therefore that some consideration be given to conducting a future test in a shield area with the shot buried deep enough to be well coupled with the rock, and that the international seismological community be fully alerted. This would afford seismic measurements along continuous profiles in any direction, and afford a reverse profile for evaluation of clandestine events."[12] In short, naturally occurring sources of signal attenuation were poorly understood. Interactions between geological formations directed and changed the strength of seismic energy, and they could delay it as well. Understanding how shock energy passed through these structures was critical if any future seismic detection system was to work with a reliable degree of accuracy.

Nuclear tests were perfect for determining the composition and location of subterranean structures; they produced a sharply timed spike of energy, and their detonation time, depth, and location were all known. They allowed the subterranean contours of the earth's crust to be precisely mapped. For the Plowshare and Vela series, the USCGS provided the seismographs and the AEC provided the nuclear charges.[13]

Gnome's revelation that salt was far more efficient at conducting seismic energy led to further interest in testing in salt environments. Salt is a crystalline substance, in some respects similar to granite, with a degree of plasticity. It has the ability to flex or flow in response to dynamic heat and pressure. It is also much easier to excavate than granite or other rocks and therefore makes an ideal matrix for a test site. Methods practiced and perfected over hundreds of years of salt mining could easily be employed to create test locations. Testifying at the 1960 JCAE hearing, Lance P. Meade, manager of Phillips Petroleum's engineering department, offered several examples of storage chambers that had been mined in salt domes. At the time of his testimony, some 250 had been created, primarily for liquefied petroleum gas storage. These ranged from 140,000 cubic feet (4,000 cubic meters) to 5,600,000 cubic feet (160,000 cubic meters). Meade proposed mining a spherical 73,000,000-cubic-foot volume chamber approximately 516 feet in diameter—theoretically sufficient to decouple a 30kt explosion. The diameter and shape thus specified, the only question left was the expense of an excavation thirteen times larger than any previous chambers. Meade provided two examples regarding the cost of excavation: one where the primary concern was expense and the other where time was the critical factor. The expense-critical (cheap) approach would last some forty-eight months and cost about $2,580,000 with a possible $500,000 to $1,000,000 in additional costs relating to site purchase and preparation, fresh water and brine disposal, and various other items. The time-critical (expensive) approach could be completed in twenty-eight months at a cost of $13,505,000.[14]

More questions needed to be answered regarding nuclear testing in a salt environment, especially concerning the residual materials created by the extreme heat and pressure of an atomic blast, and the feasibility of reusing such chambers for future tests. There was a limited number of sites that could host a large nuclear test in a salt dome in the high-kiloton or -megaton range. These sites would quickly be depleted in the course of a testing program if the plasticity of the salt could not tolerate the deformation and damage caused by a large nuclear blast.

By 1961, Project Clarion had been subsumed by the VU program. The two projects' goals were similar, although the Vela program included a greater number of chemical and atomic shots than Clarion. Lollipop, the granite shot, was never fired, at least not under that name. Instead, a test conducted on February 15, 1962, during Operation Nougat, named Hard Hat, was fired nearly 950 feet below ground at NTS in a "hard rock" structure. The 5.7kt yield and environmental similarity leads to the conclusion that it was the same test, renamed and included in a different test series.[15]

Re-designation was not unusual for test shots, test sites, and programs. The salt dome portion of the VU program was called Ripple during the survey phase and Dribble during the operational phase.[16] Six criteria were crucial to Ripple: the salt had to be pure and free of rock intrusions or ledges; the top of the salt had to be less than seventeen hundred feet down; the population around the site had to be minimal, and within two miles of the site it had to be less than one hundred; within two miles of the test site there could be no "significant oil, gas, sulfur, salt, or other mineral production"; there could be "no town within five to ten miles of the site"; and initially there had to be "firm ground" for instrumentation purposes within thirty miles—later thirty kilometers—of the site at radial intervals of forty-five to sixty degrees. If a leaching method was used to excavate the chamber, fifteen million barrels of water should be available "at a reasonable cost," and there had to be "an appropriate, economical method of disposing of the fifteen million barrels of wash water during the six months required to form the desired cavity."[17]

More than two hundred sites from Texas to Mississippi looked promising for the salt-dome shots. After further analysis, two Mississippi salt formations looked most promising: the Bruinsburg Dome, thirty miles south of Vicksburg, and the Tatum Dome. The ready availability of transportation by road, railroad, and air was a major advantage of the Tatum site, as was the absence of worry about potential effects on Mississippi River traffic. The general characteristics of both domes were well known, and deep sampling cores retrieved from them allowed further tests regarding their suitability. At the Tatum site, exploratory wells twenty-seven hundred feet deep penetrated into the dome to determine the chemical and physical composition of the caprock and salt stock.[18]

When Frank Tatum wrote to his elected representatives in late October 1960 and reported the AEC's desire to "do some atomic shooting in the salt dome," he was disturbed that the dome in question was in the middle of his family's extensive landholdings. A shrewd businessman like his father, Tatum made an offer to the Corps of Engineers: he would agree to an open lease on the land, with unlimited extension if needed, "with the proviso that they would pay an annual rental of at least equal to what we were getting from the land each year in turpentine rights and sale of the trees. They would not agree to a lease." Tatum attempted another bargain, offering to trade for an equal amount of nearby government land. This was denied, he was told, because the federal land in question belonged to different bureaus and could not be exchanged.[19]

This letter is misleading, for it portrays Tatum as a simple victim of federal action. He neglected to mention that a month and a half before he began his correspondence with Governor Barnett, Senators Eastland and Stennis, and Representative Colmer, the *Hattiesburg American* had reported the possibility that Mississippi's salt domes might be used for atomic testing, and an editorial published on September 15 further detailed scientific interest in the state's salt domes and the overwhelmingly cooperative attitude of the citizenry. The first media report mentioning government interest in a local salt dome appeared on October 7; six days later, Tatum was named to a ten-man committee to advise state officials on issues concerning the possible test program. He was better prepared to look out for his interests than he would admit.[20]

Of particular interest is a *Hattiesburg American* article published on September 12, 1960, which coupled the idea of using nuclear devices in salt domes to "produce valuable radioactive materials and energy that would be useful for industrial purposes" to the excavation of the Tennessee-Tombigbee Waterway project. The Tennessee-Tombigbee (commonly referred to as the Tenn-Tom) was to join the two river systems across northeastern Mississippi and northwest Alabama, create a water route to the Gulf of Mexico independent of the Mississippi River, and act as a major economic stimulus to the southeastern United States. The large canal that must be excavated to link the two rivers had to cut through stone ridges, where conventional blasting and rock removal was the primary expense of the project. The Tenn-Tom seemed an ideal proving ground for Plowshare, where several small nuclear devices could open the necessary passage in the rock with a modicum of radioactivity. Ultimately, the waterway was constructed, but without the use of Plowshare explosives. There was no mention of Vela Uniform in the article.[21] Linking the two projects, plus the idea of isotope creation and industrial uses of atomic shots in salt domes, further increased confusion about the programs.

As of October 1960, no firm decision had been made to acquire the property over the Tatum Dome or the minerals within it. Tatum was determined to avoid being taken advantage of by the federal government and was primarily interested in how the situation could benefit him. The Atomic Energy Commission sent representatives on October 29, 1960, to brief him fully on the plans for the Ripple tests as then conceived, and the need to assess the Tatum Dome for suitability as a test site compared with the Bruinsburg Dome:

> If the Tatum site is finally selected for these experiments it is expected that it will be necessary to acquire approximately 1400 acres. Whether this area will have to be purchased or whether a lesser interest, an easement or a leasehold, will be sufficient has not been finally determined. However, every effort will be made to interfere as little as possible with the use of the surface by the present owners. Because it is anticipated that dome salt

in the immediate vicinity of the detonation area will be made unsuitable for further utilization due to the effects of the nuclear explosion, we would plan still to purchase the mineral rights underlying the approximately 1400 acres discussed above.[22]

The mineral rights in the salt dome, noted in this assessment, would later become an important point of contention between Tatum and the federal government.

On October 31, 1960, Tatum wrote to Gov. Ross Barnett, who was still in the first year of his administration, expressing concern for the effect the proposed atomic tests might have on Mississippi's environment due to blast and radiation effects:

With further regard to the Atomic Energy Commission's program in South Mississippi on the salt domes, as you know South Mississippi is blessed with many creeks, streams, branches and springs, and practically all of our people have artesian water available. The question naturally arises as to the contamination and pollution that our streams and water resources may suffer.

We have to take into consideration not only contamination but the effect or force of the explosion and then the terrific heat. These atomic explosions seem to have a chained reaction [sic] and I do not believe anyone knows what the result might be.

He noted the possibility that the government might instead use resources for tests that they already had in their possession:

I am informed by the Humble Oil & Refining Company, one of our largest producers of crude oil in Mississippi, who have interest in many of the oil fields, especially in South Mississippi, that there is a large salt dome located on government property in the New Augusta area and on the Camp Shelby property. This dome is farther away from the oil and gas production, is already owned by the government, and has been for many years, and it seems to me should be available to the government if they need it. Humble states that the salt dome now owned by the government under their property is about the same size and conformity and depth as the one they are looking at in Lamar County and they think, from looking at their structural maps and seismograph information, that it is equally as well located structurally and probably about the same depth.[23]

Tatum thus expressed a good understanding of the geologic requirements of the proposed test site. This knowledge came from the extensive oil prospecting conducted throughout southern Mississippi prior to World War II. As he stood the chance to lose access to a substantial piece of timber land, his "not in my backyard" attitude is understandable.

Tatum found an important ally in Frederick W. Mellen, one of the most eminent geologists in Mississippi, who had discovered the Tinsley oilfield, one of the state's most productive, in 1939. Mellen's reputation for honesty and integrity led him to be appointed state geologist in 1962. He resigned that position in 1965, disgusted with colleagues who illegally diverted government funds for their own purposes and pressured him to do the same. Following his resignation, he returned to the consulting business.[24] From the beginning, Mellen was deeply opposed to the idea of nuclear testing in Mississippi, arguing that the potential destruction of the state's natural resources was too great a risk. Following a presentation by Dr. Andrew D. Suttle Jr., director of the newly created Mississippi Industrial and Technological Research Committee (MITRC), to the Oil Company Geophysicists Association, Mellen wrote a letter to Senator Stennis, dated November 22, 1961, criticizing Suttle and the AEC and requesting Stennis's intercession:

> I wrote you sometime [sic] ago, sending you a copy of a letter which appeared in one of the local papers opposing the underground nuclear testing in Mississippi. I am still just as opposed to it as I was at that time, although my reasons may have changed somewhat. I understand that you have given your tacit approval of the program, as contemplated by the Atomic Energy Commission and the Mississippi Industrial and Technical Research Board. . . . Dr. Suttle did not give one definite assurance of any economic benefit of these explosions to the State except for the pump-priming effect of spending Government money in a local area.

Mellen's concerns echoed Tatum's; he felt that Mississippi's natural resources and environment were threatened by the proposed program, and he believed that federal agencies were cavalierly planning atomic tests in a number of salt domes. The conclusion of his letter to Stennis reflects his fear of unwarranted governmental intrusion in the name of atomic security:

> It is with deep regard and concern that I find myself in the position of having to sit back and watch the destruction of our native State by a Socialistic Government. I know that it is a matter of concern to you, as it is to every thinking Mississippian, and I sincerely trust that you will continue to look into this matter at every opportunity and help us to kill this snake before it destroys us.[25]

Mellen's "Statement of Personal Opinion," widely distributed via the editorial pages of the state's newspapers, raised concern in the AEC's public-information office, which was unsure of Mellen's motives and suspected that his actions were a result of professional animosity. The Mississippi Academy of Science, of which Mellen was a member, had not been consulted during the early planning of the Dribble test series. Mellen's name and reputation carried a great deal of weight in Mississippi, and the last thing the AEC, the MITRC, and its director Andrew Suttle needed was negative publicity.[26]

Yet despite the criticism emanating from Tatum's and Mellen's typewriters, Suttle's MITRC had powerful allies in the man who had first proposed the organization, Governor Barnett, and the contracting firms in Mississippi that hoped to benefit from its creation. MITRC, spiritual descendant of the earlier BAWI program, intended to bring high-tech industry to the Piney Woods.

The Dribble test site as seen from the air, showing the roads, trailers, and derricks in the dense forest. The bleeddown facility is between the two derricks at right. *Lawrence-Livermore National Laboratory/Department of Energy.*

Close-up view of surface ground zero prior to the first test. Note the bleeddown-facility pipework just above the center of the photograph and the large "blooie" tanks nearby that would later contain radioactive solids and liquids, as well as the lined storage pit next to the derrick at right. *Lawrence-Livermore National Laboratory/ Department of Energy.*

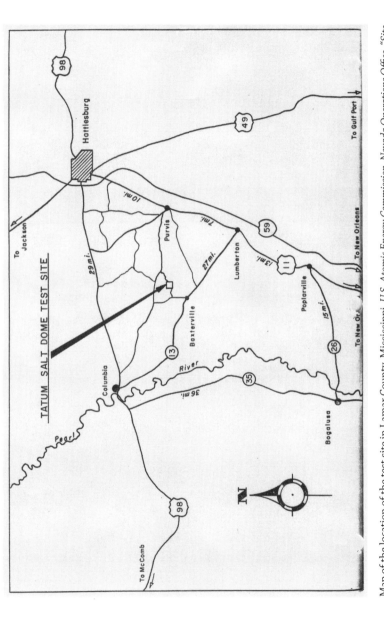

Map of the location of the test site in Lamar County, Mississippi. U.S. Atomic Energy Commission, Nevada Operations Office, "Site Disposal Report: Tatum Salt Dome Test Site (Dribble/Hattiesburg) Lamar County, Mississippi," NVO-88.

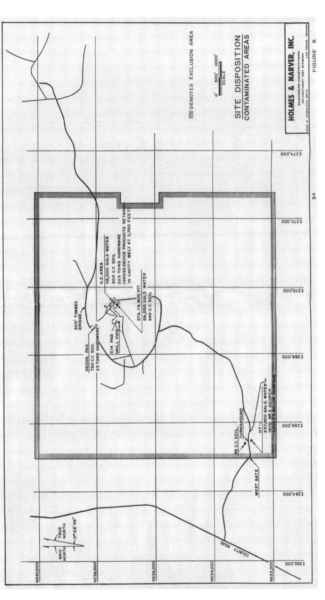

Map of areas with known radiological contamination, prepared by Holmes & Narver Engineers and included in the 1971 remediation report. *U.S. Atomic Energy Commission, Nevada Operations Office, "Site Disposal Report: Tatum Salt Dome Test Site (Dribble/Hattiesburg) Lamar County, Mississippi," NVO-88.*

Drill rig at the Salmon site. This is one of several derricks used for drilling the actual emplacement hole for the Salmon device, for drilling emplacement holes for instrument packages, and for cavity reentry. *Lawrence-Livermore National Laboratory/ Department of Energy.*

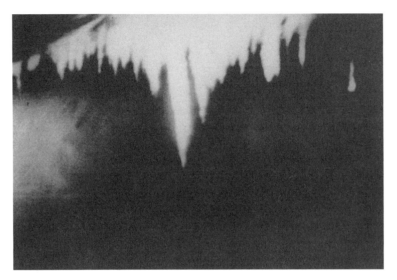

Interior of Salmon cavity. This photograph was likely one of the earliest taken after cavity reentry. Despite its poor quality, it does show salt stalactites hanging from the top of the test cavity. Unlike normal stalactites, these were caused by the trapped heat of the Salmon test, which melted the salt and allowed it to drip, forming a puddle of salt and debris at the bottom of the chamber. *Lawrence-Livermore National Laboratory/ Department of Energy.*

Salmon canister, sitting on a wheeled dolly. Both the Salmon and Sterling devices were encased in sturdy canisters that allowed them to survive being buried by tons of gravel and cement prior to their respective shots. *Lawrence-Livermore National Laboratory/Department of Energy.*

The Salmon device going down hole 001. Here, the device is being lowered into the Station 1A hole. Note the sign taped to the canister, which reads "Operation Dribble —Salmon Event." Also note the heavy attachment point at the top of the canister and the heavy-duty cable at the top, which served to connect diagnostic equipment at the surface and to relay the firing signal to the device buried some 2,700 feet below ground. *Lawrence-Livermore National Laboratory/Department of Energy.*

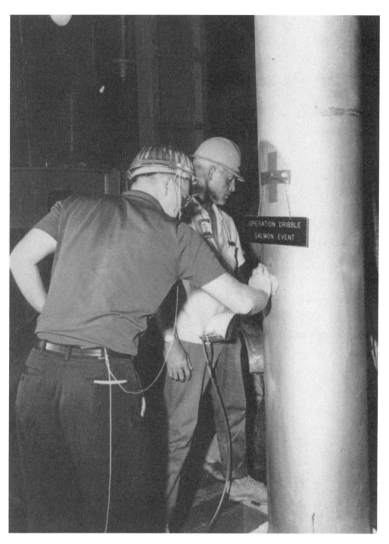

Salmon device going down hole 002. This photograph shows the Salmon canister as it is about to be lowered into the Station 1A hole. The sign taped to the casing is clearly visible. The man in the foreground appears to be wiping something off the outside of the canister, possibly cleaning it before signing it. *Lawrence-Livermore National Laboratory/Department of Energy.*

Here the heavy canister containing the Salmon device is being carefully guided down the Station 1A hole. Note the clothing on the man at left, who is wearing "flip-flop" sandals and shorts while supervising the operation. The heat, humidity, and mud at the site made such clothing appropriate. *Lawrence-Livermore National Laboratory/ Department of Energy.*

Surface ground zero following the Salmon test. The sign visible next to the center post, knocked slightly off vertical, warns of an explosive threat. The balloon at the top of the post most likely indicated surface wind direction in case of radiological release. *Lawrence-Livermore National Laboratory/Department of Energy.*

Postshot 1 following the Salmon test. A site worker strikes a dramatic pose at the lip of the Station 1A site. Note the Confederate battle flag affixed to the top of the pipe. *Lawrence-Livermore National Laboratory/Department of Energy.*

Another postshot following the Salmon test. This is the actual cap bolted to the flange of the Station 1A casing, showing the device cable attachment point. Note the culvert pipe sections that cover wiring on the ground and what looks to be a pump or generator mounted on a heavy wooden pallet at left. *Lawrence-Livermore National Laboratory/Department of Energy.*

Sterling package going down hole 001. Unlike the dramatic shots of the Salmon emplacement, this image of the Sterling device was made in daylight and without the large derrick structure evident in the previous lowering operations. Careful scrutiny shows markings on the canister, which are autographs by site personnel. Directly facing the photographer, at the middle of the casing, someone has written "See Ya"— a final farewell to the site's second and last test device. *Lawrence-Livermore National Laboratory/Department of Energy.*

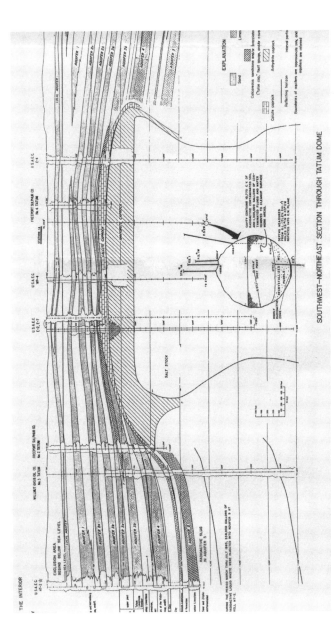

Tatum Salt Dome, Cross Section 1, showing the salt dome's general shape. Note the size of the test chamber in relation to the overall size of the dome. It is shown in exploded fashion at the center of the dome, but it is in fact that tiny circular area just to the right. This image also gives a good indication of the soil strata and aquifers at the site, as well as the deformity caused by the salt and its caprock rising toward the surface. *U.S. Atomic Energy Commission, Nevada Operations Office, "Site Disposal Report: Tatum Salt Dome Test Site (Dribble/Hattiesburg) Lamar County, Mississippi," NVO-88.*

5. MITRC, MCEC, and the Tatum Decision

FREDERICK MELLEN'S EFFORTS TO STOP THE TESTS IN MISSISSIPPI involved criticizing one of the state's newest administrative entities. The MITRC originated in 1960 in response to newly elected governor Ross Barnett's inaugural address. Barnett reaffirmed his commitment to segregation, a legacy of the state's racist past. But, looking ahead, he envisioned himself in a unique position in Mississippi history and, surprisingly, advocated high technology in his state. Noting "the urgency for this administration to direct its every effort toward raising the living standard of all our people," Barnett recommended the creation of a "Mississippi industrial and technological research center." He also advocated programs designed to increase tourism, attract industry, and improve education. This initiative was similar in some respects to Governor White's earlier BAWI program, but it would not merely focus on attracting heavy industry; instead, it would attempt to draw scientific and technological research to the state. Electronic, chemical, and nuclear industries were aggressively pursued. Barnett envisioned a large research park administered by highly qualified professionals—not politicians—as the anchor of this endeavor. This concentration on industrial and scientific expertise versus political appointees was remarkable for its ambition, especially in a Deep South state. To overcome the poverty and violence in the Delta region, and to spur development in other parts of the state, Barnett sought to attract high-tech industry. The legislature was willing to comply, and MITRC was established shortly after Barnett's inauguration.[1]

Such an organization required the stewardship of a gifted administrator. Despite Mellen's misgivings, Dr. Andrew D. Suttle proved to be an inspired choice as the first director of the MITRC. Born in West Point, Mississippi, in 1926, Suttle attended school in Starkville, where he later obtained a bachelor's degree from Mississippi State University, majoring in chemistry and mathematics with a minor in physics. He served as an aviation radio technician in the Naval Reserve in World War II. He returned to work as a research assistant in Mississippi State's chemistry laboratories; in 1949 he received an AEC fellowship to the University of Chicago. He earned his doctorate there in 1952, concentrating on radiochemistry, then went to work for the Humble Oil Company. He continued as Humble's senior research scientist while serving as MITRC director. Suttle energetically promoted MITRC and wrote numerous reports for the state's industries.[2]

Tatum and Mellen's letters to government representatives complemented each other. Mellen feared the devaluation of Mississippi's salt domes to worthless sites for testing nuclear devices; these concerns would be reprised roughly a decade and a half later. His main assertion was that, despite the depth of the Tatum Salt Dome, and of the Bruinsburg Dome, they represented the top of a slippery slope. He feared that, once Mississippi's domes were judged disposable, the state would simply become another test site, dependent primarily on the federal dole. Mississippi would, he felt, be unable to support itself through its own mineral and resource wealth; the state would be reduced to selling its salt domes as radioactive dump sites. Despite the potential global benefit of stabilizing the nuclear balance of power, Mellen was highly suspicious of the AEC's interest in the region, and he continued to protest the use of Mississippi's salt domes for atomic tests.

Mellen was in contact with Dr. Linus Pauling, a well-known scientist and opponent of nuclear testing, who feared that the proposed Vela program might harbor more sinister intentions. On December 20, 1960, Pauling wrote to Mellen:

> I agree with you that much of the destruction of our natural resources that is now going on is unwarranted. In particular, I too am strongly opposed to the use of Mississippi salt domes for detonation of nuclear explosions.
>
> Our military men may want to use even the peace-time experiments for tests of nuclear weapons, and I think that the only way to be sure that a misuse of the nuclear explosives is not being carried out is to have all peace-time applications of nuclear explosives in the hands of the United

Nations. Also, I feel that very careful thought must be given to any proposed peace-time use of nuclear explosives, because I fear that the radioactivity will damage human beings so greatly and will damage our natural resources also to such a great extent that the explosions cannot be considered justified.

I am pleased that you are active in your work along these lines, and I hope that you will continue.[3]

Tatum also expressed concern regarding environmental effects. In a letter to Eastland, Stennis, and Colmer, he spoke of Mississippi's environmental value compared to the desert southwest: "This letter is not written necessarily as a property owner but as a Citizen of Mississippi. South Mississippi enjoys many water resources in its creeks, branches, springs, and artesian wells, many grasses, plants, and growing trees, both pine and hardwood. We have vast sections in the United States that are deserts and are covered by lava rock in the western states, no water, no grasses, no trees. I have seen a great deal of these lands in two trips west and seemingly all they produce, outside of the enormous amount of lava rock, is rattlesnakes, frogs, and lizards."[4] He feared that the test program for his salt dome would ultimately be used for more nefarious purposes than "military men" merely co-opting peacetime tests to develop weapons. Writing to Senator Eastland on November 9, 1960, he stated his concern:

The Atomic Energy folks tell us the project now contemplated is what they call Project Vela, that it is a project for the *United Nations Commission*. The A.E.C. is undertaking this project to settle the question raised by the United Nations Commission who have been studying the ban of nuclear explosions and the detection of such explosions. The United Nations Commission has raised the question as to whether it is possible to set off underground nuclear explosions so they cannot be detected by our enemies or others. . . . They think by shooting off the explosions in the salt domes that the salt will so distort the shock waves that you could not tell whether it was an atomic explosion or an earthquake; that the salt mass will distort the waves of tremor and cause a different type of chart recording or a different type of wiggle or waggle. . . .

Concluding his letter, Tatum added: "with best regards and congratulations on another term. We are certainly going to need you with Kennedy elected."[5]

The Kennedy administration had few white supporters in Mississippi. Tatum was definitely not a fan of John F. Kennedy, who, with his brother Robert, the attorney general, was the focus of his anger regarding racial conflict in Mississippi. Tatum most likely conformed to the ideas of his time, including segregation as a means of maintaining social status. He saw the use of government contracts as an element to force social change from without. A June 27, 1961, letter to Barnett and to Tatum's congressional representatives may illustrate his sentiments regarding states' rights and white supremacy, although it is important to remember for whom the letter was intended:

> It seems that the Kennedy brothers have gotten together with the NAACP and similar organizations and issued new orders and directives regarding the letting of government contracts. . . .
>
> As you remember, you invited the AEC to Mississippi. We agreed for them to work on our land as a matter of patriotism and not otherwise, as we do not believe they will accomplish any good for the State, except a waste of taxpayers' money. I believe, however, if we are going to go through this sort of thing we should see that the money is spent under Mississippi law, and not under Mr. Kennedy's law or Supreme Court law. . . .
>
> It's a good time to call a halt to the whole thing and let them know that you, as the head of the State of Mississippi, are not going to put up with it. . . .
>
> As a private citizen, my position would be until we get rid of the Kennedy brothers, no government money for any purpose. I wouldn't want their projects and I would get them out of the State if I could. Untold harm is already being done to our way of life by government installations such as Keesler Field, where they [black and white servicemen] sleep and eat together.[6]

Despite his avowed opposition to the test program as a loyal American resisting UN pressure and the whims of scientific excess, Tatum wrote another letter on November 11, 1961, to Barnett, Stennis, Eastland,

and Colmer, making a case that had little to do with the environment, the threat of an internationalist government, or miscegenation via government contract. The AEC determined that it would use his land, and he wanted to be paid for it:

> The Atomic Energy Commission, I believe, now agrees with us that they can lease the land on a ten year lease, year-to-year basis. However, they still think they will have to have possession of the salt mass. When you think of a huge mass standing 40,000 to 50,000 feet high and more than a mile in diameter, you are thinking about twenty to thirty cubic miles of salt, billions or trillions of tons all of which may be useful to us as property owners, as storage basins, for the extraction of salt and for industrial purposes.
>
> We see no reason why the government could not also lease the salt mass for the period of time necessary, paying thereon a lease rental and royalty for the salt removed (1/8th of the value of whatever it may be). If the AEC and Dr. Suttle know what they are talking about, only a small portion of this mass will be used or contaminated by the project. . . .
>
> Our family has spent more time, money and energy in the conservation of our natural resources than, I believe, any other group. . . .[7]

Herein lay Tatum's ultimate argument against the federal government's plan. Despite the salt mass's location at a depth where it was not commercially feasible to mine, it had potential value that he did not want to lose. Noting that his family had invested considerable time and money in locating the dome, he felt due compensation was in order. He would happily lease the land above the salt dome, but should any of the mineral wealth be destroyed, he wanted to be reimbursed. The federal government could either buy the portion that would be affected by the tests, or they could buy the whole thing. He did not care; he wanted the money. The government saw the situation differently. It wanted to preserve as much latitude as possible in its contractual obligations to Tatum or the landholders of any other salt dome that might be chosen for the tests. As the choice was narrowed to the two domes in Mississippi, the federal government pursued an aggressive course toward acquiring land for the test site.

In late November 1960, sensing the likelihood of a major government program, directors from several prominent engineering firms formed the Mississippi Construction and Engineering Company (MCEC). This new superfirm drew upon ten million dollars' worth of assets and benefited from local expertise and international support; many of the firms represented on its board of directors had international affiliations. One of the first things the new company did was alert Stennis's office to its existence. In a letter to Stennis's aide Marx Huff, MCEC's vice president of public relations Jack Stuart threw MCEC's hat squarely into the ring: "Our company was formed in order to be large enough to handle any projects which might come to Mississippi and, to our knowledge, this is the first time so many of the large contractors have united in any single effort." The superfirm actively competed for primary, secondary, and support contracts and hoped that with Stennis's political clout it would be able to secure the most important and lucrative arrangements with the government.[8]

Meanwhile, Mellen continued his campaign against the program. In contrast to Tatum's scattershot approach, Mellen's was more like a rifle aimed at governmental impropriety and material waste. He made new accusations to Stennis, arguing that the tests were the means to justify Edward Teller's desire to end the nuclear-test moratorium. He saw Ben Hilburn and Andrew Suttle, the two most prominent officials in MITRC, as sycophantic co-conspirators. Furthermore, MITRC had refused to hire a fully trained geologist. Instead it used a graduate student who was allowed the use of state-owned equipment in exchange for rubber-stamping geological reports pertaining to the Dribble surveys. Calling for science to be "creative but at the same time conservative," Mellen concluded that "most scientists will agree that Project Vela Uniform is ultra-liberal."[9] Just a month and a half earlier, on February 6, 1961, Mellen had written that "destruction of mineral resources is tantamount to the destruction of life," and he charged Humble Oil, the AEC, and the state of Mississippi as accomplices in Suttle's and MITRC's treacherous schemes. He also feared that thermonuclear devices would be detonated in the state's salt domes. As far as Mellen was concerned, a conspiracy was growing wherein several complementary schemes were working in concert to bring a destructive program to Mississippi.[10]

Mellen was not alone in his concern for the state's role in the proposed test program. Lt. Col. James Marsalis, who was retired from the air force, also wrote to Stennis because he feared a veritable environmental apocalypse.

> I would like to bring to your attention the $16,000,000 being spent here in the State of Mississippi blowing up salt domes, by the Atomic Energy Commission.
>
> Senator, an investigation of this activity will make your hair stand on end. Ruined forest and crops—salt forming desert waste as far as the wind blows. Natural rescources [sic] destroyed. Can Mississippi stand such an act? No, not when we are on our way to becomming [sic] a manufacturing and agricultural paradise. There are other places to detonate these expremintal [sic] explosions, with little harm to man or beast.
>
> You have heard of Fred Mellen, who discovered oil at Tinsley. He is a product of our own State and is recognized as one of the foremost scientest [sic] in the United States. It would be amazing for you to hear him.[11]

Marsalis's letter is similar in tone to Mellen's "Statement of Personal Opinion," which had raised the AEC's concerns about Mellen's influence. But what Marsalis and Tatum alluded to was not environmental at all. Tatum's earlier letters portrayed Mississippi as an unspoiled region; Marsalis's letter referred to salt that lay beneath the surface. Possibly Marsalis was referring to plans to bring salt to the surface during excavation, and the potential gain from that, but his argument that Mississippi was a near paradise was far from accurate. Still, his letter indicates the reach of Mellen's opposition to atomic testing in the state.

Mellen's animosity toward Suttle continued. While the MITRC director continued to try to bring atomic energy to Mississippi, Mellen continued to rail at Dribble in general and Suttle in particular, as when he wrote to Stennis on April 12, 1961.

> I may be naïve in not suspecting that the Defense Department had no more than a casual interest in the outcome of Project Vela Uniform, a sub-project of Project Plow Share [sic], supposedly set up for peaceful uses of atomic energy. You will note that the Clarion Ledger article of April 29 stated that the detonation in the Tatum dome and, or in the Bruinsburg dome will be conducted by the Defense department. In other words, the

Defense department is more than a cooperative agent in this undertaking, although Dr. Suttle has told us that the present testing was part of Project Plow Share. If there were any evidence that a decoupled nuclear shot would be of any aid in development of scientific detecting instruments, the project might be a little understandable. It still appears to most of the people that I know over the State of Mississippi that Drew Suttle simply wants to start setting off some nuclear firecrackers just for the sake of seeing what happens, irrespective of the adverse effects, the moral implications and the financial drain on a weak economy.[12]

Mellen was mistaken in his connection of the Vela Progam to Plowshare, although it is understandable why this occurred. Both were non–weapons-testing programs using nuclear devices, and they were commonly confused with each other.

Meanwhile, Suttle was engaged in several important pursuits during the first half of 1961. He was determined to bring Dribble to Mississippi and wanted to prepare the ground as much as possible to prevent last-moment relocation to another state. He also wanted to increase the benefits of the Dribble tests beyond seismic detection to experiments regarding the production of isotopes and heat for electrical-power generation. Suttle's interest in radioisotope generation is unsurprising, as this was his area of expertise. In essence, he wanted to engage in a program similar to what Gnome ultimately became: a combined Plowshare/Vela test wherein materials of industrial importance might be produced. More important, Suttle believed that hydrocarbon and petrochemical experimentation valuable to state industry could be performed in combination with the AEC program. To Suttle, it only made sense to utilize the tests to their utmost economic potential. He could not still every disapproving tongue, but a financial windfall for the state and the region would win the MITRC converts from the ranks of its detractors.[13]

His other ambition focused on the Tenn-Tom Plowshare project. Noting a twenty-five-million-dollar cost savings on the proposed waterway, he pointed out that the size of the waterway could be enlarged with the use of nuclear explosives. It could be upgraded from a unidirectional channel, with periodic expansions along its course to allow opposing river traffic to pass, to a true bidirectional watercourse. He wrote to Stennis:

At the present time . . . it is the feeling of the most competent physicists in the United States that devices which are relatively free of fissile fuels can be constructed and operated with good efficiency and great economy. . . . But I would also emphasize that the peaceful utilization of nuclear explosives is a separate and distinct activity which, I believe, should be completely divorced from the weapons development program and regardless of the decisions reached in that field, that this peaceful utilization should move forward without delay.[14]

Depending upon one's point of view, the news concerning Dribble was promising for the Piney Woods, or it was a looming disaster. On January 1, 1961, a ten-year lease went into effect for the land above the Tatum Dome, with annual extensions negotiable among the AEC, Frank Tatum, and the Bass family.[15] Tatum believed that the agreement had been made under duress: "Some time ago I had a letter from Senator Stennis in which he stated he thought we were in favor of the Atomic Energy Commission's experiments in Mississippi. . . . We did lease to the AEC 1430 acres of land for the experiments, as we were told they would probably condemn it if we didn't." Tatum received $7,344.00 per year, and an additional one-time $7,500.00 payment for expected tree and growth damage at the site. The Bass family, who grew paper-shell pecans on one hundred acres near the dome, leased a parcel of their land to the AEC, receiving $650.00 per year. In all, this amounted to 1,470 acres.[16]

A February 8 newspaper story reported that AEC engineer and Mississippi project engineer Ray C. Emens had stated that the Tatum Dome fully met the technical requirements for the Dribble tests. A week later, Nevada Test Site director James E. Reeves visited the area. Addressing a civic-club meeting in Hattiesburg, he outlined the AEC's past experience with underground testing. He told the group that the only injury caused so far by underground tests had been due to a large kettle of soup overturning and scalding a person at the Nevada site. During the meeting, one waggish reporter asked Reeves whether anyone had considered detonating the subterranean shots beneath the United States Supreme Court building, to which Reeves replied, "That's a heck of a thing to ask a Yankee."[17]

At the Tatum Dome site, once the lease was concluded, roughnecks began drilling into the caprock and the salt below. At one location, twenty-four men employed by Texas Water Wells operated a derrick engaged in drilling exploratory holes and retrieving core samples. Only four men were from the company headquarters in Houston; the rest came from the oilfields of southern Mississippi. It was the same type of hole many of them had dug before, but one driller remarked, "It's the first time I ever worked on one where everybody, from the start, hoped and prayed that it was a dry hole." For the men on the platforms, it was more work in a dwindling oil region. Mississippi's big strikes were playing out, and oilfield work was welcome, although they were fairly certain they would not strike oil. Ironically, an oil strike could have eliminated the Tatum Dome from the list of possible sites listed in the Ripple criteria.[18]

More than anything else, what the men on the derricks did not want to hit high-pressure water. At various depths, sedimentary layers contained large aquifers that could prove problematic. The region's aquifers had long been used as a water supply for people and livestock. Despite standard drilling procedures that lined the drill holes with an impermeable casing as the hole extended downward, water might travel down along the casing to the salt, creating brine that might contaminate several aquifer layers. There were also concerns about the release of radioactive materials. Although the depth of the shots would eliminate the possibility of an atmospheric release, water could scour its way into the test chamber along the casing and convey highly radioactive materials away from the test site and into public contact. Water was trouble.

Operation Concerto had been planned to employ six atomic test shots in different locations and environmental conditions. Dribble would test at one location. The Concerto devices would have ranged in yield from two hundred fifty tons to fifty kilotons. Because of the two primary candidate locations for Dribble, the device sizes would not range as widely in yield. From July 25 to 27, 1961, a special JCAE hearing took place wherein the VU program was first addressed as a whole and the Dribble component fully defined. VU's program manager Theodore A. George outlined a six-shot test program. The devices were code-named Record, at one hundred tons yield; Hayride at five hundred tons yield; Hermit at one hundred tons yield; Gaucho at five kilotons, the highest yield shot; Greenbean at twenty-five kilotons; and Tipsy at five kilotons.

"These tests will furnish us with information on the effectiveness of concealment of an underground explosion by decoupling," George wrote. "All of these tests will be conducted at a depth of 2,500 feet."

First we have three small underground nuclear explosions. Record is to be fired in the center of an underground cavity which will provide for complete decoupling. It will be followed by Hayride having a yield five times as much as Record, but fired in the same cavity. This will provide data on the effects of partial decoupling. Both of these shots will then be compared with Hermit with the same yield as Record, but fully tamped. These three events are expected to take place in the Tatum Salt Dome in Mississippi.

The next three events are also intended to furnish data on decoupling but at a much higher yield level. Here we have Gaucho a 5-kiloton event completely decoupled; Greenbean a 25-kiloton event partially decoupled; and Tipsy the comparison shot of 5 kilotons, tamped.[19]

The Dribble site, which George noted was likely to be located in the Tatum Dome, would require several test locations. At least two chambers would need to be excavated, with a corresponding pair of test tunnels for the two tamped shots. Fortunately, the Tatum Dome was large enough to accommodate this, despite the high-yield series having an explosive force fifty times greater than the low-yield series. Reflecting on one of the questions raised by Cowboy, no one knew what the effects of even a small atomic test in salt would have—specifically, whether the test chamber would be reusable as it would have to be during the Dribble series. Nor did anyone know how the walls of a pre-excavated chamber reacted, or if the salt might fissure and allow high-temperature gases to escape. The first shots in the two series were decoupled, and there would be blast effects on the chamber walls. Furthermore, the second shot in each series would seismically overload or "overdrive" the test chambers with explosive energies five times as powerful as the decoupled shots. Overdriving the chambers would explore insufficiently decoupled devices in shot-created cavities. The chambers had to be structurally sound enough to withstand the stress; it would be five months after the hearings before Gnome gave any indication as to how salt held up to an atomic blast.[20]

World events caused VU and Dribble to quickly regain international importance. On September 1, 1961, the Soviet Union broke the voluntary test moratorium that had been in effect since October 1958 with a sixteen-kiloton atmospheric test of a tactical missile warhead. In September alone, the USSR conducted twenty-six atomic and thermonuclear tests ranging from subkiloton to multimegaton yields. In all, the Soviet Union conducted fifty-nine tests from September 1 through November 4, 1961, including the awesome *Tsar Bomba* on October 30, with an estimated yield of fifty to sixty megatons. On several dates, up to three tests were conducted in a single day; on one day, four devices were detonated. In many cases, these multiple tests were fired at the same test site.[21]

The American nuclear testing program had been dormant for the thirty-four months the moratorium lasted, but on September 15 it roared to life, first at NTS, and later at several sites in the Pacific. Until November 4, 1962, the majority of the American nuclear-testing program had been conducted in the atmosphere. The final Soviet atmospheric test was held on December 25, 1962.During fourteen months of tests by the two superpowers, one hundred were conducted by the United States, and one hundred forty-one by the Soviet Union. The tests were conducted above and below ground, under water, and at high altitude, before the end of atmospheric testing. These tests were carried out regardless of delicate international events; they included seven American and at least four Soviet detonations during the Cuban Missile Crisis.[22]

In early October 1961, the AEC and ARPA selected the Tatum Dome as the site for Dribble, removing the Bruinsburg site from contention. The criteria having been met, field activity was put on standby status, and the Dribble program was further refined.[23] The biggest battle between Tatum and the AEC, over the salt dome itself, was beginning to take shape.

Earlier in the year, Tatum had started to feel that his correspondence to Barnett and others was making the rounds of the AEC. They seemed to know too much about his objections to the way operations on his land were proceeding. For instance, in a letter to Mellen on March 31, 1961, he had railed against the United Nations, "[W]e are not for world government or world court and had thought that the United Nations should be moved to some distant point beneath the ocean." He had also requested that his correspondence be limited in exposure: "[O]ne thing we have found out is, everytime we write, the letter always ends up with the Atomic Energy Commission." Ironically, this letter did end up with Stennis, with a penned notation at the bottom, reading, "Senator: I thought you might want to take note of this—Fred M."[24] This request from Tatum became increasingly common in his correspondence to his elected representatives. His paranoia was warranted; his letters were shared by their recipients with the AEC.

Tatum understood that he was agreeing to a lease on the land and that the mineral-rights question had yet to be addressed. For nearly a year since its decision to locate Dribble at the Tatum Dome, the AEC had believed that a fight with Tatum over the salt was inevitable. Earlier letters from Tatum and Mellen had argued the importance and value of the large salt deposit to the future of Mississippi and, by extension, of the United States. Tatum was not going to mine it, as it would be economically foolish to try to retrieve it. But that did not mean that he would allow it to be devalued. If the salt was going to be used or ruined by the AEC, he wanted fair compensation; he offered to accept one-eighth of the market value for any salt used or destroyed.[25]

The AEC's position was twofold. First, only a portion of the salt was likely to be made radioactive, but a large quantity of salt would be mined during the creation of two enormous test chambers twenty-seven hundred feet underground. This salt would be excavated in one of two ways: by brine mining, in which water washed away the unwanted salt and the resulting brine was pumped to the surface for storage and removal; or by mechanical means. Either way, hundreds of thousands, possibly more than a million, cubic meters of salt would be brought to the surface by contractors employed by the AEC, not by Frank Tatum. Paying Tatum for the salt would amount to undue enrichment at taxpayers' expense. Second, several large shafts would have to be drilled into the salt dome for equipment insertion and salt extraction. These were also regarded as undue enrichment, as they would open the Tatum Dome's resources to easier mining, again at the taxpayers' expense. There would be no investment by Tatum, yet he wanted the salt—or to be paid for it. Tatum replied that would accept condemnation of 2 to 3 percent of the salt mass and all the shafts excavated by the government. But this was unacceptable to the AEC.[26]

The effect of the Tatum salt on the global market was another element in this conflict. Tatum recounted a 1961 visit from a worried representative of the Morton International Salt Company who inquired what would be done with the enormous amount of salt, estimated at two million tons, that would be brought to the surface. Tatum had his own ideas, while NTS director James Reeves offered another possibility: trucking it south and dumping it into the Gulf of Mexico. Estimates of sixteen million dollars for the salt were bandied about, although Tatum considered the figure far too conservative. Before talk of cavernous excavations and atomic testing, Tatum had considered the salt practically worthless because it held no oil or gas. Ironically, it was extremely valuable to the world salt market only if it remained undisturbed; if it was suddenly made available, salt prices would plummet.[27]

The standby period at the Dribble site stretched on for nearly a year. Livermore Radiation Laboratory (LRL) announced on August 15, 1962, that it was ready to take over control of the activities at the site and to appoint a technical manager. Most important, during the standby the configuration of the test program had drastically changed. The number of test shots was halved, from six to three: a five-kiloton tamped shot named Salmon; a hundred-ton decoupled shot named "Sand" that would be fired in a fully excavated test chamber; and a control shot, a hundred-ton tamped blast named Tar.[28] The proposed test program was expected to last a year, from May 1963 to May 1964. The months between October and April were not considered feasible because of a seasonal increase in seismic noise due to atmospheric storms and wave noise from the Gulf of Mexico. The newly configured program would require only one small chamber to be excavated, saving on construction and salt-disposal costs.[29]

In September 1962, the AEC made its move, filing to acquire the mineral rights in the Tatum Dome through condemnation. A letter from AEC general manager Maj. Gen. Alvin R. Luedecke to Senator Stennis explained the government's reason for initiating condemnation proceedings, including the need to control the area where radioactive debris would be contained, and possible damage to surrounding mineral deposits due to tunnels, shafts, and the placement of experiments. In addition:

[O]wnership of a large part of the mineral interests in the land is in dispute, and several parties have indicated that each owns, and will claim title to, the same salt mass within the Tatum Dome. The time required for legal action to clear title to the mineral interests would be incompatible with the current schedule for execution of the series. For this and other reasons, it is the opinion of the Corps of Engineers, acting for the AEC in this matter, that condemnation will be necessary to obtain some or all of the mineral interests.[30]

Tatum was outraged. The claimants to the mineral rights were Tatum, the Bass family, and the Hibernia National Bank in New Orleans. The relationship was complicated: Tatum and Bass laid claim to the surface land, which they acknowledged they had leased to the AEC. But, they said, this did not extend to mineral rights; nor could it, because Tatum had bought the land over the salt dome from Hibernia in 1937, and the bank retained the mineral rights. But, as Tatum wrote, "our attorneys and we, ourselves, have always construed this as it is written to mean Hibernia retained only the oil and gas minerals and that the salt mass belongs to us. We drilled the land and discovered the salt mass after extensive seismographic operation."[31] Luedecke realized that this Gordian knot needed to be severed quickly, or the Dribble site would likely remain in limbo for years as lawsuits dragged on. Tatum was a headstrong man from a powerful family, and such suits would be fought on his home turf to his advantage. While condemnation was distasteful, Tatum would at least be minimally compensated for mineral resources he had no plans to exploit, the surface lease would function as signed, and later the land would be returned. The salt would belong to the government. Of course, Tatum saw this as further evidence of unwanted government intrusion. As usual, he blamed the Kennedy administration's efforts to build "facilities in South Mississippi where the negro and white will have to eat, sleep, bathe, etc., together."[32] Tatum favored a mineral lease, and he continued to demand from the government terms more favorable than condemnation.

On October 15, 1962, a memo went out naming Dominic Magnetti as the temporary project officer for Project Dribble. Magnetti, normally an operations officer at the Nevada Operations Office (NVOO), was transferred to the Hattiesburg Project office and from there began to prepare for the bidding process. The AEC's primary contractor Holmes & Narver (H&N) sought subcontractors to carry out the work at the Dribble site.

Magnetti held his post for only a month before he was replaced by Leonard J. Yelinek, who would be the permanent manager of the Dribble site. Yelinek had worked at NTS in 1956 as a project engineer; in January 1962 he was area engineer for Pacific operations in Honolulu. His duties were primarily administrative, while men such as Jim Reeves did the publicity work, traveling from NTS to answer questions from local residents at civic meetings.[33]

In late October, Holmes & Narver issued a notice to mining and engineering firms, calling for bids to excavate the underground chamber for the decoupling test at Dribble. This was the most lucrative of all the contracts at the site, and five firms ultimately submitted proposals: the Dravo Corporation in Pittsburgh; Kerr-McGee Oil Industries in Oklahoma City; Brown and Root in Houston; the Camay Drilling Company/Patrick Harrison in Los Angeles and Golden, Colorado; and the Mississippi Construction and Engineering Company.[34] This contract was the reason the MCEC had been formed; it would keep much of the project money in Mississippi while furthering Barnett's promotion of the state's technical development. Stennis went to work immediately to promote the superfirm's bid, telegraphing Reeves and meeting with Mike Manatos of Kennedy's staff to agitate for their cause. Stennis claimed that he was not seeking special favors for the group, but "with everything being like equal, this Company is entitled to a break and that is the reason for the Senator's call."[35] This was not true. Stennis took a strong personal interest in the success of the MCEC and continued to lobby on its behalf.

In the end, their efforts failed. The first notification of the decision came on the evening of Monday, December 3. Reeves called Stennis's office in De Kalb, Mississippi, to notify him that not only was the MCEC's bid not chosen, it was "low on the list." Reeves acknowledged Stennis's lobbying efforts and said that "if Senator wanted to take it up higher in Washington, of course he could."[36] Defeated, the MCEC waited for the opportunity to bid on future contracts. Despite the proximity of the member firms, their apparent familiarity with the region and their international affiliates, MCEC lost to the Camay/Patrick Harrison (CPH) partnership. Camay had established itself as a competent drilling firm; prior to the contract, it had been working for the Pan American Petroleum Corporation, prospecting for oil in Utah. Little is known of Patrick Harrison, Inc., except that it was also engaged in mine and tunnel work.[37] CPH prepared to excavate the ninety-five-foot-diameter spherical test chamber, as well as a vertical forty-two-inch-diameter shaft drilled next to the location of the chamber and connected by an "uphill drift," or inclined connecting tunnel, that would allow mined salt to be removed for surface storage. Other ventilation and auxiliary shafts, drilled to the test chamber approximately two thousand feet below the surface, would also be excavated by the CPH. It would later prove to be a pyrrhic victory for CPH; it was a lump of Christmas coal for the MCEC.[38]

A little more than a month later, an important contract was issued to another outside firm. Six ten-inch-diameter shafts, ranging from one thousand to four thousand feet deep, needed to be drilled at the site; oilfield veteran Big Chief Drilling Company of Oklahoma City won the bid. In business since the mid-1930s, the company had a reputation for achieving previously unheard of depths in the Oklahoma oilfields; in 1956, one of its wells had reached a depth of sixteen thousand feet. Beating out seven competitors, Big Chief was to create the deep holes required by the two tamped tests and the accompanying shafts for monitoring equipment. Big Chief would become an increasingly important subcontractor at the site.[39]

One bright spot for Mississippi industry in relation to Dribble came on March 9, 1963, when a firm from Laurel, the Studdard Workover Company, contracted with Reynolds Electrical and Engineering Company (REECO) to rework five instrument holes at the site to prepare them for use in the tests. REECO had long been associated with America's atomic-testing program. Like Holmes & Narver, it was a primary contractor for the AEC; H&N assumed responsibility for the physical preparation of the test sites, while REECO and another firm, Edgerton, Germeshausen and Grier (EG&G) took care of the electrical and electronic tasks, respectively. The cofounder of this firm, Dr. Harold Edgerton, developed remarkably synchronous timing and firing circuitry for both atomic devices and recording equipment.[40] Studdard Workover's contract with Reynolds was an encouraging development; it was important work and, though unrelated to device emplacement or chamber excavation, refurbishing the previously drilled instrumentation holes saved the Dribble program money and put a Mississippi drilling firm to work at the site.[41]

The MCEC might have been defeated, but Frank Tatum was not. His next destination was the chancery court in Lamar County, where he conceded the oil rights at the Tatum Dome but claimed that the salt had been discovered three years after he bought the land. Since he had discovered the salt, he maintained, it was completely and totally his. Furthermore, he charged that the government condemnation was an expedient wholly designed to avoid a hearing on the matter. The AEC had filed Civil Action 1765 in the United States District Court, seeking to obtain all mineral rights in the salt dome for $32,235.00. Tatum countered that his family had spent $125,000.00 in the process of discovering the salt dome; furthermore, the $32,235.00 would have to be divided between Tatum and the Hibernia Bank. Tatum estimated that he would receive between $1,400.00 and $1,500.00.[42]

On December 21, 1962, the federal court in Jackson issued an order of possession condemning the salt dome. Tatum attempted to ameliorate his losses by arguing that only part of the salt should be condemned—the portion that contained the tests. If it would satisfy AEC chairman Glenn Seaborg, Tatum's political representatives, and his attorneys, this could also include any shafts, excavations, or anything else that could constitute undue enrichment. This proposal, too, was rejected by the AEC, which felt that an all-or-nothing approach was preferable to partial condemnation, thus removing the possibility of further wrangling over salt. By April 1963, the issue was largely decided. Tatum would have little to do with proceedings at the Dribble site while it remained under government control. His compensation exceeded his expectations; the AEC paid him $142,164.25 for the mineral rights to the salt dome. The land was leased, the salt belonged to the government, and that was that.[43]

6. Salmon Run

WHILE THE SALT UNDER THE DRIBBLE SITE WAS CONTESTED IN the courts, Hattiesburg began feeling the effects of the impending test program. Well drillers, necessary for site surveying and sampling, had been active since late 1960, sinking shafts into the caprock, salt, and surrounding soil to chart the location of aquifers and sedimentary strata. The Dribble program's schedule had set the first nuclear shot for May 1963. This gave the contractor, Camay/Patrick Harrison, barely five months from awarding the contract to complete the job of excavating the ninety-five-foot-diameter decoupling chamber. The wells drilled through the caprock and deep into the salt dome had to penetrate numerous layers of sand, clay, and gravel. Within some of these layers were aquifers, some containing fresh water and some containing brine. Like underground rivers, the aquifers generally flowed at constant rates. Farmers and residents of the region knew the aquifers well; they had tapped them for fresh water for themselves and their livestock for many years. Eventually, water would lead to a reappraisal of the whole Dribble site; for a time it appeared that the AEC might have to leave Mississippi prematurely.

The flip side of this dilemma was a benefit to Hattiesburg, because the longer the crews worked at the site the longer they would stay in the city and contribute to its economy. Despite the hubbub raised by Tatum over the condemnation of the mineral rights, the city was eager to do business with the federal government. Hattiesburg had long been an intersection of road and rail lines, and it had a commercial airport. Southern Airways and Delta Airlines operated regularly out of Hattiesburg; with the need to transport equipment and personnel to and from the test site, the air force anticipated operating from there as well. To do this, the air force needed to fly its mainstay transport aircraft, the Lockheed C-130 Hercules, from the Hattiesburg airport. The Hercules was designed for relatively short takeoffs and landings. Its six-wheel under-carriage maximized the aircraft's "footprint" or weight distribution. Still, the Hattiesburg public-works commissioner, C. B. "Pat" Patterson,[1] and air force personnel were concerned about whether the city's existing strip could handle the large transports. The aircraft were attached to the Air Force Technical Applications Command (AFTAC), which had been created long before Vela as the primary military department dedicated to atomic-test detection. In addition to transporting equipment and personnel, AFTAC aircraft would observe the Dribble tests from the air; the Hercules's long range and endurance were a benefit for extended loiter-time observation.

In mid-May 1963, AFTAC notified Patterson of its desire to oper-ate from the Hattiesburg airport. AFTAC sent a packet of information, including a pilot's manual for the C-130A, to provide operational and technical specifications, as well as loading tables that showed the Her-cules's weight distribution was similar to the older, more familiar C-47. Patterson replied that consultation with airport engineers led to some concerns that would be diminished by drier weather, because wet soil beneath the runway could lead to damage from heavily laden airplanes.[2] AFTAC was certainly welcome to operate from the Hattiesburg airport, wrote Patterson, but, "[W]e would grant our permission for landing your aircraft on the condition that if any damage is done to the runways, we would expect your agency to reimburse the City for the cost of repairs." Wishing to simplify operations and keep expenses down, AFTAC opened an operations office in Hattiesburg on May 27. On June 3, AFTAC no-tified Patterson that it would stage its aircraft from Brookley Field in Mobile, Alabama. This removed any possibility that AFTAC could be held liable for damage to the Hattiesburg airport, including normal wear and tear on the facilities.[3]

The dates of the airport correspondence reveal the official decision to push the date for the first test, the five-kiloton Salmon, from May to the week of July 8, 1963. That was still within the one-year window, and the extra two months gave the excavation crews precious additional time considering the fickle spring and summer weather in the South. Other important work had already been conducted in relation to the Dribble tests. Between April 1 and 10, some twenty chemical high-explosive tests had been conducted within a one hundred twenty-mile radius around the test site. Ranging from five hundred to four thousand pounds, the blasts were conducted to investigate further seismic anomalies that could affect the shock wave from the nuclear tests, and to calibrate recording equipment.[4]

While AFTAC and the airport were negotiating the use of the Hattiesburg airport, nine single-story structures were erected at distances varying from three-fifths of a mile to three and one-half miles from the Dribble test site. Two of these were cement-block buildings, while the other two were of frame construction. They were arrayed along two axes: one toward Baxterville to the south, and one toward Purvis to the east. These structures were instrumented and used to assess the ground movement from the five-kiloton Salmon test. Although noted as an experimental program in their own right, test buildings had less to do with the scientific observation of ground motion caused by a test in a salt dome and more to do with indemnification of the AEC, which knew that many structures in the area were vulnerable to damage or collapse. The experimental buildings would act as controls when the expected claims came rolling in after the Salmon test. While safeguarding citizens, the AEC was reducing its own liability.[5]

An April 5 memo from Alvin Luedecke to Gen. Austin W. Betts, director of the AEC's Department of Military Applications following Starbird, noted that the Dribble program was on schedule. According to Luedecke, the program had "now reached the point where it is considered essential to initiate a rather intensive public information program in order to assure continuing public acceptance of the program and to initiate actions required so that the proposed mid-summer detonation schedule for the initial shot may be met." This comprised an area-wide structural survey to be conducted by Holmes & Narver engineers; contacts between local residents and United States Public Health Service (USPHS) representatives attached to the Dribble program; and the drafting of form letters to local residents who would have to either evacuate the area or be outside their houses during the test. Timetables specified certain points of contact with Governor Barnett, local officials, and the AEC. As it turned out, this schedule was wildly optimistic, but in April and May 1963, a July date for Salmon looked possible.[6]

As Frank Tatum had previously explained to Barnett, the region around the Tatum Salt Dome "is blessed with many creeks, streams, branches and springs, and practically all of our people have artesian water available." That water proved difficult to drill through. The sites where CPH had begun operations struck water on the way down to their target depth. This was not unexpected, as core samples revealed the existence of several aquifer layers between the surface and the top of the caprock. Oil drillers were experts at keeping overlying water from flowing into oil wells. The most common method was to line the hole with a metal casing extending to the bottom of the well and puncture it at levels where desirable materials—natural gas and oil—had been located by core-sample analysis. The contractors drilling at the salt dome found it excessively difficult to prevent water from entering their boreholes because of the large diameters of the wells. This threatened the most important test at the Dribble site, the decoupling test. For the ninety-five-foot-diameter chamber to be excavated at a depth of two thousand feet, some twelve hundred feet of overlying soil, clay, sand, aquifers, and caprock had to be penetrated before even reaching the salt. Then the hole had to continue for almost eight hundred feet before reaching the excavation site. There had to be at least two such holes, and they had to be absolutely watertight to ensure the safety of those excavating the chamber. In a best-case scenario, a water leak into the chamber would hamper the excavation; in a worst-case scenario, a catastrophic leak could kill the excavation crew hollowing out the subterranean cavity and ruin the salt dome beyond further use.

Water posed another threat to the test itself. If any was present in the test chamber, it would immediately flash into steam when the decoupled shot was fired, adding mechanical energy to the test and potentially affecting the data. Steam caused by a tamped test could work its way through fissures that occurred naturally in the dome or that were caused by the detonation of the test device. It could also blast the plug of concrete and gravel into the atmosphere like a giant cannon. The water had to be contained or another option had to be found. The vent shaft to the chamber—penetrating to two thousand feet, cased with thirty-inch-diameter pipe one hundred fifty feet into the dome, and sealed with cement grout and other materials—defied all efforts at waterproofing and caused months of delay. Although it was pumped dry on November 1, 1963, eighteen days later it was found to be filled with water that reached "within several hundred feet from the top." The thirty-inch-diameter ventilation shaft was the smallest of the three needed for the cavity excavation; the seventy-inch production shaft had been abandoned at nine hundred fifty feet because of casing failure.[7]

James Reeves, the Nevada Operations office manager, stayed up to date on the bad news. Despite the best efforts of the engineers, drillers, and hydrologists, all three shafts were constantly flooded by pressurized water that forced its way past the grouting materials and casing. In December, ordering a "thorough study by highly qualified authorities in the country of the engineering problems that have been encountered in construction work at the Project Dribble site," Reeves cut back the operations at the site "to a status of minimal activity." In short, the Dribble tests would not be conducted soon, if at all. The year 1963 ended with Dribble again in limbo while the AEC and its consultants scratched their heads. It was cold comfort that environmental factors would only allow for the testing window to open again in April 1964, when accurate seismic data could again be recorded.[8]

The problems at the Dribble site did not stop the overall progress of the VU program. On October 26, 1963, the first atomic test of the series was fired at Fallon, Nevada. Yielding twelve kilotons, the device, code-named Shoal, was a tamped shot detonated twelve hundred feet below ground in a shaft. Shoal was a fully contained seismic experiment. Although it was initially planned to follow the first Dribble test, there was no reason to hold it up—especially in light of increasing competition for funding. Already Vela had been reduced in size, and it could potentially be further dismembered by the accountant's ax. By proceeding with the series, the AEC could show some return for the money and planning that had been spent on Vela and the doomed Concerto series.

The flooding problem at the Dribble site condemned the shafts for the excavation of the chamber for the decoupling test. This experiment was one of the primary reasons for choosing the Tatum Dome; the other was that it could accommodate both phases of the originally proposed series. If it could not be used for the decoupling tests, they would have to be moved elsewhere. During the lull in activities at the test site, several other salt domes that had originally been considered for the Ripple/ Dribble program were reappraised. Environmental conditions limited the time when seismic data could be clearly received to the period between April and November, when weather-related and other seismic noise was relatively low. This pause in activities at the site gave engineers time to examine what course should be followed. Salmon was a less troublesome shaft to drill. Due to its yield, it had to be detonated where it would have a lesser effect on the surrounding population. Sand and Tar were much smaller and could be staged in a greater variety of locations. The Dribble program started with six atomic tests, then dropped to three; the growing likelihood was that the Tatum Dome would be the site of only one shot.

Ross Barnett had actively encouraged high-tech industry in Mississippi, and he had supported segregation during his administration. The 1963 gubernatorial campaign saw the end of Barnett's political career. His lieutenant governor Paul Johnson Jr., the son of former governor Paul Johnson Sr., was elected governor. While campaigning, the younger Johnson had expressed segregationist sentiments that accorded with Barnett's rhetoric, but upon his inauguration, his tone changed dramatically. Despite his efforts to keep James Meredith out of the University of Mississippi, and his gubernatorial tenure's being tarred by the disappearance of civil-rights workers, Johnson was a man of conscience who realized that Mississippi would never progress if gross racial inequalities were permitted to continue. Johnson managed to anger just about everyone during his time as governor because he actively refused to segregate or desegregate Mississippi. Most important, he did not stand in the way of the changing social situation in his state. He would not oppose change, preferring a laissez-faire approach coupled with continuing efforts to bring technologically advanced industry to the state. That proved to be a wise choice, as demonstrated when Litton Industries decided to locate its Shipyard of the Future in Pascagoula in 1967. The challenge to southern governors in the age of expanding federal defense contracts was to maintain a connection to the old ways while changing their tone enough to satisfy Washington.[9]

While weather and budgetary threats loomed, construction at the site resumed in earnest in April 1964, as a second shaft for the Salmon device, designated Station 1A, was begun. This new hole, seventeen and one-half inches in diameter, progressed steadily as new methods of grouting the casing avoided the water problem from the previous year. The target depth for Station 1A was twenty-seven hundred feet. The first twenty-two hundred feet would be cased with steel and the final five hundred feet excavated directly into the salt stock. This uncased portion of the hole was to eliminate the casing from the region where the maximum predicted "chimney" area would be located. The chimney was expected to develop where the material fractured and loosened by the detonation collapsed into the blast cavity. Because the salt was rigid, and the upper limit of it was buried 1,469 feet below caprock and overlying strata, a subsidence crater would not form. Instead, a spherical chamber would initially be created by the blast, and shortly thereafter molten and fractured salt would drop to the bottom of the chamber, giving the expected cavity an egg-like shape, with the lower part partially filled with melted and crumbled debris. The prediction of the chimney's maximum height was 435 feet. The absence of the steel casing enhanced the blast's ability to help stem the emplacement hole as fractured materials were blasted up toward the surface. This worked in concert with the materials poured from the surface down the hole, a mixture of pea gravel and concrete, added shortly after the device was emplaced. In addition, should the casing extend into the chimney region, it would likely be seriously damaged and would complicate or completely frustrate any efforts to utilize the Station 1A shaft for chamber reentry.[10]

In addition to Station 1A, numerous other shafts were sunk into the salt dome. Along with reopened and reworked instrumentation holes, several new shafts for instrumentation and water sampling were drilled at various locations around the 1,750-acre site. The depths for the instrumentation holes varied greatly, ranging from near-surface emplacements to those below the Salmon emplacement depth. All the holes within an 1,100-foot radius of the detonation point were stemmed in the same fashion as the Salmon emplacement hole, using gravel and concrete to block the escape of highly pressurized gases from the detonation. The sampling wells were drilled to the depth of their respective aquifers, with several wells assigned to each aquifer to detect the quantity, direction, and speed of any radioactive contamination, if it was released.[11]

Satisfactory progress also continued at the Dribble site where NVOO manager Reeves issued more timetables and technical information to the parties involved in the test. Along with enhanced safety procedures, and concerns regarding nearby oil and water wells, Salmon was finally assigned an official operational period, beginning on July 10, 1964, and indefinitely continuing into the postshot period. A second test phase was planned for 1966. Salmon was projected to be ready for early September 1964.[12]

Still, there was the question of the other two Dribble shots, Sand and Tar. Salmon's emplacement was comparatively simple, because keeping the water out of Station 1A was proving effective, but the larger holes needed for chamber excavation were not technically feasible in the wet environment over the dome. Thirty-nine salt domes were originally considered candidates for the Ripple/Dribble program. Of these, eight domes in Texas and Louisiana were reappraised for the decoupling test. The resulting report pointed to the Hockley Dome thirty-five miles northwest of Houston. Because it was a salt mine, it had a large sixteen-by-sixteen-foot shaft that ran 1,650 feet deep into the dome. It had lift and hoist equipment to handle the removal of large quantities of salt, and it was fully ventilated. It had originally been approved for the Phase I low-yield tests of the Ripple/Dribble program. Excavation and instrumentation of a decoupling chamber could be accomplished relatively quickly. The main piercing points at Hockley were free of aquifers, so water intrusion would not be a problem. The tamped Tar shot would require a shaft similar to Salmon's, about two thousand feet deep into the Hockley Dome. The Sand cavity could be excavated from within the mine, requiring about twenty-five hundred feet of new shafts. Hockley would be cheaper than the Tatum Dome; it was estimated to cost $13,195,000 versus $13,860,260 at the Mississippi site. Strangely, this figure did not include the cost of buying the actual site. The trade-offs included the proximity to a major metropolitan area (not considered a hazard due to the very low yield but problematic in terms of public opinion), and the effect on the seismic program caused by the use of two test sites for Dribble. Program managers recommended continuing the investigation into relocating the two small shots to Texas.[13]

Back in Mississippi, ground-motion surveys and predictions led to the delineation of a 1.6-mile radius around the test site, where an additional force equal to gravity (1G) was expected. James Reeves returned to the site in July and August to address the sixty people who lived in this area. As part of the site preparations, H&N surveyed residences and other structures and prepared detailed drawings of each to brace them against the expected shock. The USPHS ordered pads and blankets to protect furniture and packing materials to safeguard delicate possessions. Propane tanks were braced and secured, and ten house trailers were set aside as emergency housing in case homes were damaged and uninhabitable. An ample amount of water was contained in tanks and trucks to supply thirty-two of the sixty-two families in the two nearest zones to the detonation, as well as their livestock. Ten three- to five-kilowatt generators could supply electricity in the event of damage to power lines.[14]

The preshot evacuation plan was complicated by the wind. Before the test, some residents would be asked to evacuate the area, while others would be advised to remain outside their homes until the test was concluded. Three areas around the test site were designated A, B, and C. Zone A was described as being "irregularly shaped" and covered all homes out to 1.6 miles from ground zero. These people would evacuate the area; their proximity to the site not only left them vulnerable to the shock of the blast, but accidental failure of the stemming could lead to their being fatally irradiated. Zone B extended from the outer boundary of Zone A to 2.6 miles from ground zero. These people would be allowed to remain on their property but were advised to remain outdoors until told otherwise, to prevent injury from a house or chimney collapse. Ground-motion analyses by the Roland F. Beers firm suggested that the region should receive a sharp jolt. Although the intensity would be milder than the shock expected in Zone A, it could be more than enough to turn shelf contents and wall decorations into missiles. Zone C was the downwind sector that would be determined on the day of the shot by meteorologists. It incorporated part of Zone B and would be extended outward as dictated by wind speed. Like Zone A, Zone C would have to be evacuated until it was determined that the stemming had held and radioactive leakage was unlikely.[15]

Securing the test site and the surrounding area was the responsibility of private and public safety officials. Private security guards patrolled the site itself, while local and state police were slated to man roadblocks and safeguard houses in the region. Perhaps the most important security service was that of radiation-safety (rad safety) officers whose job was to detect and monitor any radiation release from the test. Fanning out over the area before and after the shot, these crucial safety personnel could quickly evacuate endangered civilians in the path of an atmospheric release. The rad-safety personnel also monitored wells and aquifers, taking preshot baseline radiation readings for comparison with postshot conditions. Naturally occurring radioactive substances are commonly found in well water in minute quantities. Knowing what already was present would help allay public fears and allow precise detection of any radioactive leakage into underground water sources.

With the holes for device emplacement and instrumentation nearing completion, final site preparation began in July. Further delayed by a couple of weeks, Salmon was rescheduled for September 22, 1964, at 10:00 a.m. Before it could be fired, several auxiliary and support structures had to be constructed. Outside of a 1.7-mile perimeter from the Salmon surface ground zero (SGZ), a control point (CP) was established. The Technical Director's Manned Station (TDMS) was constructed a mile from Station 1A. The detonation party and site reentry teams would be stationed there during the test, and access would be highly restricted during the maximum-security phase of the test program. This phase of operations was designated by the arrival of the test device at the site— ideally five days before the test date—and was expected to last for three days after the shot. This maximum-security period could be extended as needed. An observer area three and one-quarter miles from the shot was developed for media, interested civilians, and personnel not essential at the CP or TDMS. A one hundred fifty-foot radio repeater tower would also be located at the observer's area, along with a support trailer. An electrical facility, including a transformer and distribution station, was constructed at the site under the control of REECO.[16]

Not far from Station 1A, the assembly area—large enough for a trailer —was graded, leveled, and surrounded by a security fence. Here, the Salmon device would be prepared following its transportation from LRL. Nearby were several earth berms erected for high-explosives handling and assembly for the immediate preshot high-explosive test series. These areas were tightly controlled and, during the maximum-security phase, would be the most inaccessible parts of the site.[17]

Near the Salmon emplacement hole, a "bleeddown" plant was built. This facility was crucial to the chamber-reentry phase of operations at the site, which was scheduled to begin within several days of the shot. The bleeddown facility would be connected to the well head as the reentry hole was drilled. Once the shot point was reached, any pressurized gases produced by the blast would be diverted to a large condensation and holding tank, called a "blooie tank," at the facility. The gases would then be cooled and scrubbed of as much radioactive material as possible and diluted with air; the resultant efflux would be released into the atmosphere. Once pressure had been equalized, air would be injected into the cavity to remove the remainder of the gases, which would likewise be scrubbed at the bleeddown plant, diluted, and released. Air monitors surrounded the test site, and any spike in radiation would be immediately noticed. The radioactive contaminants collected in the condensation tanks would then be disposed of. Depending on the levels of radioactivity, the waste might be stored on site or shipped to a disposal facility such as Oak Ridge, Tennessee. After the cavity was purged of hot radioactive gas, cameras and sampling equipment could be lowered into the resultant cavity. One of the goals of the original Dribble program was to find out whether the cavity created by a five-kiloton test could be reused to decouple a twenty-five-kiloton shot. Reentry and inspection of the cavity would suggest whether this was possible.[18]

On August 6, the nineteenth anniversary of the bombing of Hiroshima, a public-information meeting was held at the Baxterville School. It was attended by James Reeves; director of AEC public information Henry Vermillion; Hattiesburg office director Leonard "Buck" Yelinek; Lawrence Radiation Laboratory project director Dr. Phillip Randolph; director of AEC project operations William W. Allaire; and Mississippi Research and Development Commission director Dr. Robert Dye. Also at the meeting were Phil Allen of the Meteorological Service; Joseph Lang of the USGS; Mel Carter, director of the United States Public Health Laboratory in Montgomery, Alabama; Roland F. Beers; and Tom McCormick from H&N. The shot date was a month and a half away, and despite the increasing pace of preparations on and off site, the project administrators displayed a relaxed, easygoing attitude during the meeting. Following Vermillion's introduction, Reeves declined to revisit project information reported by the *Hattiesburg American* and other news sources, concentrating instead on the impending actions planned for the area. He believed that the delay in the Salmon test was a positive situation; the extra time spent solving the engineering and construction problems at the Dribble site meant the Salmon test would be safer. Still, the two causes for concern were accidental radiation release and ground motion. Admitting that there might be "some damage to structures, cracked plaster, [and] broken windows" and that "maybe a chimney or two will fall down," Reeves noted that claims would be settled either by repairing the damage or with monetary settlements.

Allaire arrived late to the meeting, having gotten lost en route to the school. Reeves joked that Allaire had either gotten lost or had run afoul of the local police. Allaire's sense of direction may have been poor, but his timing was perfect; he was to brief the assembled residents on evacuation plans for the forthcoming test. The plan for September 22 was to evacuate all residents within the 1.6-mile radius of the test, Zone A, at 7:30 a.m. They were expected to be away from their homes for most of shot day, as were those who lived in the downwind sector, Zone C, which was assumed to be the northern quadrant of Zone B extending out to five miles from SGZ. The downwind sector would not be specified until the day before the test. All residents would be allowed back as soon as monitoring personnel were certain that no radioactive leakage had occurred. While the evacuation was in effect, helicopters would patrol for unauthorized persons and emergency situations such as fires. For their inconvenience, each adult who evacuated these sectors would be paid ten dollars, and each child under twelve would receive five dollars.

The people in Zone B who were not in the downwind sector would be asked to remain outdoors during the shot but would then be allowed back into their homes. Allaire suggested that people who lived in an area from the outside perimeter of Zone B, 2.6 miles, to a farther distance of 4.6 miles, might also remain outdoors to avoid falling objects indoors; while it was not necessary, it was "just an extra precaution."

Once the all-clear was given, probably in midafternoon, public health personnel would escort heads of household to their properties to check that their homes were sound. Damage would be radioed to the CP, and assessors would be dispatched to survey the damage and compare it with H&N's preshot surveys of all the dwellings and buildings in the area. The General Adjustment Bureau, a "professional claims adjustment group," would then handle the paperwork and expedite the claims. The five-thousand-dollar limit on individual damage claims was set by the Atomic Energy Act; Allaire doubted that any damage would reach that amount. One reason for this was the preparations for structural bracing made by H&N. Structures in the A and B zones were slated for aggressive bracing. Tom McCormack of H&N noted the concern for bracing "foundations and chimneys and porches and anything that's susceptible to ground motion." Residents within a 4.6-mile radius were divided into five groups according to their distance from the shot point. Following the meeting they were invited to see the bracing suggestions and plans that H&N had created for each structure. H&N would contact each homeowner before bracing homes and other structures. Finally, Vermillion advised that a public observation area had been established at the Dawson Johnson farm between Baxterville and the Tatum Dome. He made the cryptic statement, "I don't think anybody is going to see anything because I don't think there will be anything to see; but nevertheless, there will be a place from which you could see something if there were anything to see at all."

After the presentation, residents were invited to ask questions. Most were expected and quickly answered. Emergency water for humans and animals would be available nearby if needed; livestock was not expected to be heavily affected because the evacuation would be of short duration; structural bracing, not mandatory but strongly advised, would be paid for by the AEC; packing materials would be provided, but it would be up to the homeowners to safeguard their household possessions. Plastered walls and ceilings could suffer damage; the AEC would fix or pay for any damages. Structural changes made since the original H&N surveys would be accounted for and new surveys made so that buildings could be correctly braced.

Some questions were surprising. One concerned the ability of tele-phones and televisions to pick up AEC radio transmissions. A REECO en-gineer explained that the problem was more likely related to the televi-sions than to the AEC's equipment. The REECO engineer was at a loss to explain the telephone interference and referred the frustrated resident to the phone company. The unnamed resident replied that the phone company was of no help, and that the reception of AEC radio traffic was especially annoying during expensive long-distance conversations.

Another question, involving ground motion, prompted a response from Roland Beers, whose firm had consulted for the AEC for years and was widely recognized for its experience in ground-motion prediction and analysis. Using a large map of the area, he estimated the shock effects in terms of units of gravity (Gs), and the relationship between shock forces equivalent to fractional amounts of gravity and damage. The area within the 1.6-mile radius was expected to experience forces equivalent to an additional 1 G, if not slightly more. At 4.5 miles, the shock was expected to be 0.1 G, and the shock would likely not produce any damage. Beers was then asked to "describe in words people would understand about how much the ground would shake." Beers responded that "everyone within this radius of four and one half miles will get a tingling in the toes. It won't hurt you. It may be fun." For those closer to the test, within 1.6 miles, they "would get a jolt which would be comparable to jumping off a curbstone, for example. You could, of course, jump off a curbstone and turn your ankle so that it would hurt, but that is about the extent of it. If you landed squarely on your feet, the force of gravity would not hurt you, and if you translate this feeling on or into what your house might do, perhaps you would have an understanding of how we feel about the predictions."

Vermillion also fielded a question regarding future activities at the Dribble site. He noted that two "much considerably smaller" tests were scheduled, but it was unclear if they would be fired at the salt dome; if they were, it would be much later, and they would be far smaller than Salmon. Once the question-and-answer session ended, those attending were divided into groups and invited to look over the H&N bracing plans for their structures.[19]

Many scientific recording instruments were scheduled for emplacement during the Salmon test. Four deep instrumented holes surrounding Station 1A contained seventy-one instruments belonging to Sandia Corporation, designed to record subsurface and surface motion. Vertical accelerometers emplaced at one thousand and at nineteen hundred feet in seven different holes were the responsibility of the Stanford Research

Institute. LRL, the stewards of the Salmon device, would also monitor crystal pressure gauges emplaced within the salt to measure the stresses on the salt from the blast. The United States Coast and Geodetic Survey was responsible for several seismic stations. Linear seismograph arrays stretched east and south from the shot point, consisting of six recorders at distances ranging between three-quarters of a mile and four miles. Other stations were located at the Baxterville oil field five miles to the southwest, the Pontiac Eastern Refinery three miles north of Purvis, and one each at Purvis, Wiggins, Ellisville, Beaumont, Prentiss, and Tylertown. Another station was located at Bogalusa, Louisiana. Several other stations were operated by the USCGS about seventy-five miles from the shot point, and one of their research ships operated a submarine seismograph off the coast of the Yucatán Peninsula to record the Salmon shot.

The USGS operated three seismic stations at a range of seventy-five miles from the SGZ. ARPA operated five seismic stations that would actively monitor the Salmon test. They included Vernal, Utah; Fort Sill, Oklahoma; McMinnville, Tennessee; Baker, Oregon; and Payson, Arizona. Geotech Corporation, acting under the supervision of AFTAC, operated some forty seismic stations located more than twelve hundred miles from the Dribble site. Although seismological development was the primary goal of Salmon, other nonseismological programs would be conducted with Salmon, including detection of visual and photographic effects of the shot, electromagnetic research, piezoelectric and solid-state changes in rock strata, and seismic-noise research.[20]

In addition to these programs, many others were interested in monitoring Salmon. Seismographic stations from around the world anxiously awaited the shot, including several within the Soviet Union. Newspapers openly reported the proposed shot date and time as well as the device yield, depth of emplacement, and precise geographical location. In a surprising break from typical atomic-testing secrecy, Salmon was a public spectacle—that is, as public as an underground test could be.

Seismic departments at colleges and universities around the globe looked forward to the test. Instead of waiting for unpredictable earthquakes, an expected seismic source of a known magnitude would allow further calibration and synchronization between stations. One of these independent stations was located some one hundred miles from Dribble at Spring Hill College in Mobile, Alabama. The small Jesuit college had benefited from the order's attention to seismology after the 1906 San Francisco earthquake, which it undertook as a service to humanity. The college also benefited from the presence of its one-man seismology department and innovator, Father Louis Eisele. His contributions to the field included the development of an electronically coupled seismograph that recorded on paper in ink that would not clog the recording pen with fungal growth. This replaced the standard method of using mechanical seismographs that recorded on photographic paper. In 1962, Spring Hill College joined the World Wide Network of Standard Seismic Systems (WWNSSS), adding six more machines for Eisele to care for. They were of the older photographic type that Eisele had replaced with his 1952 development of paper-and-ink machines. He was the first to report to the world the tremendous magnitude 8.6 earthquake in Prince William Sound in Alaska on March 27, 1964; the event was so strong it nearly broke his recording equipment. The data recorded at the technologically advanced seismic station at Spring Hill College would be particularly valuable because the Louann Salt that spawned the Tatum Dome extended deep beneath the college.[21]

In August, invitations went out to local officials and media personnel to witness the Salmon shot. A press brief from the AEC to news reporters and editors cautioned that "news media representatives should be aware that they probably will not see any effects of the detonation at shot time. It is probable that there will be noticeable ground motion at the observer area which is located about three and one-half miles from the explosion point." The brief also mentioned the evacuation and compensation of local residents and the plans for structural bracing and damage compensation.[22]

Hattiesburg mayor Claude F. Pittman and city engineer Pat Patterson received identical letters from Jim Reeves:

> As you know, the Advanced Research Projects Agency of the Department of Defense and the United States Atomic Energy Commission are scheduled to detonate a nuclear device deep underground at the Commission's Project Dribble site near Hattiesburg on Tuesday, September 22. We would like to take this opportunity to invite you to participate in Project Dribble as an official observer.

We would like you to be aware, however, that we do not anticipate any visual effects to result from the detonation. It is also possible that there will be delays on an hour-to-hour or day-to-day basis due to unfavorable weather conditions, technical considerations, or for other reasons. We will inform you in advance of any delay in the schedule if time permits, though this may not be possible in the case of last minute changes.[23]

Senator Stennis received his personal invitation from AEC Chairman Glenn Seaborg on August 28:

As you have been informed by advance copies of the press releases, the SALMON event of Project DRIBBLE has been scheduled for September 22, 1964. This experiment is a 5-KT nuclear detonation at a depth of 2700 feet in the Tatum Salt Dome near Hattiesburg, Mississippi.

Since this event is an unclassified Department of Defense-Atomic Energy Commission seismic experiment, appropriate public information activities and announcements are planned before and after the detonation. News media representatives and local residents will be invited to observe the surface effects of the detonation from a designated observer area.

Although venting of radioactive debris is not expected, safety considerations require precautions against this possibility. The wind must be steady and from a direction which would carry any radioactive release toward a closely prescribed, previously evacuated sector. A delay of several days is possible in obtaining the desired conditions for your optimum safety.[24]

As experts stated, there would be little to see of the Salmon test. Persons looking for the effects of the detonation might see a toppled chimney or two. Looking elsewhere, as Winfred Moncrief did, one would see the effects all around the region. A photographer for the *Hattiesburg American,* Moncrief compiled a collection of photographs of the events. Now housed at the Mississippi Department of Archives and History in Jackson, the photos offer a window into events at the site and in the area. In one photograph, four-year-old Martha Saul peeks around a heavy timber bracing the chimney on her house. Additional lumber props up the timber, firmly anchored in place. Heavy wire further secures the bracing to the chimney and the house. In other photographs, Martha appears beside her mother, who is carrying her younger brother. The sturdiness of the bracing work added by H&N contrasts with the braces on the boy's legs—he may have suffered from polio or another disease. The family looks otherwise robust and well kept.[25]

Though no record is immediately available, in early or middle September a convoy from LRL made its way down the narrow roads to the test site. Within the convoy was a truck carrying the Salmon device. It parked at the assembly area, and technicians inspected the device after its transit from the stockpile to its ultimate destination.[26] Diagnostic equipment was attached to test whether the sensitive components in the device were functional, and the nuclear components were further checked. Salmon was a complex machine; despite Jim Reeves's feelings about extra time equaling extra safety, it also meant extra money. Salmon was to be emplaced at the bottom of a shaft, twenty-seven hundred feet deep, that would then be backfilled with pea gravel and concrete. If it failed to function when the firing switch was triggered, it would be practically irretrievable and would represent a significant waste of material and money. Once Salmon was thoroughly examined, it was attached to lifting equipment and lowered to the bottom of Station 1A.

Salmon's pedigree is still top secret. It was not a weapon—although at one time it may well have been. It was an oversized seismic charge, much the same as the bundles of dynamite that were used as seismic charges before high explosives became common. At the heart of the Salmon device was a core of radioactive material, either plutonium or highly enriched uranium. There was no assembly line for nuclear-test devices; only weapons were produced in quantity. In April 1960, the AEC had realized that the testing moratorium would not become permanent and that it was important to have devices on hand to resume testing immediately upon its cessation. This led to an examination of America's nuclear stockpile for older weapons that could be converted to test devices. Two fit the requirements: the Mark VI and Mark VII fission weapons. The Mark VI was thirty-nine inches in diameter and operationally yielded thirty to sixty kilotons. It remained in the United States stockpile from 1951 until it was phased out in 1962.

The Mark VII, twenty-seven inches in diameter, was America's first truly multipurpose warhead. It could be configured in several ways by varying the high-explosive detonators and nuclear cores. The inter-changeability of different critical components gave it a wide range of yields, from one to seventy kilotons. Although it remained in the stock-pile from 1952 until 1967 and was still an active weapon in the inventory, older models of the Mark VII had been withdrawn from active service before 1964. The seventeen-and-one-half-inch diameter of the Station 1A hole seems problematic when compared to the twenty-seven-inch diam-eter of the Mark VII; it is probable that much of the ten-inch difference would be accommodated by the size of the smaller of the interchange-able pits and explosive assemblies, and the ballistic casing, fins, and other components necessary in weapons systems would be unnecessary in a seismic-test device. The Salmon device was likely an older Mark VII tactical nuclear bomb, stripped of its weapons components and recycled into an atomic seismic charge.[27]

Whereas a bomb relies on internal barometric switches, radar altim-eter triggers, or impact switches to detonate the high-explosive lenses that initiate the compression and fission processes, the Salmon device would be dependent on a system designed by EG&G to fire the bomb accurately. The detonation signal would be sent via cables from the sur-face, and the firing station itself would be triggered by radio, allowing the firing party to be a safe distance from SGZ. The device would require a strong shell, as it would be topped with tons of gravel and concrete; it was encased in a cylinder that was 2.32 meters (7.6 feet) long and 40 centimeters (15.75 inches) in diameter.[28]

On September 13, 1964, Salmon was hoisted from its truck and low-ered into the Station 1A hole. Slowly dropped down the shaft, the de-vice was constantly subjected to diagnostic tests via its attached cables when, at a depth of twelve hundred feet, it registered an undisclosed malfunction. It was returned to the surface for analysis. The shot date of September 22 was scrapped, and a new shot date was set for Septem-ber 28. The Salmon device was fully lowered to the bottom of the shaft on September 21 and was finally emplaced. The shaft was stemmed with six hundred feet of concrete poured on top of the device, and the rest of the hole was filled with pea gravel. Despite the apparent safety of the stemming procedures, the *Hattiesburg American* questioned whether the Dribble site might become an enormous shotgun if the force of the blast could not be contained.[29]

Salmon was the first atomic test to be conducted east of the Mississippi River. This was not its only distinction: it was the most postponed nuclear shot in the history of American nuclear testing. The delay caused by diagnostic readings during the canister's descent to the bottom of the emplacement hole merely added a few days to the schedule. It was late summer in Mississippi, and the predictable wind patterns failed to materialize. Salmon was repeatedly postponed because of unfavorable winds. A major problem was the method used to predict the winds; forecasts originated almost twenty-four hours before the conditions were expected. The AEC still clung to September 28 as the date for Salmon. But September 28 came and went, as did the next scheduled attempt, September 30. The winds refused to cooperate.

Far from the Dribble site, well into the Gulf of Mexico, towering cumulonimbus clouds formed and sustained themselves on a diet of warm water and high pressure aloft. Growing in strength, they reached hurricane force by September 30. Hurricane Hilda intensified rapidly. Over twenty-four hours on October 1, 1964, she almost doubled her wind speed from eighty to one hundred fifty miles per hour. Sparking an evacuation of more than fifty thousand people along the Gulf Coast, Hilda bypassed the Texas coast in favor of central Louisiana, making landfall near Morgan City. Within a week, the storm had claimed at least thirty-eight lives, twenty-one of them from a tornado that hit Larose in Lafourche Parish. As she died out, Hilda hugged the Georgia-Florida border, flooding the region. But in her wake disturbed winds continued to plague Salmon.[30]

Hilda was a catastrophe for residents of the central Gulf Coast and the planners of the Salmon test—and as soon as Hilda exited the scene, there was another tropical storm to contend with. On October 13, Tropical Storm Isbell was reported to be threatening Cuba; ironically, American hurricane-tracking aircraft were prohibited from closely monitoring the storm because of the deterioration of American-Cuban relations. Isbell strengthened into a hurricane on October 14, making landfall in southwest *Florida*. Despite her distance from Mississippi, she stirred the atmosphere over the southeast. Given the unpredictable nature of tropical weather, Isbell could have suddenly made a beeline for the test site. As far as the seismic teams were concerned, Hilda and Isbell were noisemakers. The large waves generated by storms pounding the beach created a seismic cacophony that prevented a clear reading of signals generated by the test. Turbulent winds and high waves meant that the test would have to be delayed.[31]

Salmon's firing date was delayed six days because of technical problems with the device. Then came a series of wind delays. Postponement followed frustrating postponement. Twelve shot days had come and gone by Monday, October 19, when Salmon passed the previous record for test delays—twenty-nine days. Eleven times, the weather bureau had forecast that the winds would cooperate and blow south to north at around five miles per hour. Twice, the Mississippi Highway Patrol had set up barricades and residents had been urged to leave their homes. Twice they had been given reimbursement chits, and twice they had been paid. A one-shot, one-evacuation test program was promising to become a windfall for larger families. Meanwhile, men in hardhats and khakis lounged in the sun around the observation points, eating sandwiches, Eskimo pies, and Honey Buns, and consuming coffee and cold drinks. On October 8 and 11, the observation areas were populated, and people left muttering. News reporters with television cameras waited, but nothing newsworthy happened.[32]

Tuesday, October 20, also proved unsuitable for the shot—the wind was coming from the wrong direction. It still refused to come out of the south around the big Bermuda High; instead it blew in the opposite direction, north to south. In a situation reminiscent of Teller's and Starbird's decision to save money at NTS by carrying out shallower tests to spare the atomic-testing budget, meteorologists quickly put together a plan that would accommodate a north wind. Instead of evacuating residents in the northern sector of the B zone, evacuation would take place in the corresponding southern sector. But there was a problem: to the south of Dribble lay Biloxi and Gulfport. Should the worst happen at Dribble, those populated areas could be irradiated. If a contaminated plume rose high enough and did a quick turn to the south-southwest, Slidell and New Orleans could be affected. On the other hand, if the test did not proceed, no one knew what would happen; the device would not remain viable forever. The AEC and LRL did not want to leave an expensive five-kiloton device at the bottom of a hole, but the testing budget only allowed for certain expenditures for personnel, materiel, and compensation for residents. Developing a new set of protocols for the experiment was the expedient solution, and it worked. The rest of the week looked increasingly favorable. The new Zone C was designated on Wednesday and prepared for evacuation the following morning. At 7:30 a.m. Thursday, October 22, evacuation of Zones A and C began for the third time. Aerial patrols took off to secure the region, joined by sampling and observation aircraft. Rad-safety personnel took up their stations, ready to sound the alarm if necessary. Around the world, seismographs awaited the first motion of Mississippi's premier atomic blast.[33]

SGZ was deserted, of course, although signs of human presence were everywhere. The ground was crossed in several directions by cables connecting buried and surface instruments to recording trailers and telemetry equipment. Temporary plank walkways spared shoes and socks from summer mud, and a sign warned of an explosive hazard twenty-seven hundred feet below. A large Confederate flag flew overhead, beneath which an unknown airman had reenlisted several days before. The flag had been raised not by locals but by imported Dribble personnel, as a good-natured joke and a salute to local hospitality. Other souvenirs marked Station 1A, including a sign bearing a defiant southern slogan left "by an AEC wag." Just before 10:00 a.m., the countdown began, and for the first time, it did not stop. At the Dribble test site near Purvis, Mississippi, on October 22, 1964, in keeping with the spirit of the flag and the sign, the South did rise again—by approximately four inches.[34]

7. Shoot That Damn Thing

CLAUDETTE EZELL IS LAUGHING IN THE PHOTOGRAPHS, OBVIOUSLY enjoying the attention of the photographer and the reporter. The October 1, 1964, story in the *Hattiesburg American* focused on preparations for the Salmon test, which had already been postponed three times. Mrs. Ezell was worried about the safety of her plaster of Paris plaques, which she had begun collecting after undergoing cancer surgery. More than a thousand hand-painted plaques, many with religious motifs, hung on the walls of her house, in her father's corn crib, and inside the Gulf Café and Service Station in Baxterville, which she operated. She lived less than three miles from SGZ and was determined to leave the area on shot day. There was no official need for her to evacuate, but she figured her business would be nonexistent that day. She showed the reporter the chemically treated cloth patches that the AEC had distributed to area residents; a heavy dose of radiation would turn them purple. As she talked, her laughter masked fear of the unknown results of the impending test. One mile closer to the test site, Martha Saul's mother waited for site activity to conclude so her husband could hook up her new electric clothes dryer. Her fragile possessions were packed in padded crates, and she accepted frequent visits from monitoring personnel who sampled water from her well. "We're used to being pestered," she said.[1]

A resident of Lamar County, invited to join the official observers at the Saucier farm near the test site, demurred, saying, "If it comes off as quietly as the AEC says it will, there won't be anything to see, and if it doesn't work that way I don't want to be around."[2]

Others eager to see what they could see were repeatedly disappointed. One mother was overheard saying "They're not going to shoot that damn thing" as she rounded up her children and loaded them into her car. Her identity was unknown; she was likely one of many evacuees who had left home early on shot day and returned once the test was cancelled. Sunburns and large nests of fire ants were the immediate hazards at the observation area, where reporters and civil-defense personnel mingled, families picnicked, and the AEC-run canteen experienced a curious lack of interest in its barbecued-beef sandwiches. Before the wind-protocol change was approved on October 20, it seemed that they would never "shoot that damn thing."[3]

Mrs. Clifford Jones wrote from Philadelphia, Pennsylvania, to Hattiesburg mayor Paul Grady to inquire about the status of the tests and express her outrage:

> I read in Closer Up—(a small periodical from Florida) that our U.S. Government had made an announcement of the decision to explode a nuclear bomb near Hattiesburg Miss on Sept. 22, 1964.
>
> Not one word of this have I read in any of our newspapers or the Wall St. Journal or N.Y. Tribune.
>
> I am curious to see if it was done. Do you mind answering and let me know?
>
> Never have I heard of such a thing and I am furious. What are we coming to on this earth? . . .
>
> Our actions now are worse than the Carpet Baggers times. That [?] Amendment is not part of the U.S. Constitution. . . .
>
> I want to God to bless you [sic] all thru this trying experience which Washington has thrust on you.[4]

Mrs. Jones's connection to Hattiesburg is unknown. She apparently lacked direct contact with the area, where newspaper stories kept close tabs on the development of the Salmon test. She saw the federal government's presence at the Dribble site as an outsider's intrusion and a crime against the people of the region. Her outrage is notable for its contrast with the sentiments of those living near the test site.

The general consensus among locals was the desire to get the Salmon test over with. Despite the holiday mood at the observation stations, fear of the unknown continued among those living near the test site. Their lives were on hold until the test took place. Metaphorically, it was like hearing the distant thunder of a slowly approaching violent storm and anxiously waiting to see what debris would have to be cleaned up afterward—but this particular storm had been thundering for a month, and the first raindrop had yet to fall. It was annoying.

Flooding, a hurricane, device problems, and uncooperative winds had stalled Salmon for thirty days from its planned shot date; given more time, fire ants might have found their way onto this list. The AEC sought to control the ants with the same degree of success they had with conducting the test. There was nothing in the air that marked October 22 as "the day"—apart from favorable winds. Evacuees and the still curious assembled once again at the observation station that Thursday morning. Advised by loudspeaker that the countdown continued and that conditions remained favorable, news cameramen checked their equipment, official observers and evacuees left the precious shade of trees, and all focused their attention on the test site three and one-half miles away. The countdown reached zero, and a cloud of dust rose into the air over the Dribble site.

The energy equivalent of fifty-three hundred tons of TNT exploded at the bottom of Station 1A. The intense heat instantly converted a large mass of salt into ionized plasma, while a shock wave formed and propagated outward. The shock hammered the cement-stemming plug, which held, causing a spherical cavity to form in less than a second. The ground bounded upward and then fell back, ending up roughly four inches above where it had been. More important, the shock wave shook the entire salt dome. As the blast forced the ground upward, it also pushed the enormous finger of salt downward, and because it was not at the radial center of the dome, it caused the enormous saline protuberance to vibrate. Within a few seconds of detonation, the plasma cooled to form salt vapor. Fractured and molten material fell to the bottom of the chamber, forming a rubble pile of vaporized device components and molten salt.

All over and around the test site, seismographs recording the motion were promptly knocked over. Wooden housings for the sensitive USCGS recorders leaned precariously, threatening to dump thousands of dollars' worth of machinery onto the ground. At least one was saved by its bulk, wedging it into place so that it stuck precariously out of its box. At the zero point, anything not staked into the ground was thrown up into the air—the vertical surface displacement was 30 centimeters, or 11.8

inches—falling to earth shortly afterward. The expected acceleration at SGZ was 10G, while later measurements recorded acceleration almost three times as strong: 28G. Dust filled the air.[5]

The dust was the only thing to see until the ground shock reached the manned positions and the observation area. Several noticeable ground waves propagated outward for nearly three minutes. Cars rocked on their springs and equipment trailers shook. The vibrations raced out in all directions—"three good tremors" rocked Purvis; the *Hattiesburg American* building swayed; and numerous other locations reported ground motion. Clearly the "tingle in the toes" that was expected several miles from the blast was far more perceptible than first thought.[6]

Twenty-five seconds after the blast, the shock wave reached Father Eisele's seismographs at Spring Hill College. Examining the data, Eisele said that Salmon "recorded comparably to a major earthquake." Seconds later, the shock wave reached the University of Michigan's experimental seismic stations. At the university's botanical gardens, the blast registered 6.0 on the Richter scale; at its Fulton County, Ohio, station it registered 5.8. Salmon was far stronger than anyone had expected, and its effects were unanticipated. Later radiochemical analysis of chamber debris verified that the device had performed as specified, with the expected yield, but it had shaken the earth like a larger device. The reason this had occurred was the unique geology that allowed the Tatum Dome to form. Recalling the process of diapirism, the hot, fluid salt forced its way toward the surface from several miles below. If one mentally removes the surrounding strata from above the Louann salt bed and around the dome, one is left with a long finger of salt, shaped like an inverted teardrop, connected to the Louann bed. The top mushrooms out, though not dramatically. The sedimentary strata pierced by the salt diapir are not rigid like stone but are more like pudding. If one sticks a finger in water, gelatin, or pudding and wiggles it quickly, the wave effect can readily be seen. At the immediate area, a vertical bound and several rebounds were recorded. But the diapir also vibrated horizontally, causing a sympathetic "sloshing" of the surrounding ground that amplified the seismic effects.[7]

No underground radioactivity escaped from the Salmon explosion. The chamber created by the blast contained all of the fission products deep underground. Still, safety protocols dictated that a full sampling sweep be conducted to make certain that an unknown fissure somewhere was not spewing radioactive gases into the atmosphere. Fifteen minutes after the shot, a helicopter transported personnel back to SGZ to take readings from several devices there. At noon, USPHS personnel began escorting residents from evacuated areas to their homes to check for damage.

Claudette Ezell got good news: her treasured plaques had survived. Three miles from the shot, her home and business were subjected to a strong shock, but the plaques remained just where she had left them. At the other extreme, two miles from Station 1A, Horace Burge returned to find a mess. A fifty-one-year-old tung-tree farmer, Burge, his severely asthmatic wife, and their four children lived in a three-room frame house. For all intents and purposes, it was uninhabitable—the fireplace and chimney were destroyed; his refrigerator had been jolted open, dumping food from the shelves; and bricks and debris littered the floor. Making matters worse, his pipes had burst, spewing water all over the kitchen floor. Winfred Moncrief's photographs for the *Hattiesburg American* show a crew-cut Burge, clad in shirt and striped overalls, dejectedly surveying the damage to his home.[8]

Most of the damage around the site was slight, with cracked masonry and plaster most commonly reported. Damage complaints flooded into the AEC's Hattiesburg office; 205 had been lodged within three days. By November 17, some 700 complaints had been reported and 267 claims filed.[9] At the beginning of December, the AEC reported that the Hattiesburg office had recorded 835 complaints and that 358 claims for damages had been filed. Of these, 97 had already been settled. Residents of the affected area, which spread well beyond the five-mile radius initially predicted, rapidly grew impatient with the AEC because they found the process too slow. Along with their anxiety over being paid in a timely fashion, they were critical of the AEC's "clamming up." Before the Salmon test, news and announcements had been issued almost constantly from the Hattiesburg Joint Information Office; after the test, much less information was forthcoming. Official announcements concerning damage complaints and claims were made on December 1, almost six weeks after the test; additional announcements came a week later. The next

AEC announcements related to the reentry operations at the site. By March 25, 1966, some 1,189 claims had been filed for damages from distances as much as twenty-five miles from the site. These claims totaled $2,178,713.78. The majority of the claims, 1,018, were settled for a total of $547,498.03. Four claims, well in excess of the $5,000.00 limit, required approval by Congress for a total of $44,288.73.[10]

The disparity between the amounts claimed and the amounts paid was appreciable—roughly 25 percent. Despite H&N's structural surveys and bracing, some structures could not be thoroughly inspected. Buildings that had seemed solid could actually have been on the verge of collapse due to a number of factors, including termite or other insect damage, weak foundations, or poor construction. Regardless of the severity of the shock, the structures would have suffered damage. Some complaints and claims were filed for questionable reasons. Lavern P. Smith wrote to the AEC concerning a strange event.

> I think that you all want to know everything that happened during the explosion so just think you should know this. My wife and I were sitting in the car listening to the radio, and as soon as the blast was over & the car stopped shaking we shut the radio off and I stepped on the starter and all of the water in my battery just boiled all over the place and the battery was dead as it could be. Please don't think I want a battery because I don't as I already have one. I don't know what could of [sic] happened because it was an almost new battery. I just thought you would want to know.

Frank Ingram's reply from the Joint Office of Information was polite, but he insisted that the battery trouble was a coincidence not directly linked to the Salmon test.[11]

The AEC and Roland Beers clearly erred in their predictions of ground motion caused by the test. The shock wave was stronger and propagated farther outward than anticipated. Following the test, some residents were optimistic that test damage could benefit them. The *Hattiesburg American* reported that a Baxterville woman had said of her house, "I was hoping the whole thing would fall down."[12] A five-thousand-dollar house could be an improvement over an older structure, especially in 1964 dollars. As 1965 began, the presence of an atomic-test site in the

Piney Woods was increasingly considered a nuisance. Patriotic or not, the residents of the area felt growing resentment toward government agencies that had the power to dislocate them at will, threaten their homes and lives, and delay payment on legitimate damages to private property. The initial excitement was wearing off, the metaphoric storm had passed, and the aftermath was frustrating and tedious.

While adjusters worked over the mass of claims following the Salmon test, personnel at the site began working toward reentering the shot cavity. With shots Sand and Tar on indefinite hold, efforts concentrated on the long and hazardous process of investigating the products of the 5.3-kiloton blast. Initially the plan was to begin reentry a day or two after the shot. This idea was soon discarded, as there was no way to know the pressure of the gases in the chamber, although it was certain that they would still be extremely hot. Salt retains heat—a property that allowed salt diapirs to form. When the cavity was opened, hot, pressurized radioactive gas could conceivably overwhelm the bleeddown facility and escape into the atmosphere. This would be an environmental disaster requiring an emergency evacuation of people living near the dome. All of the radioactive materials created by the test were trapped deep within the dome, and they were not going anywhere. Rad-safety monitoring continued all around the site. By holding the known contaminated gases and materials in the dome, the AEC ensured that radiation-leak detection would be far more accurate. Chamber reentry would bring contaminated matter to the surface, potentially affecting readings.

A work order issued on January 3, 1965, named REECO and the Oklahoma firm Fenix and Scisson (F&S) to perform new tasks at Station 1A, with REECO assuming the duty of radiation monitoring. Almost one-quarter million dollars in contracts was allocated for private firms, with one hundred seventy-five thousand dollars available immediately for chamber reentry, rad safety, and "contingency engineering and construction." Once again, Big Chief, also from Oklahoma, drilled into the salt dome. Contracted before Salmon, the firm's workers began the task of drilling a hole called Postshot 1 parallel to and thirty feet distant from Station 1A. Despite Big Chief's experience with the Tatum Dome, work was slow due to radiation-safety concerns. The initiation of a second hole, Postshot 2, began in February about 105 feet away from Postshot 1, in order to allow a different method of material assessment. The second hole was planned to be sunk to twenty-nine hundred feet, where sample cores could be retrieved. The hole would then be filled to twenty-two hundred feet. An angled shaft would be dug from that depth at twenty-five degrees to enter the top of the chamber, allowing further sample collection from the area near the top of the void. Angled drilling, or "whip stocking," a procedure perfected in the oilfields, allowed drilling rigs to explore promising pockets of oil and gas that were not accessible by drilling straight down.[13]

Postshot 1 drilling started, or "spudded in," on January 2, 1965. Carefully checking for leaks in the new casing via television cameras lowered periodically into the hole, the Big Chief drilling team slowly closed the distance to their target. At 2,655 feet, drillers detected radioactivity; a foot deeper, high levels of gamma radiation showed that the cavity was close. Drilling at a speed of roughly a foot every half hour, they reached the Salmon chamber, at a depth of 2,660 feet, on March 4. Remote probing showed that Salmon had created an alien world that resembled Venus more than Earth. Nearly four and a half months had passed since the blast, yet the chamber temperature was a nearly uniform four hundred degrees Fahrenheit. Highly acidic fluid accumulated in the bottom of the shaft where it met the chamber, a boiling concoction of concentrated hydrochloric acid, brine, and ferric chloride. This delayed the chamber interior survey with a television camera until the fluid could be removed.

Despite the temperature, a partial vacuum existed in the chamber; the bleeddown plant kept the pressure at a steady level, 310 millibars, while the monitoring technicians performed a cavity-gas sampling operation. Radiation levels averaged 100 milliroentgens per hour, with higher levels encountered at the bottom of the chamber and in a layer three feet into the salt. Put into perspective, this meant that every hour, an exposed human would receive a little less than one third of the annual exposure average of 360 milliroentgens. The corrosive atmosphere in the chamber required that air be introduced to dilute the mixture and flush it from the cavity. During this process, calculations of the volume of the chamber showed it to be in the vicinity of 380,000 cubic feet. On March 7 and 8, a television camera was lowered into the chamber. The cavity created by Salmon measured about 120 feet in diameter, was spherical, and had a flat floor. The video from the camera was telling. It was still hot as an oven inside the chamber; wisps of smoke appeared on the television monitors as paint burned off the camera casing. Following the television survey, the platform crew installed a device called a bridge plug in the Postshot 1 hole at the chamber intersection. It would guide the drilling tools down into the layer of slag and debris at the bottom of the cavity and penetrate deeper to sample the salt below the chamber.[14]

The sampling operations were extremely complicated, relying on technology and equipment developed in the oilfields. Onsite innovation, a hallmark of the petroleum industry, also became a hallmark of the operations at the Dribble site. The actual work in the cavity was performed by roughnecks and engineers one-half mile from the action, connected only by a thin metal pipe. Any mistake required a tedious removal of tools through the drill casing, which was slightly less than nine inches in diameter. The drilling pipe, or thread, accessed the bottom of the cavity by a bridge casing connected to the bridge plug. The bridge casing was crucial to add rigidity to the drilling thread as it crossed the chamber from top to bottom. Without it, the drilling thread with its attached coring tool would flex and whip around as it was sunk into the material at the bottom of the chamber. It was like feeding a plumber's snake into a drain from several feet above. But with the snake, the shaft lashes back and forth and will not break. In the case of the drilling thread, the heavy steel tubing would flex beyond its maximum stress point and snap off, losing the tool and the important samples located therein. One sample core hole through the bottom of the chamber reached a depth of 2,908 feet, more than 200 feet beneath the zero point of the Salmon test. To obtain further seismic readings below the chamber, technicians added, or "spotted," brine in the hole to allow seismic energy to be transmitted through the material below the cavity when an explosive charge was detonated.[15]

Two documentary sources report an incident that followed this sampling and spotting operation. One is a project manager's report published almost two years after the Salmon test; the other is an undated, handwritten draft report that has been partially "sanitized." The two suggest that an accident occurred at the site on March 22 during a coring operation—in fact, it may have been the deep penetration below the cavity floor. On that date, at 4:15 a.m., the crew retrieved a core sample from the dome. Once the sample cleared the hole, Postshot 1 became a man-made geyser of water and steam. For seven minutes, the geyser reached an estimated forty feet into the air before the blooie line could be attached; for five hours the efflux diverted into the bleeddown plant. Fourteen men were near the hole when it blew; two were drenched by water from the chamber. All affected personnel proceeded with decontamination at onsite facilities; clothing was handled by a specialized laundry at the Dribble site that functioned as part of the decontamination facility. The director's report mentions nothing of this event—but it does note that the bridge casing broke away from the bridge plug at an unspecified date, requiring twenty-two days to retrieve.

The incident occurred as a result of a steam event in the chamber— the pressure in the chamber as the core sample was taken indicated approximately one pound per square inch (psi) above atmospheric pressure (approximately 15psi); this was estimated to have risen to 12 or 13psi above atmospheric pressure when the water flashed over to steam. The water could only have come from one of two places: either the brine injected into the hole bored beneath the chamber floor, or an aquifer somehow leaked through a section of damaged well casing and poured into the salt dome, flashing into steam as it encountered the hot salt. The second possibility seems unlikely, because there are no reports of this problem's being repeated, as it would have been with a leaking casing. Either way, Postshot 1 was rendered unusable for some time as workmen plugged the hole with cement for later redrilling, while additional casing was inserted down the hole to replace the damaged casing that required drilling out and removal.[16]

The omission of this event from the manager's report is significant. It was an uncontrolled release of radioactive material at the site. Although several people were exposed and mildly contaminated, what was reported appeared to be a routine radiation release. The report notes that there was no radioactivity evident one thousand feet from Postshot 1; but until the crew diverted the efflux through the wellhead to the blooie line and tank, the water and steam blew into the atmosphere and collected on the ground. Fortunately for those near the well, previous ventilation with compressed air allowed the processing of the corrosive vapors through the bleeddown plant. Samples of water from the blooie tank showed minimal radiation. Two important radiological readings emerged from the contaminated water around Postshot 1 and from the blooie system, showing a mystery isotope whose identity has been erased from the handwritten memo. The concentration of this isotope, 65.6 microcuries per milliliter of water, existed in the ground sample; 3.85 microcuries per milliliter was present in the blooie tank. Once the groundwater sampling was complete, it was washed into a collection pond and later collected and disposed of as radioactive waste.[17]

What was the mystery substance? Although its identity does not appear in the handwritten report, several clues point to a logical conclusion. The fission device that created the cavity was efficient—that is, the fissile material reacted in such a manner that it was consumed in the reaction, with little residue remaining from the detonation. Forcibly injected into the salt by the blast, the metallic bomb residue and fission products existed as a rind around the cavity embedded a few feet deep into the salt. Although such material could exit the chamber in a steam plume, widespread dispersal was not felt to be a threat. Also, fissile materials are severe inhalation hazards and were recognized as such even in 1964. There was a localized evacuation of the drilling rig at Postshot 1, but there was no site-wide evacuation, so it may be concluded that the material was considered less hazardous. Therefore, plutonium or uranium, their heavier "daughter" elements, and device-casing debris were not likely to have been the materials deleted from the report.

The Salmon test did produce a radioactive and water-soluble substance in sufficient quantity to pose a health risk, an isotope of hydrogen called tritium. Possessing a half-life[18] of a little more than eleven years, it emits beta radiation, which can penetrate skin and cause burns. It has several industrial applications and is widely used in rifle scopes as the illuminated pipper and reticle. The steam eruption would have brought substantial quantities of tritium to the surface in the hot water and steam. Despite tritium's radioactivity, it could be easily washed from clothing and skin, as the report noted before the contaminated water was directed into disposal pits. With all the creeks and aquifers in the region, the water solubility of tritium posed the greatest contamination hazard. If any material could migrate off-site, tritium was the most likely culprit. The Salmon test caused no detectable contamination to the environment beyond the perimeter fence, but the drillback operations produced a sizeable quantity of contaminated drilling fluids and "chips," or solid debris, and they released additional tritium onto the site.

Upon resolution of the steam incident, further investigation of the chamber continued. The Salmon device had excavated a chamber slightly larger than the one CPH had contracted to excavate. It did not need ninety-inch shafts for access and excavation. It required no additional site negotiations, nor would it require relocating personnel to Texas. The Salmon chamber looked to be a promising site for the decoupling test. Sand and Tar were indefinitely suspended, although the AEC and ARPA still wanted them conducted. The primary problem facing their execution at the Dribble site was size. The Salmon cavity was thirty feet greater in diameter than the chamber planned for the one-hundred-ton Sand test. Tar could be conducted as easily as Salmon, because it was slated to be a tamped test. Further analysis showed that device sizes were inappropriate to study the magnitude of the decoupling effect because of the chamber volume. Sand and Tar remained in limbo, but plans for reutilizing the cavity continued to develop.

With the successful test of the Salmon device, Mississippi still hoped to become a center for nuclear research. The seismic-detection program was important, but it also achieved one of the goals of Plowshare—a potentially useful salt cavity had been excavated in less than a second by an atomic explosive. But it was not the only nuclear-research program that interested the state in 1965. Upon his inauguration, Pres. Lyndon Johnson had issued a "Policy for National Action in the Field of High Energy Physics," authorizing construction of a two-hundred-billion-electron-volt (BeV) proton-accelerator facility. Having a nuclear test site in the state and enjoying a short-term financial boost was one thing, but gaining an advanced scientific facility in the Piney Woods near Hattiesburg was quite another. It would bring long-term financial benefits to the region and be the ultimate reward for MITRC's efforts to champion Mississippi's technical and scientific potential. Dr. Andrew Suttle was no longer the director of MITRC. In 1962, he had joined Texas A&M University as vice president for research before leaving to work with Dr. Harold Brown in Washington. Dr. Robert F. Dye assumed the MITRC directorship, having been with the organization since its formation. Winning such an accelerator facility would vindicate Suttle and Dye's work to bring high technology to the region. Suttle's close ties to the AEC and its chairman Glenn Seaborg, developed during his work in Washington, between 1962 and 1964, was a further advantage. By mid-1965, forty-five of the forty-eight contiguous states were vying for the contract; near the end of the year, the list had shrunk to forty-three states, with Mississippi suggesting locations near Jackson, Scott County, and Perry/Forest County. The latter location was close to Hattiesburg.[19]

The requirements listed by the AEC and the National Academy of Sciences (NAS) were broad in nature. At least three thousand acres were necessary, preferably already owned by the federal government or easily procured. The soil had to be firm enough to provide a solid foundation for the one-mile-diameter apparatus, and preferably it would be fairly level to avoid earth-moving operations.[20] Furthermore, a suitable location should be free of faults and seismic activity. Several hundred megawatts of electricity should be available, and there should be a ready supply of fresh water for the facility. The site should be near a major airport and have access to highways and railroads for materiel and personnel transportation. In addition, the AEC wanted a commercial industrial center nearby for easier access to specialized technical personnel. The AEC wanted research facilities that would allow "opportunities for desirable interaction of scientific and engineering personnel," suitable housing for several thousand people who would form the permanent staff at the facility, and "proximity to a cultural center that includes a large university [that] will provide intellectual and cultural opportunities attractive for staff and families." Always desiring to save money, the AEC was conscious of "regional wage and cost variations as well as labor surplus areas" in its decision-making process. Thus the South, with its traditionally anti-union sentiment and large number of under-employed skilled laborers, appealed to the selection committee.[21]

According to those specifications, the Hattiesburg area was a strong contender, and the city fathers knew it. The University of Southern Mississippi was in Hattiesburg, Camp Shelby was just to the southeast, and fresh water abounded. Thanks to the Salmon test, the entire area had been more seismologically and geologically surveyed than practically any location on the planet. Although AFTAC had demurred on using

Hattiesburg's airport, it received moderate commercial traffic and could be enlarged to a more suitable size if necessary. Roads and railways, the source of Hattiesburg's nickname Hub City, were more than sufficient. Cultural activities unavailable in Hattiesburg could be found in New Orleans, Mobile, or the state capital in Jackson, all within one hundred twenty miles. Gulf Coast beaches were only an hour away. At the Tatum Dome, air compressors cooled the atmosphere in the Salmon chamber, while in Hattiesburg and Jackson excitement heated up.

Dreams of advanced research facilities and further activities at the Tatum Dome were dampened when the hurricane season slapped the Gulf Coast with another deadly storm. From September 1, 1965, until landfall on the night of September 9 and the morning of September 10, Hurricane Betsy carved a path of destruction that confounded meteorologists with her refusal to follow a consistent track. Betsy made two complete loops in the Atlantic before hitting the tip of Florida and entering the Gulf. From there, she headed steadily toward Louisiana, striking the mouth of the Mississippi River and charging inland, passing southwest of New Orleans. In the worst hurricane to hit New Orleans up to that time, the waters of Lake Pontchartrain inundated neighborhoods throughout the city. Forty years later, Katrina would flood the same neighborhoods to devastating effect, but Betsy's death toll barely exceeded eighty persons.[22] The storm occasioned sharp criticism from Edward Teller, who was addressing a meeting of the Louisiana-Arkansas division of the Mid-Continent Oil Association. In words that would resound two generations later, he asked, "Why weren't the people of the inundated areas evacuated? . . . Your city had hours of warning. Why wasn't it anticipated that the levee of the Industrial Canal might break? In any storm the size of Betsy, tidal wave action can be anticipated." Understandably, New Orleans mayor Vic Schiro gave this criticism a less than cordial reception. The scope of the damage eliminated the city from consideration for the particle accelerator.[23]

But Mississippi remained guardedly optimistic that it had a chance to land the particle accelerator. Things proceeded well at the Dribble site, too. One problem the testing program encountered was how to deal with hundreds of thousands of gallons of liquid waste generated by the reentry program and by the release of steam and water. Project management considered collection and transportation of these wastes too expensive and hazardous and deemed an onsite disposal method necessary. An uncontrolled release of radioactive substances into the aquifers around the site raised serious concerns at the Dribble site because area residents and their livestock depended on well water. But there were aquifers that locals did not use because they contained nothing but brine. Project engineers realized that the fifth aquifer layer below the surface, which lay at an average depth of twenty-five hundred feet, was isolated between heavy clay layers and consisted of brine. Liquid injection from the drillback operations into the brine aquifer through the HT-2 well isolated the waste. Monitoring stations ensured that the waste remained where it belonged until its radioactivity decayed.[24]

Meanwhile, an extensive program of water, air, and milk sampling tracked any entry of radioactive materials into the environment. The USPHS office in Montgomery, Alabama, constantly monitored calcium (Ca), potassium (K), strontium isotopes Sr-89 and Sr-90, an isotope of iodine (I-131), an isotope of cesium (Cs-137), and an isotope of barium (Ba-140) in milk samples from 1963 on. These isotopes presented special health hazards, and because they were direct-fission products they indicated a serious problem at the site linked directly to the Salmon explosion. The worst threats, strontium, cesium, and iodine-131, sparked an international demand to stop atmospheric testing. These substances were especially dangerous if consumed by children, because the body processes strontium like calcium, storing it in the bones, where the radiation kills and weakens bone cells. In large enough doses it could cause tumors and cancer. Cesium concentrates in muscle tissue, and iodine-131 mimics beneficial iodine and is concentrated in the thyroid gland. Cesium and iodine are water-soluble; surface water and milk were constantly checked for the presence of these substances. From the beginning, all sites reported the presence of these materials in minute quantities, the legacy of nearly twenty years of atmospheric nuclear testing.[25]

The public-safety program considered water-well monitoring crucial. Monitoring personnel periodically took samples from both purpose-drilled and private wells and transported them to Montgomery for testing. Water wells were a source of concern to local residents because, along with sporadic damage to their homes, well water was a visible sign that something had happened at the salt dome. One hundred fourteen sites within thirty miles of the Dribble site reported water-quality issues—in most cases the water had been agitated deep in the aquifer by the shock from the test and had picked up sediment. The shock also affected the filter screening of some pumps, leading to clogging with sediment or rust. None of these complaints was considered serious, except by those affected. Still, the water looked different, and the Hazleton Nuclear Science Corporation (HNSC) conducted continual monitoring, both to ensure that cavity materials had not contaminated the water supply and to reassure local residents.[26]

On the anniversary of the Salmon test, the *Hattiesburg American* reported noticeable changes on and around the test site. Government vehicles were no longer omnipresent on the roads around the site, and human activity was minimal. Compressors continued to cycle air through the chamber, but from all indications things were on hold. Unknown to the reporter, estimates had already been submitted for the purpose of reopening the Station 1A hole and putting the Dribble site back on a nuclear-test footing. The chamber was too big for the paired Sand and Tar decoupling/baseline tests; instead a reverse extrapolation suggested an appropriately increased device yield for the cavity volume. The first step to a return to testing was to reopen Station 1A, as it was larger than the postshot holes and led directly down into the Salmon chamber. A second device would be lowered into the chamber and suspended in the exact center of the void. The cost of reopening Station 1A was estimated at three hundred thousand dollars, with a sixty-one day timetable. Furthermore, there was no guarantee that the casing had held against the aquifers when Salmon detonated: engineers estimated that there was only a 25 percent chance that the shaft was dry to a depth of twenty-two hundred feet. If they reached that depth and the shaft was dry, they estimated that there was a 75 percent chance that they could extend their reopening operations into the chamber. The Tatum Dome had stymied them before, and no one was betting that it would not do so again. Finally, on January 3, 1966, the AEC issued a work order to reopen Station 1A.[27]

A week after the anniversary of Salmon, the third and largest VU test was conducted. Called Long Shot, the eighty-kiloton shot exploded in an excavated shaft twenty-three hundred feet below the remote island of Amchitka in the Aleutian chain. The test was conducted there because of regional seismic activity and the isolation of the site. Long Shot was the first nuclear test at Amchitka, which would see two thermonuclear tests: the one-megaton Milrow in 1969 and the five-megaton Cannikin in 1971, the largest underground test ever conducted by the United States.[28]

Meanwhile, news regarding the particle accelerator was less than positive. Having survived the process of elimination thus far, the Piney Woods received official visitors on December 1; four AEC advisers arrived and were feted throughout the day. Their morning arrival in Hattiesburg was followed by a press conference, a country-club luncheon attended by most members of the Chamber of Commerce, a tour of two possible sites for the facility, and a dinner reception at the Holiday Inn. The local paper whipped up enthusiasm for the visit, and editorials espoused the importance of bringing more research-and-development assets into the area. Beginning in September, the *American* regularly featured articles arguing that Hattiesburg should ride the crest of high-tech industrial development. Mayor Paul Grady was determined to bring the facility to the region. "Anything this big could smash many of our problems," he said. "It would be a magnificent development for the entire trade area. We're keeping our fingers crossed." Others advised caution. Les Wood, chairman of the Mississippi Power Company's industrial-development department, was not "overly optimistic."[29]

After the visit came the exchange of obligatory thank-you notes. The AEC team wrote to Mayor Grady on December 27 after finishing their tour of possible sites; Grady's response followed more than a month later, still arguing Hattiesburg's case. He contended that an easily ar-ranged plan for temporarily housing workers at Camp Shelby offset the shortage of housing noted by the AEC visitors. Road improvements had progressed substantially since construction workers had been stationed there during World War II, when Hattiesburg had little public hous-ing. Grady pointed out that before the war "there was only a two-lane highway that carried the traffic from Hattiesburg to Camp Shelby. Now there is a beautiful four-lane highway, separated by a wooded median strip which provides for faster, safer, and more effective movement of traffic from Hattiesburg to either of the two sites we visited with your team." It was no use. The AEC wanted its particle accelerator, but it was part of a financially burdened government faced with the rapidly growing expense of the Vietnam War. Then there was the political problem. Mississippi continued to defy the national Democratic Party and gave Barry Goldwater an overwhelming 87.1 percent of the vote over Lyndon Johnson in the 1964 presidential election. As Bruce Schulman pointed out, acting against the will of the federal power structure bore the potential consequence of losing federal programs. Citing Hubert Humphrey, he noted the power that bureaucrats held when locating federally funded research programs at universities, "making a vast intellectual wasteland out of America by having R&D contracts concentrated as they are in limited geographical areas."[30]

Ultimately, a 200-BeV particle accelerator was constructed at Texas A&M University in College Station. AEC chairman Seaborg told Suttle that he wanted the school to become a center for research in chemistry and physics despite competition from other institutions; this certainly influenced the selection process. The new particle accelerator became known as the Texas A&M Variable Energy Cyclotron, or TAMVEC. Suttle continued as assistant director of research at Texas A&M until 1971, when he was dismissed from his post as director of the cyclotron institute. TAMVEC began operations in 1967, narrowly missing the contraction of the AEC's largesse in funding particle accelerator research that occurred in the 1970s.[31]

The particle accelerator project sought by sites across the nation almost certainly became the TAMVEC; Seaborg's wishes were evident before the official site selection began. Texas A&M had entered into a contract with the AEC on April 24, 1964, to develop a particle-physics facility. The inescapable conclusion is that the selection process was a mere formality; despite its citizens' hopes, Hattiesburg had never stood a chance.[32]

These developments disappointed city leaders, but another nuclear test planned for the Dribble site promised more government activity in the region. But once again the program had changed; a decoupling test would be conducted at the Tatum Dome, but it would be different from the proposed and cancelled Sand test. The device yield would be increased, from one hundred tons to more than three hundred tons to compensate for the larger diameter of the cavity created by the Salmon test. There was also the issue of the chamber itself, which was blast-formed instead of having been excavated; no one was sure how it would stand up to further use. Still, scientists were determined to test the de-coupling theory, and the Dribble site offered the best location for their important experiment. The new atomic test shot was called Sterling.

8. A Silver Lining and a Miracle Play

PROJECT DRIBBLE HAD UNDERGONE SEVERAL CONFIGURATION
changes since it had first been announced in 1961. As originally conceived, it incorporated two phases of operation at the Tatum Dome. The
series lost its higher-yield tests in 1962. This was a fortunate change, for
if the five-kiloton Salmon shot shook houses in the region, the planned
twenty-five-kiloton detonation would likely have leveled them and
caused damage far beyond Purvis and Hattiesburg. Instead, the five-
kiloton shot and the two one-hundred-ton decoupling tests, Sand and
Tar, remained on the active shot list until water problems forced ARPA
and the AEC to consider executing the two smaller tests elsewhere.
They remained in limbo and eventually died there. Sterling simply replaced them. As far as the question of decoupling was concerned, it was
the more important test; Sterling would be detonated in the chamber
Salmon had created. Though Sterling was in effect a consolation prize to
the Dribble program managers, because it was not the program that was
originally desired, it still addressed the important aspects of decoupling
in underground-test concealment.

The high-explosive Cowboy tests had clearly shown that the decoupling effect could be significant when an explosive was detonated in
an excavated chamber. One of VU's primary tasks was detecting large
decoupled nuclear tests when their seismic signals dropped below the
generally detectable threshold of five kilotons. Below that yield it was
unlikely that an underground shot could be reliably detected because
of the masking effect of natural seismic noise. In a large enough salt
formation, decoupling chambers could be excavated that would allow
large weapons to be secretly tested while generating seismic signals that
remained below levels that would betray their origin. In other words, salt

could allow an unfriendly country to hide its weapons tests. Should a treaty be signed between nuclear nations creating a threshold yield for underground tests, one side could violate it with impunity. This was the problem faced by scientists and diplomats alike.

Originally, the ideal decoupling chamber was to be mined in the Tatum Dome as part of Project Dribble—in fact, there would be two chambers, one for each phase of the operation. But water-control problems quashed any possibility that the large-diameter shafts needed by the excavation crews could be successfully sunk into the salt. So the Salmon emplacement by a narrower shaft was far easier to seal against water intrusion, and the resulting void appeared to meet the needs of a slightly larger decoupling test.

In fact, Sterling was far more practical and ideal than anyone initially realized. Plowshare, the "peaceful atom" program, used nuclear charges for excavation and earthmoving. As Salmon demonstrated when the chamber was reentered in March 1965, a nuclear device was useful for creating a sizeable, dimensionally uniform void in solid salt. On top of that, there was no salt to dispose of that could reveal excavation efforts. This made secret testing feasible for several reasons. There was no threshold limit for underground tests; a device of any size could create a test chamber that could be used to hide later tests. By 1966, the Soviet Union had conducted several underground tests that created underground cavities. In addition, a country that wanted to be truly devious could cloak its tests using diplomatically acceptable means. A country could announce an internationally acceptable Plowshare-type test, detonate the device, and end up with a ready-made decoupling chamber. The size of the void would be determined simply by the device yield. The seismic signal would thus be explained as an acceptable detonation, and no repercussions from the creation of the test chamber would follow.

The real problem lay in the properties of salt once it had been exposed to the effects of an atomic blast. In a mined chamber, the cavity walls are smooth. The only cracks or fissures are those that have occurred naturally as the salt pushed upward from deep within the earth. If brine-mining is used, the solution can actually fill any small cracks; the chamber will have a perfectly uniform surface, almost like glass or marble. In salt mines, striations and ripples are clearly visible in the ceilings and walls of the excavations, allowing geologists to track where smaller upwellings in the overall diapir have occurred over time.[1]

The Salmon chamber was a different story. The device created a hellish environment with heavily fractured cavity walls. The heat released by the test remained trapped in the void for months before reentry and ventilation cooled it down. Sample cores drilled into and near the void revealed that three distinctive salt conditions were present after the test, layered like a hollow onion. The cavity radius was some seventeen meters, or about fifty-five feet. The innermost layer started at the wall of the chamber and extended about twenty meters, a little more than sixty-five feet. The second shell or layer extended from twenty meters to sixty meters, nearly two hundred feet from the cavity center. The third distinct layer extended from sixty meters to one hundred twenty meters, or nearly four hundred feet. The innermost layer was highly distressed and deformed. The blast shattered and melted the salt immediately surrounding the Salmon device and heaved it outward. Radioactive gases were injected into natural and newly created fissures. The intense heat caused the shattered mass to remain viscous; as it slowly cooled, material fell to the bottom of the chamber, forming the flat floor. Large and small fractures in the salt existed throughout this layer.[2]

The second layer consisted of microfractured salt created by the mechanical action of the chamber's creation. When Salmon detonated, a void formed where solid salt had once existed, and during its creation there was an immediate period of expansion followed quickly by a rebound of the cavity walls. The mechanical action shattered the crystal structure of this second layer. The third or outermost layer was partially microfractured and transitioned into the natural salt stock that made up the dome.[3]

The fracturing, microfracturing, and gas injection were serious. They did not affect the structural integrity of the chamber —which, though heavily deformed, was sound —but they did affect the transmission of seismic energy. Estimates varied as to how much the shot-formed cavity would decouple blast energy from a nuclear test; the consensus was that it would diminish the decoupling effect. But this seems illogical, for the chamber was surrounded by a loosened layer of salt that would allow the chamber to flex when a subsequent device exploded, and it would dampen the shock before it traveled farther into the salt dome and into the surrounding earth. Most desirable was a uniform salt body with no microfractures that would flex uniformly, distributing the blast wave evenly along the walls of the chamber in all directions. The Salmon chamber was spherical except for the floor, formed from an aggregate of melted material and device debris. The floor was flat and would not allow blast shock to expand uniformly. The heavily distressed chamber walls concealed mechanically created weaknesses that could allow blast energy to find an easier transmission to the more solid salt. No one knew for sure. Estimates of the decoupling effect ranged from a factor of one hundred sixty to a factor of twenty.[4]

Sterling was to be the second nuclear shot at the Dribble site. A third shot was also being considered: a decoupling shot detonated in a mined cavity to compare with the Salmon and Sterling data. Despite the problems with water control in the shafts leading to the mined chamber site, engineers felt that innovations would eventually allow the mined chamber to be created with a thirty-six-inch-diameter shaft to a depth of twenty-seven hundred feet. Called Payette, the five- to ten-kiloton shot would explore the possibility of fully decoupling a five-kiloton blast and reusing a mined test chamber. Unlike the Sand shot, Payette's chamber-mining operation was not on a rigid timetable; it was expected to proceed at a much slower pace. Long before Payette, Sterling would test the reusability of the Salmon cavity, with an estimated yield of three hundred fifty tons.[5]

Sterling's pedigree is not as easy to estimate as Salmon's. Unlike Sterling, Salmon was a militarily obsolete device. Subkiloton devices have existed in the nuclear arsenal of the United States only for specialized functions. Before advanced designs allowed small-diameter thermonuclear weapons with megaton yields, device size corresponded with device yield. Thus, if one wanted a big explosion, one had to deliver a big bomb. For specialized uses, such as the Davy Crockett recoilless rifle or the nuclear-armed version of the Falcon air-to-air missile, the small weapon size corresponded with a small device yield. The same could be said of the new Small Atomic Demolitions Munition, or SADM. These three devices shared a common warhead based on the W-54 design that allowed for a yield between 0.02 and 1 kiloton, depending on the weapon configuration. All three were actively in the stockpile in 1966. In fact, the W-54 was a relatively new design. Sterling probably used the fissile core of an active weapon and thus was far closer to a weapon test than Salmon, which made sense for a decoupling experiment. Another possibility is that Sterling was the fission primary from a retired thermonuclear weapon. This is almost impossible to discern, because all pertinent information regarding the Sterling device has been "sanitized" from the project documentation.[6]

Beginning on October 8, 1966, United States Public Health Service personnel began contacting residents near the test site. Concentrating primarily on a five-mile radius around the site, they collected pertinent information regarding residents of the area in order to create a viable evacuation program. Despite Sterling's comparatively puny yield compared to Salmon, no one could predict the amount of decoupling that would occur—or whether the chamber's integrity would fail and allow a radioactive leak into the surrounding countryside. As with Salmon, evacuation procedures would be followed, as would other interesting measures. A November 17 meeting at the Baxterville school informed residents of the upcoming test and asked if those within a two-mile radius of the test site would again leave their homes. Sen. John Stennis kept abreast of the developments and was advised that the AEC had determined a shot date of November 29, 1966, at 6:00 a.m.[7]

The early timing of the Sterling shot presented different challenges from those of the Salmon test. Salmon's 10:00 a.m. shot time had allowed residents to leave in the morning and wait for the all-clear signal. Sterling's early shot time led USPHS workers to advise residents within a two-mile radius to leave the night before. Of the 31 families in the area, comprising 127 persons, all agreed to follow the recommendation save for one family that ran a poultry farm. They elected to leave at 3:00 a.m. on shot day in order to tend to their chickens. Instead of paying each adult and child a daily compensation for evacuating, the AEC based the payments on four-hour blocks of time; adults would receive six dollars for every four hours they were dislocated, and children would receive two dollars.[8]

The reason for pushing the schedule up was seismic noise. Sterling was a small device, and the chamber was expected to decouple its seismic signal and make it hard to detect. Six o'clock was about dawn, when people stirred and began their day. Because of the unique nature of the regional geology, commuters added significantly to seismic background noise. Father Eisele at Spring Hill College noted the inability of his relatively sophisticated seismographs to collect accurate seismic data due to the traffic in Mobile during daylight hours: "[A] problem in the operation of sensitive instruments in this Gulf Coast region is the absence of solid rock upon which to mount the seismographs. . . . It is so easy to vibrate this kind of sediment that the local traffic patterns of Mobile are clearly recorded on our records. In fact, from about 6 a.m. to 6 p.m. our records are almost useless because all we are recording are 'wiggles' caused by commuting Mobilians." The early test time would avoid noise generated by the morning commute and diminish the possibility that road and rail traffic would affect the ability of distant recording stations to detect Sterling. Road and rail traffic would be temporarily halted in the area around the test site on the morning of shot day. Newspaper reporters, granted full access to the progress of the Sterling operation, called it "the sneak test."[9]

The only thing that sneaked by anyone on November 29 was the Sterling test. In a depressing reminder of Salmon's month of weather delays, program managers rescheduled the shot for December 5. Whether the device was retrieved following the aborted test and re-emplaced or was allowed to remain in the decoupling chamber is unknown. What is certain is that something went wrong between November 28 and December 2. A coolant system designed to regulate the device temperature while it was suspended in the still-warm chamber began to fail. Nuclear devices seem infinitely powerful, as they are capable of wiping out targets in less than a second. Yet they are also delicate, relying on precise mechanical geometry that ensures the proper progression of the shock wave from the high explosive that compresses the fissile pit. The pit itself must be kept within a certain temperature range so that fission propagates properly through the fissile mass: the warmer the pit, the greater the distance between atoms, making them harder to hit with neutrons. The physical distance seems small, but on the atomic scale this spread can mean the difference between a full fission reaction and a partial reaction or "fizzle." Temperature readings from the Sterling device indicated that the cooling system was not functioning and the temperature of the device was not being maintained. Instead of delaying the test to retrieve the device and repair the cooling system, the decision was made on December 2 to begin evacuation procedures for the area around the Dribble site in preparation for firing the following morning.[10]

Local law enforcement and the state highway patrol policed the area that night while USPHS caseworkers tallied residents as they departed. At 3:00 a.m., the AEC took control of the roadblocks. Alerted by radio, a Southern Railway freight train on the Picayune-to-Purvis main line stopped. The last family left the area just before 3:00; the roads around the test site were empty, save for law-enforcement and government vehicles transporting detection teams and rad-safety personnel. At 6:15 on the morning of December 3, 1966, Sterling's firing circuit closed. The control personnel stationed a mile from the epicenter of the test reported a rumble; cattle grazing near the area also likely felt a mild tremor. Reporters stationed at the observation location debated whether they had felt anything at all. The only people who were certain that something had happened were monitoring seismographic instruments, and they clearly saw that the blast had occurred. Sterling was later found to have exceeded its planned yield by the equivalent of 30 tons of TNT, for a total yield of 380 tons, or 0.38 kilotons.[11]

Sterling's seismic signal was decoupled by the Salmon chamber. Despite uncertainty over the effect that the distorted and distressed salt surrounding the chamber would have on the shock wave, its effect on Sterling was substantial. The postshot assessment found that the decoupling effect was roughly a factor of seventy, exactly in the middle of the range predicted before the test. In other words, in a shot-created cavity of appropriate size that had been excavated by a nuclear blast, a seventy-kiloton blast could register as yielding as little as one kiloton. Though far lower than the predicted effect of a mined chamber due to the inelastic nature of the microfractured salt layers, this was a significant reduction in signal strength. The other important finding with Sterling was the seismic-frequency range produced by the test in relation to Salmon. Sterling, and a high-explosive shot fired in a shaft in the salt at the same depth, produced longer-lasting high-frequency seismic waves, whereas Salmon's seismic energy was concentrated in lower frequencies; it was the difference between a "boom" and a "bang." It pointed the way to the ability of a seismic-detection network to determine whether a shot was coupled or decoupled. Furthermore, the floor of the chamber improved the elasticity of the salt in that portion of the chamber and possibly added to the decoupling effect.[12]

Shot-generated decoupling chambers clearly offered an effective means to attenuate seismic signal strength. Mathematically, the Salmon chamber was appropriately sized for a shot in the two-hundred-ton range, but as the margin of safety in Albert Latter's decoupling figures was a factor of two, a three-hundred-twenty-five-ton-yield device and later a three-hundred-fifty-ton-yield device were approved. As Sterling fell precisely in the middle of the expected range for the decoupling effect, it suggested that mathematical scaling laws and other means of extrapolation were adequate to explore the size of a shot-created decoupling chamber needed to hide a five-kiloton blast from detection. As technicians behind the Iron Curtain would later discover, duplicating the effect that Sterling produced was difficult.[13]

Sterling benefited from the extensive seismic-monitoring program that was emplaced for Salmon. Seismometers placed in deep holes around the site augmented surface stations radiating outward from the test site to a distance of roughly twenty-five miles. The reuse of equipment was cost-efficient and logical. Without the extra expense of drilling and emplacing new devices, the program could remain closer to the overall budget. Reusing the same devices also allowed those monitoring the data to correlate readings from the test site that had passed through a common filter. This simple expedient further aided the employment of scaling laws to model different-sized decoupling effects.

There were no plans to reenter the Salmon cavity for at least eight months after Sterling. Meanwhile, the recording equipment was recovered; USPHS personnel monitored the wells and the milk produced in the area around the test site; and residents returned to business as usual. But there was a difference; the excitement surrounding the Dribble site was increasingly replaced by feelings of resentment. The Sterling test required little extra work from contractors, so it generated less money than the Salmon test. In addition, further talk of Project Payette made people nervous. Salmon, at five kilotons, had caused damage over a greater area than anticipated, although most of it was minor. Payette was to be from five to ten kilotons, despite its being planned for an excavated decoupling cavity. To people living near the Tatum Dome, it seemed that the AEC wanted to set off devices in the salt dome while they still had it. Science and future treaties be damned—they were tired of the inconvenience and wary of damage from future tests.

By May 1967, Payette had Frederick Mellen and Frank Tatum fully riled up. Letters from both criticized the AEC's further exploration of the salt dome for the test. Tatum argued that the drilling could be performed by private companies from Louisiana or Mississippi for much less than the two hundred seventy-five thousand dollars that the *Jackson Clarion-Ledger* reported was to be paid to Fenix and Scisson of Oklahoma. Citing the vast experience local firms had gained by creating underground storage chambers for hydrocarbons and petroleum, Tatum was convinced that activities at the salt dome were outlandish federal waste.

> On every hand, where there is a government project, you see an enormous waste of material, time and effort. As an example, the AEC has paid $150,000 to $300,000 to get a well drilled 2500' into the salt mass at the Tatum Salt Dome and I am sure private industry could have done it for $25,000 to $40,000. As a matter of fact I drilled the first well into the Tatum Salt Dome with a small drilling rig from the Jackson Gas field and drilled 600' into the salt at a cost of about $15,000.[14]

Mellen was concerned with more than government waste. Writing to Sen. George Murphy concerning the AEC's activities at the Dribble site, he argued:

> Never in the history of the United States of America has an agency been given such broad sweeping authority and such unlimited funding with which to carry out its direct and lateral objectives. This authority is abused (1) in the unwarranted seizure of private property under eminent domain procedure; and (2) in distorting true scientific objectivity of other agencies and contractors through liberal funding of these groups. Thus, the U.S. Geological Survey, for example, receives much direct funding through the AEC, a procedure which Congress should never permit, consciously.

Mellen protested that damages from the 1964 Salmon test had not been fully settled. Like Tatum, he wanted local firms to work at the site: "[T]here are many competent people in Mississippi who might perform this study [the assessment of the Tatum Dome regarding Payette] objectively—but it is obvious that objective evaluations are not sought." Furthermore, Mellen feared an all too cozy relationship between F&S and the AEC. He worried that F&S was working on a method of salt-cavity excavation under a government contract that F&S would later patent and use to monopolize the subterranean salt-dome storage-chamber industry. Mellen urged Murphy to conduct a Senate hearing on the AEC's conduct in Mississippi and to investigate whether there had been misappropriations or abuse of federal money in the Dribble program.[15]

Payette would also force the lease the AEC had signed with Tatum to last longer than originally planned. It was estimated that it would take four years from the issuance of the order to begin site preparation to the actual shot. Two years was budgeted for excavation of the cavity alone. The chamber would be deeper than that created by the Salmon test and deeper than the planned Sand chamber. Also, intensive surveys had to find entry paths to the salt dome that would avoid as many aquifer layers as possible. Payette called for a substantial investment in simply creating the test site, and Mississippi would reap little benefit from the program.[16]

Thanks to events several thousand miles away, Payette was ultimately stillborn. The escalating hostilities in Vietnam drew billions of dollars away from the defense budget, including money intended for nuclear testing. While America's conventional forces fought in a futile attempt to quell the communist insurgency in that nation, the fiscal burden was such that expensive programs were delayed and later terminated. Payette was also a victim of advanced mathematics. Because Sterling had behaved exactly as predicted, and because it correlated with data collected from the excavated-chamber, high-explosive tests of the Cowboy series, it was less necessary to fire decoupled shots in an excavated salt chamber. The Piney Woods would experience no further nuclear tests. Activities at the Dribble site, however, were far from over.

More than a year after Sterling, in January 1968, the AEC solicited bids to reopen the Salmon chamber to inspect the effects of the Sterling test. This was not the only activity related to the VU program, as the fifth test of the series, the six-kiloton shot Scroll, exploded in a shallow shaft at NTS on April 23, 1968. No more VU tests were planned for Mississippi, but that did not mean that the AEC was ready to surrender the Tatum Dome. The Salmon cavity proved useable for future tests, but due to the expense and safety concerns attached to nuclear shots, more atomic testing there was immediately dismissed. A data set regarding a nuclear test in a shot cavity had been created, and duplicating the results of Sterling with another nuclear shot was unnecessary. Suspending several hundred tons of high explosives in the chamber center to simulate the blast generated from a Sterling-sized device was also impractical. If a means were discovered that correlated to the Sterling blast wave, using conventional explosives, accurate decoupling tests could be conducted in areas unsuited for the risk of accidental radioactive release. The AEC decided upon a simple explosive mixture of methane and oxygen that could be accurately measured and administered into the shot chamber with little or no chance of radiation if something went wrong.[17]

On November 25, 1968, the AEC announced the new test program for the Dribble site; it was called Miracle Play. It would consist of two, or possibly three, methane-oxygen detonations in the Salmon chamber. The program configuration was well defined from the beginning, unlike the previous atomic tests. The plans called for the two initial tests to yield three hundred fifteen tons, with the third yielding just short of a kiloton, at eight hundred ninety tons. This third test was optional; it depended on whether the chamber was strong enough to handle the blast following the first two shots. The AEC code-named the Miracle Play tests Diode Tube, Humid Water, and Dinar Coin.[18]

Using methane and oxygen for the explosive mixture had advantages and drawbacks. The components were relatively cheap, and a simple manifold allowed easy piping of the gases into the test chamber. Ignited from a central point, the blast wave raced through the mixture, applying a nearly symmetrical shock wave to the chamber walls. The amount of stemming needed to guarantee safety for a nuclear test was unnecessary with gas explosions. A plug of cement grout and sand prevented the gas detonation from reaching the surface. The Salmon cavity became a combustion chamber. The drawback to the methane-oxygen mixture was that the reaction generated water, which could eventually further degrade the salt walls. Diode Tube was a straightforward test of the chamber and gas-handling apparatus; Humid Water, as its name implies, investigated the deleterious effects of water on the chamber and on the decoupled seismic signal. If all went well, Dinar Coin would partially overdrive the chamber, generating energy too large for the cavity to fully decouple. This could generate unexpected seismic noise and give test monitors parameters to determine whether a foreign test had been unsuccessfully decoupled.

As it had done with Salmon and Sterling, the AEC convened a meeting to inform the public about the new program to be conducted in their area. Unlike at the previous two meetings, AEC officials met with some resentment. On December 17, 1968, about sixty people attended the meeting at the Baxterville school. The AEC laid out its case for the test program and its location at the Tatum site. Because of prior tests at the site, the gas tests had an excellent baseline with which to compare the data. As with the Sterling test, reuse of instrumentation holes, combined with the cheaper gas detonations, made the Miracle Play program extremely cost-efficient.

That was not enough to placate residents who felt that the nuclear-testing program's issues had not yet been resolved. Since the Sterling meeting two years earlier, people had reported subsidence that resulted in several buildings sustaining serious damage. The AEC cannily applied a one-year limit on damage claims; it was ready to settle on acute damages, but chronic damage caused by factors like subsidence was excluded. Obviously, the AEC felt that subsidence was not its problem. But the excessive ground motion from Salmon revealed the water-laden quality of the soil and underlying layers. Should an aquifer have been diverted by the test so that its hydrostatic pressure did not aid in supporting the overlying strata, the resulting subsidence could have been attributable to the AEC's activities. To investigate this, more exploratory wells were needed, and wells cost money. William Allaire, now deputy test manager of the Nevada Operations office, promised engineers to investigate the subsidence. With the one-year limit, it was an empty promise. One attendee at the meeting finally asked why the AEC still remained in the area and why they could not conduct their tests at NTS instead of in the

Piney Woods. David Miller of the NVOO public-affairs office explained that there were no salt domes at the Nevada site—at least none approaching the size of the Tatum Dome. If the AEC had similar formations in Nevada, it would use them, because it would be far cheaper. This invited the retort, "It would be cheaper for us, too." This sentiment was probably a key to why the AEC increased its isolation from those living near the test site. Atomic testing bore certain responsibilities, but gas explosions did not. The Miracle Play tests were small and non-nuclear. There was no reason to embark on a public-relations crusade among a population that was tired of the AEC's presence.[19]

Diode Tube, the first test of the Miracle Play series, was scheduled for January 6, 1969. To no one's surprise, it did not take place. Equipment delays and changing construction requirements pushed the date back a week, then two, then three. The valves for the piping system that injected gases into the chamber arrived late to the site. For increased safety, the cement-grout plug increased in depth from sixty-five feet to four hundred feet. Originally the sand backfill extended upward three hundred forty-five feet from the top of the grout plug. This was increased as well, to reach ground level. Problems with the firing circuitry caused Diode Tube further delays. The mixed gas stayed sealed in the chamber while technicians traced the wiring faults. No one expected any perceptible motion from the detonation, just as experts had predicted before Sterling. But not everyone was reassured. Talmadge Saucier, circuit clerk for the city of Purvis, circulated a petition to stop the tests, citing safety concerns and problems with building subsidence in the area. This petition and several letters were not enough to halt Miracle Play, but they underscored citizens' growing resentment of the AEC's presence at the Tatum Dome.[20]

At 7:15 a.m. on February 2, 1969, the test finally took place. As with the Sterling shot, observers nearly a mile from Station 1A felt a slight motion, but the real proof of success was recorded on paper by seismographs placed around the site. As expected, Diode Tube yielded about three hundred fifteen tons of explosive energy. Thanks to its low yield, its nonradioactive nature, and the integrity of the salt dome, the test was conducted without costly evacuations or roadblocks. Ironically, this probably added to the growing antipathy of the residents. During Salmon and

Sterling, they had been active (and paid) participants. Despite Salmon's repeated delays, it was an occasion for picnics and trips to observation points; it was an opportunity to mingle, enjoy cold drinks, and meet news reporters. Salmon was a big story that was important to the world, and thus the people around the test site felt important. Some had their pictures in the newspapers and their very lives opened up to the world. People read about Claudette Ezell's plaster plaques and Mrs. Jones's waiting until Salmon was finished to have her new clothes dryer connected. The papers covered the Saul family anticipating the results of the shot and the mess on Horace Burge's floor. That personal touch was missing from Diode Tube. There was little local participation; what happened at the site had little to do with the people around it. Scientists and technical personnel were now intruders, conducting further tests on an enclosed site and having little effect on those around it. Most of the personnel involved in such defense work were imported from elsewhere; locals held "manual and custodial positions." Although the Dribble site had employed local drillers during its construction, later site operations relied on non-Mississippians. The outsiders may as well have been tinkering in a secret laboratory somewhere. The benefits of the AEC's presence in the Piney Woods were more questionable by the day. Diode Tube was done. Humid Water was scheduled to quickly follow it, and then, if feasible, Dinar Coin. This third shot was the only one for which people living around the site might need to prepare or evacuate.[21]

Humid Water, the second Miracle Play test, was originally planned for mid-February. A month-long delay stretched to well over a year. The test was finally scheduled for April 21, 1970, following reentry, ventilation, and inspection of the cavity. The bleeddown facility handled the waste gases and the radioactive materials freed by the Diode Tube explosion, and site personnel recharged the cavity with its explosive mixture. Once again nature stepped in. The Dribble site had originally been selected for its geology, not its weather. Hurricanes, tropical storms, and unfavorable winds had all delayed the tests at the Tatum Dome, but this time the weather accelerated the pace of testing. On April 19, two days before the planned test, a particularly violent spring thunderstorm blew up over the test site, complete with high winds, heavy rain, and at least one unfortunate bolt of lightning. Immediately after the flash, security guards at the site felt a low rumble under their feet. The lightning had discharged into the chamber and ignited the mixture. Fortunately, some of the seismographic equipment was operating and managed to catch the shock waves from the blast, allowing the AEC to confirm that Humid Water had indeed detonated. But it quickly became clear that lightning posed a threat to any gas detonation, and lightning is common in the area all year long. An expensive war, a declining national economy, and a growing desire to move operations to a centralized location caused the AEC to reassess its offsite testing. Save for the Plowshare tests and the two tests conducted in Alaska, America's atomic-testing program retreated to NTS, where the AEC conducted the sixth VU test, Diamond Dust, on May 12. There the relative ease in conducting actual nuclear tests, rather than relying on gas detonations, rendered Dinar Coin unnecessary. The AEC released news of its cancellation on June 23, 1970.[22]

The fate of the Dribble site had been determined before the Diode Tube test, on January 31, 1969, when the DMA notified the Defense Atomic Support Agency (DASA) and NVOO that ARPA would have no further use for the Tatum site after the conclusion of Miracle Play. Decommissioning and disposal procedures outlined well in advance would begin following either Humid Water or Dinar Coin. They were intended to bring the site back to a condition in which it could safely be returned to the Tatum and Bass families. The AEC lease on the 1,430 acres over the Tatum Dome was set to expire on June 30, 1971, although it was subsequently extended for a year. The AEC planted trees and other vegetation to control erosion around the site. It also removed or dismantled most of the buildings on the site and removed excess machinery and hardware to be reused or sold as surplus. Foundation slabs and roads on the site were left in place. Cleanup personnel incinerated or buried nonradioactive trash and debris. Once it was finished at the Tatum Dome, the AEC had no desire to leave tangible evidence of its presence.[23]

As for other evidence of its activities at the Dribble site, the AEC noted several locations where radioactive materials were present. Because all of the contaminated materials had resulted solely from drillback operations, AEC personnel disassembled all of the contaminated drilling equipment, storage tanks, piping, and valves. These items were partially decontaminated and sent to NTS for storage. Low-level radioactive waste, including rags, coveralls, contaminated paper, and other debris, was packed in drums and removed to NTS. The real problem was the quantity of contaminated soil, mud, and water. The water was primarily disposed of by pumping it into the HT-2 well and injecting it into the deep brine aquifer that had served as a receptacle for drilling wastes from the Baxterville oilfield. Whether collected in the drilling sump, the bleeddown tank, or the blooie tank, contaminated water was relatively easy to handle. But it had also collected in a large storage pond. In addition, the large "slush pits" used to hold spent drilling fluids and other debris were unlined. This had created contaminated mud that migrated slightly into the surrounding clay.[24]

Drillback activities and the 1965 water/steam incident had contaminated the soil at surface ground zero. Slight contamination was detected in the soil around the decontamination pad. Soil materials were not as easy to dispose of as the waste water. Most of the heavily contaminated material generated by the tests remained encased in the melted salt at the bottom of the Salmon chamber. Like the convenient brine aquifer, the test chamber itself became a waste repository. The AEC simply dumped the more heavily contaminated materials and soil down the Station 1A hole. Once they were pumped dry and emptied of their radioactive burden, the storage pond and holding pits were filled with uncontaminated soil. After all of the radioactive debris had been deposited in the chamber, the Station 1A hole was plugged for the last time; a granite marker and plaque were placed at the site. By April 1, 1972, the Atomic Energy Commission was ready to hand the land over the salt dome back to the original owners, with the proviso that personnel from the Environmental Protection Agency (EPA) be allowed to visit the site regularly to monitor it for radioactivity. No future excavations would be permitted at the site, thus ensuring the integrity of the chamber and isolating radioactive waste.[25]

In addition to returning the site to its original owners, the AEC announced that it was terminating its presence in Hattiesburg, save perhaps for one or two personnel. This resulted in the layoff of at least a dozen people; the drilling firms that had played such a critical role in the program were long gone. Mayor Paul Grady managed to put a happy face on the situation in a letter to AEC manager Robert Miller:

Thank you for your nice letter informing us of the complete closeout and cleanup of the Tatum Salt Dome operation near Baxterville. Working with your people during this project was most enjoyable and they were all good citizens while in our community.

You are to be commended for the type of personnel you must have especially screened for this project. Please convey to them that our community is a richer place by having shared this portion of their life with them.

Should we be able to work with you in the future, in any matter, please inform us accordingly. Warm personal regards.[26]

VU was finished, too. The ARPA program that had begun in 1960 ended on July 1, 1971, in an eight-hundred-seventy-five-foot-deep shaft at NTS. Like the two previous VU shots, the Diamond Mine test is listed as being less than twenty kilotons. A period of unprecedented seismic research had led the way to the 1975 Threshold Test Ban Treaty (TTBT), limiting all underground tests to no more than one hundred fifty kilotons. The VU program had ended, but the sealed Salmon chamber at the Tatum Dome would play a crucial role in another important debate.[27]

9. Nuclear Waste

BY THE TIME OF ITS DECOMMISSIONING, THE DRIBBLE TEST SITE had changed from an enormous laboratory to a massive liability. Slated for six nuclear detonations, it had seen only two. It was then to host three methane-oxygen detonations, of which only two occurred. The cavity excavated by the Salmon shot of 1964 proved reusable, yet it showed deterioration after the second Miracle Play shot. When the methane was oxidized in the chamber, it produced water vapor, which worked its way into the cracks and microfractures in the cavity walls. As a result the walls, weakened by blasts and water, threatened to crumble. This did not affect the overall integrity of the Tatum Dome because, compared to the size of the overall diapir, the Salmon cavity was tiny and buried deep below the surface. It did mean that the chamber was useless for further research. Unless the AEC intended to excavate another cavity by means that had already proved useless, or by detonating another device and risking further damage claims from residents living near the test site, the agency would only extend its lease of land over the salt dome for as long as it took to perform cleanup and remediation activities.

Radioactive contamination had first reached the surface during the 1965 reentry of the Salmon chamber. Salt from the immediate vicinity of the chamber was radioactive, which was one way the work crews knew they were reaching their target. Drilling fluid or "mud," an oily material containing clays and other minerals, cooled and lubricated the drilling head. Mud also played a critical role in drilling, because it constantly washed away the cuttings created by the drilling head. The mud then flowed back to the surface through the shaft, was filtered to remove the spoil, and then reused if needed. Radioactive mud was a different story, because it could not be reused. It was collected in large storage pits near the drilling derrick. Because it was not intensely radioactive, storing it in the large pits seemed safe. But the unlined pits, although excavated in thick clay, were not the most secure place to store these fluids. The Piney Woods region has always experienced occasional heavy downpours. The test site had several creeks and ponds not far from surface ground zero. Surface and underground water was plentiful, as were water-soluble radioisotopes. Storing radioactive mud in unlined pits would be analogous to locating a maximum-security prison next to a mass-transportation station. Security might be good, but should a convict get out, he would have numerous routes of evasion and escape; returning him to his cell would be difficult, if not impossible.[1]

In order to combat the possibility that radionuclides could escape containment, the AEC initiated a large cleanup beginning in May 1971 that quickly outstripped its estimates. Soil, water, and vegetation analyses indicated that the primary contaminants at the site were tritium (3H) and radioactive antimony-125 (Sb-125). An on-site monitoring laboratory staffed by eight personnel continually assessed samples collected from different locations and soil depths to identify where more active decontamination measures needed to be taken. Initially, the AEC thought that fourteen hundred cubic yards of soil would require removal and disposal; in actuality more than eleven thousand cubic yards of soil were taken from the surface and the disposal pits and fed through a shaft into the Salmon chamber. Large clods of earth that were too big to fit down the shaft required breaking by hand. The process was expensive, costing roughly forty dollars per cubic yard for removal and disposal. The AEC likewise underestimated the volume of liquid wastes and contaminated water; it originally estimated 77,000 gallons, but ultimately more than 1,300,000 gallons poured into the Salmon chamber. This increased volume of material was due in part to stringent decontamination standards imposed by the AEC. It was also due to cross-contamination of previously cleared sites which then required further excavation. Ultimately site-remediation workers filled these excavations with clean soil and leveled them with the surrounding soil. On occasion, workers were mildly contaminated due to soil and fluid contact, but it required little more than soap and water to remove the materials from their skin.[2]

In other areas of the site, personnel prepared larger objects from Dribble, including contaminated drilling equipment and chemically jelled liquid wastes, for rail shipment to Oak Ridge National Laboratory (ORNL) in Tennessee for disposal.[3] The preparation of these materials included beating the scale and rust off the metal parts and spraying them with a protective material to keep the surface isolated from the environment during transportation. Pipes and tubing had end caps attached to ensure that no contaminants escaped. ORNL's ability to handle contaminated materials from Dribble was limited due to the quantity of waste it received from other sources. The AEC then considered the Savannah River site in South Carolina for permanent storage of the coated drilling threads, contaminated casings, derrick components, valves, tanks, and miscellaneous other objects. In the end, public opinion nullified this plan. The sight of trucks bearing black and yellow radiation-hazard markings hauling contaminated loads over public highways was not desirable. The AEC also had to consider the risks of barging the contaminated steel through the Intracoastal Waterway, around Florida, and up the East Coast to the Savannah River, an estimated journey of nine days. A sunken barge would create both navigation and environmental hazards. Ultimately, contaminated materials from the Dribble site arrived at NTS via eighteen railroad flatcars, a low-visibility alternative that allowed the AEC to sequester the artifacts for long-term desert storage with a minimum of risk. As far as the AEC was concerned, it was a case of "out of sight, out of mind." Overall, the 1971 decontamination effort in Mississippi cost $1,080,000.[4]

Radioactivity was only part of the problem for crews restoring the test site. The site had hosted numerous ground vehicles and a number of helicopters when test operations were active. Vehicles and machines required fuel and lubricants, and occasionally they broke down and had to be repaired. Field equipment required cleaning with powerful degreasers and solvents. There was an electrical substation at the test site; when transformer equipment failed or cracked, the oils inside could leak into the soil. The oils contained high levels of polychlorinated biphenyls, or PCBs, which were considered a health risk. Generators at the site used diesel oil, and the cabling insulation contained copper and chemicals. While teams conducted radioactive decontamination at the Dribble site, they frequently encountered more conventional types of chemical pollution. Many of the contaminants were known by the Environmental

Protection Agency to be carcinogenic as well as water-soluble. Radiation was not the only hazard at the Tatum Dome; industrial chemicals presented their own threats to the environment.[5]

The Dribble atomic tests answered many Americans' questions regarding decoupling. But theirs were not the only questions that required addressing. A little more than half a year after the AEC began its remediation activities at the Tatum Dome, the Soviet Union embarked on its own decoupling experiment utilizing a large salt dome. On December 22, 1971, the Soviets fired a fully tamped device yielding sixty-four kilotons in a salt formation at Bolshoy Azgir in Kazakhstan at a depth of 987 meters, or 3,238 feet. The result of this shot, which was designated A-III, was similar to the Salmon shot of seven years earlier but on a larger scale; the blast formed a nearly spherical chamber 36 meters (119 feet) in diameter. A-III was part of a series of tests designed to explore the capability of nuclear devices to create usable subterranean storage cavities. Comprising ten tests in total, this program was notable in that six tests were conducted in a shot-generated cavity created by the detonation of the twenty-seven kiloton A-II test that had been fired in 1968. Once the cavity was filled with water, the six later shots were used to test methods of isotope generation. The chamber created by A-X, the last of the series detonated in 1979, was ultimately used as a nuclear-waste receptacle, like the Salmon chamber.[6]

On March 29, 1976, Soviet researchers initiated a decoupling test designated A-III-2. At 8 kilotons, the blast was one-eighth the yield of the shot that created the A-III chamber. It was detonated at the center of the void, as Sterling had been in 1966. In contrast, the Sterling test at the Tatum Dome yielded 380 tons, not quite a fourteenth of the 5.2 kilotons that created the Salmon cavity. The results could not have been more different. Where the Salmon/Sterling decoupling test produced a decoupling effect of 72, the larger Soviet decoupling test produced an observed decoupling effect of 11.7. Theories as to why this discrepancy was so pronounced centered on the thermal effects caused by the larger yield of A-III. Its blast would have caused the same microfracturing as in the Salmon chamber, but the overall heat released by the blast was far greater, and it remained in the chamber far longer. Thus the chamber walls were hotter when A-III-2 was detonated. This had the effect of allowing the seismic energy from the 8-kiloton shot to radiate outward more efficiently, overriding the chamber's ability to decouple the seismic signal. Clearly, shot-generated cavities behaved unpredictably; the only way to raise the likelihood of full decoupling was to excavate the shot chamber; that would produce detectable evidence.[7]

The A-III-2 decoupling test may have been preplanned or it may have been driven by diplomatic developments. The TTBT was a direct result of research conducted during the VU program and bolstered by the Soviet tests at Azgir. Representatives of the United States and of the Soviet Union signed the treaty on July 3, 1974, and submitted it to Congress two years later. VU assumed critical importance with the diplomatic efforts to create the 1963 LTBT. VU developed methods so that seismic signals from underground Soviet tests could be detected and analyzed for technical development and prevent the hiding of nuclear tests. Technical means developed and tested during the VU series bolstered the TTBT, making it possible to enact treaties limiting the yields of underground testing. When testing moved underground in 1963, there were no yield limits. Megaton-sized underground shots were uncommon, but both sides conducted them. Primarily, these consisted of weapons tests: America's largest underground test, the 5-megaton Cannikin shot in November 1971 in Amchitka, Alaska, tested a warhead for the proposed Spartan antiballistic-missile system. The largest underground Soviet nuclear tests on record were likely twice this yield. The TTBT put a ceiling of 150 kilotons on all testing, although combined-device tests were allowed a 1.5-megaton yield limit.[8]

Such was the desire to cooperate in limiting their arsenals and testing programs that the treaty signatories obeyed the TTBT provisions even though they did not take full effect until 1990. The Soviet Union's last test officially to exceed 150 kilotons was in late October 1975; the last American test to do so was in late March 1976. The reason the TTBT's provisions were prematurely honored was twofold: first, the Soviet decoupling experiment showed that shot-generated cavity decoupling was unreliable. The vast difference between American and Soviet results showed that cheating was far too risky. Though poorly decoupled, the 8-kiloton Soviet test produced certain frequencies that indicated a probable decoupling attempt, despite the apparent success of the Sterling test in decoupling the device signal. A detected low-yield test accompanied by those particular signals would tip off the other side that something covert was going on. Consequently, the international uproar caused by solid evidence of such cheating would result in the sort of negative public relations that neither side wanted to risk, especially while both superpowers continued to align developing nations with their respective blocs.[9]

The second reason for the success of the TTBT before its official enforcement was that warhead size was shrinking due to the dramatic increase in the accuracy of ballistic missiles between 1964 and 1976. Initially, yields for intercontinental ballistic missile warheads (ICBMs) were in the high kiloton or megaton range. This was a function of accuracy, or rather inaccuracy. To destroy a city or a military installation with a missile that likely would not strike closer than a mile from the target required an enormous yield. This was a wasteful way to conduct a nuclear war, because it meant area destruction instead of target destruction. In addition, it could not guarantee target destruction if the target was sufficiently hardened against weapon effects, or if it was underground. Missile-guidance improvements, and the development of multiple individually targeted reentry vehicles (MIRV), moved both nations away from the brute-force approach. The 1972 Strategic Arms Limitation Treaty (SALT) limited the number of delivery vehicles, not warheads. Thus it was possible to increase a nation's nuclear-warhead count while maintaining or lowering the actual number of missiles by the simple expedient of putting multiple warheads on each missile. To do this, the warhead weights needed to be lowered. Guidance improvements, which allowed individual MIRVs to impact much closer to their targets, aided the process. Militarily, it is foolish to expend a megaton on a target that can be destroyed by a 100-kiloton warhead. Accuracy and MIRVs led to smaller, lighter, and lower-yield warheads; large weapons did not need further testing to prove they worked, but the newer and smaller ones were the products of innovative weapons designs and needed testing. High-yield single-warhead ICBMs remained in smaller numbers in both arsenals for use against special targets, such as the North American Air Defense (NORAD) command center in Cheyenne Mountain, Colorado. Paradoxically, the increase of smaller weapons made nuclear war more dangerous and more likely. But it also meant that there was little reason to test anything above 150 kilotons.[10]

While the superpowers cautiously worked toward the TTBT, the Dribble site slowly returned to its pre-test condition. The return of the land over the Tatum Dome to its original owners was not without special provisions. There were quarterly visits from the EPA and the USPHS for well-water sampling and there was annual radiation monitoring. Once the fences came down, the land reverted to its original state. Deer and other wildlife roamed freely, and curiosity seekers and hunters had free access. Except for the granite marker and a bronze plaque at the site, which occasionally caught a hunter's bullet, and signs indicating the locations of monitoring wells, the Tatum land began to look as it once had. EPA monitoring noted the presence of tritium and other contaminants at the site, but nothing raised much concern; most of the radiological pollution was interred in the Salmon chamber and the remainder was staying safely on site.

Less than a decade after the Tatum family had regained possession of its land, radiation fears thrust the salt dome back into the center of public debate. The rush to build nuclear-power plants in the 1950s and 1960s had led to a rapid buildup of nuclear-reactor waste by the 1970s, and there was no place to dispose of it permanently. The massive salt diapirs along the Gulf Coast, which had proved effective for natural gas and petroleum storage, offered an environment where reactor waste could be stored indefinitely. But the growing environmentalist movement sought to restrict locations where nuclear waste could be stored. The Tatum Dome ultimately became an unlikely battlefield where science and public opinion clashed over the usefulness of Mississippi's salt domes as nuclear-waste repositories.[11]

America's nuclear industry generates copious amounts of radioactive waste. Foremost are the residues from nuclear weapons material production and spent fuel assemblies from reactors. Highly radioactive and corrosive, these are some of the most dangerous man-made substances on the planet, but they are not the only source of radioactive pollution. Everything that was contaminated, from paper towels used to wipe up small radioactive spills to contaminated coveralls, shoe covers, air filters, steel tubing, machinery, vehicles, and decommissioned reactor components had to be especially disposed of. Low- and midlevel wastes were occasionally packed into marked fifty-five-gallon steel drums and dumped into landfills or into the open ocean. High-level wastes were either stored at nationally run repositories such as ORNL, Hanford, Washington, or NTS. Spent reactor-fuel rods were generally stored on site at the plant that had used them for producing electricity. The growing focus on indiscriminate nuclear-waste dumping in the 1970s caused the Department of Energy (DOE) and the Nuclear Regulatory Commission (NRC), successors to the AEC, to evaluate numerous and varied geologic formations for their suitability as long-term nuclear-waste repositories. Several factors involved in the process of selecting such candidate sites, such as geologic isolation, stability, the possibility of water intrusion, and the likelihood of tectonic activity, excluded many locations. But salt domes looked promising for waste-isolation purposes. Ideally, an older, stable, and moderately deep salt dome could contain a repository for thousands, if not tens of thousands, of years. Eight salt domes along the Gulf Coast were selected for special study in 1978. Three were in Mississippi: the Cypress Creek Dome, the Lampton Dome, and the Richton Dome. The DOE further investigated the Cypress Creek and Richton Domes through sample core and water-well drillings. To avoid the problems encountered at the Tatum Dome, quarterly monitoring of the water wells indicated the flow rate and direction of local aquifers.[12]

Public reaction to the program was not positive. The most favorable location, Richton Dome, was two miles from the center of the town of Richton, which would have been within the security-exclusion area for the waste site. The same pitch was delivered to the citizens living near the salt domes as had been given to the residents of Lamar and Forrest Counties—that a government installation meant jobs and income. But the AEC and other organizations at the Dribble site wore out their welcome by becoming quiescent after the first test. It was unlikely that periodic bulletins would accurately report the classified contents and their status in a salt-dome repository. Except in the case of an accident, the chosen site would become a black hole, as the Dribble site had become during the Miracle Play series.

Two events within days of one another in March 1979 virtually killed the initiative to build a waste repository in Mississippi's salt domes. One was a little-reported incident involving *Bufo terrestris,* or the southern toad, while the other was America's worst nuclear-reactor accident at the Three Mile Island power plant near Harrisburg, Pennsylvania. On

March 22, Dr. Edmund Keiser from the University of Mississippi's biology department reported finding disturbing evidence that all was not well at the Tatum Salt Dome. Part of the remediation at the former test site involved collecting and analyzing biological specimens, especially those with a high propensity for environmental-contaminant absorption. These were collected from various locations around the area in conjunction with well monitoring and soil analysis. Small fish and minnows, low on the food chain, effectively concentrated any contaminants found in surface waters. Farther up the food chain, amphibians such as frogs, toads, and salamanders accumulated not only toxins found in the water but also soil-borne contaminants. Amphibians absorbed these materials from food as well as through their skin. In essence, they were canaries in the coal mine; these living biological alarms reflected the slightest change in their environment. Any contaminants present would be concentrated in their livers. Keiser and his assistants collected several specimens that week around the Tatum Dome, noting what appeared to be skin irritation and a few cases of toads with deformed feet. When they returned with their collection to the biology department, they received a major shock. One of the sampled toads appeared to be dangerously radioactive, and initial analysis showed it to contain the element americium, which is formed when plutonium atoms capture extra neutrons without undergoing fission. Like plutonium, americium does not occur in nature.[13]

All of the radioactive contaminants at the Dribble site originated in the test chamber. That chamber had been reentered after each test shot for analysis and sample collection. Anything on the ground or in the water that issued radiation beyond background levels came from the two nuclear tests. Except for the steam event following the Salmon test, contaminated solids and liquids produced during reentry drilling proceeded through the bleeddown plant for processing and storage. Technicians retrieving samples from the Salmon chamber knew those materials to be radioactive and handled them carefully. For americium to be present in a toad's liver, it had to have come from the test chamber—an extremely unlikely source. Americium production is the result of slow neutron bombardment, such as in a reactor. It is not the result of intense high-energy neutron bombardment, such as one finds in a nuclear explosion.

In addition, the level of radioactive emission from the specimen was intense—one thousand times the allowable level set by federal guidelines for environmental samples. It appeared that the Tatum site was venting highly radioactive materials into the environment.[14]

Keiser and his graduate assistants found the samples shocking. As members of the environmentalist group Sierra Club, the parent organization of Greenpeace, they passed the word to fellow members. These included Ron Lewis, one of the leading antinuclear activists in Mississippi. Lewis spoke to Keiser, who confirmed the findings but requested that Lewis not publicize the information until further analyses could be performed on the contaminated frog. Lewis ignored him and passed the information all the way up to Gov. Cliff Finch, who eventually sounded a general alarm. At 3:00 a.m. on May 26, Lamar County sheriff's deputies evacuated residents living near the test site. Finch declared the area off limits. Despite the later realization that the radiation was not from americium, but from a highly radioactive isotope of sodium known as sodium-22, the samples continued to emit dangerously high levels of radiation.[15]

On March 28, the same day that news broke about the Three Mile Island reactor accident, the *Jackson-Clarion Ledger* printed a letter to the editor expressing one resident's concern for the future of the state.

> I see that the U.S. Department of Energy has approved plans for further tests to determine if salt domes in Perry and Marion counties can be used for nuclear waste dump sites. DOE officials also met with Mississippi state officials, and the group reviewed the plans and found no reason why the field geologic tests should not be carried out.
>
> Well, you don't have to be a genius to know that after the tests are carried out the group will determine that Mississippi salt domes will be just great for nuclear waste dump sites.
>
> The U.S. Energy Department is an agency of the same government that used the Tatum Dome as a nuclear testing site and then walked away leaving Tatum Dome radioactive for maybe the next 10,000 years.
>
> From now on you don't have to call us the "Great State of Mississippi" and you don't have to call us the "State of Mississippi" and you don't have to call us "Mississippi," just call us the "Radioactive Waste Dump for the U.S.A."[16]

This letter expressed the growing sentiment of many in Mississippi who feared the federal effort to place dangerous materials in salt domes. The perception of the DOE's efforts at the Tatum Dome is especially poignant. Site-remediation reports, although available, were not front-page news. As far as most citizens knew, the site was still heavily contaminated, despite work to safely inter the waste and monitor the site for further contaminants. The contribution to global nuclear-arms control was ignored or forgotten, and the Dribble site was publicly perceived as a scar on Mississippi's image. The discovery of the contaminated toad further underscored the threat to the people and environment of Mississippi from any proposed nuclear-waste repository located in a salt dome.

Yet something did not seem quite right to the DOE office in Las Vegas. Troy Wade, deputy director of the Nevada Operations Office, found the readings puzzling. Noting that the toad contamination at the Tatum Dome was unlike anything previously reported, he visited the site to collect more information and assist in the investigation of contaminated animals.[17]

The mystery became more puzzling when other portions of the toad were analyzed and showed only trace amounts of radioactivity. Several scientists at the University of Mississippi laboratory and an FDA facility verified the radiation levels from the liver samples. The discrepancy between radiation levels in the liver and in other organs revealed a serious error: the toad itself contained no sodium-22, but the sample dish did—it was heavily contaminated. The liver had been transported to various facilities and subjected to measurement by several methods, all indicating strong levels of radioactivity. The liver remained on the same sample dish the whole time, completely confusing the readings. At least one journalist had a hearty laugh at the expense of Keiser and the Ole Miss biology department. Keiser asserted that the error would have ultimately been discovered. But under media and political pressure, they had missed it entirely. The incident made Keiser and those monitoring the former test site look incompetent.[18]

What was worse, and apparently not thoroughly investigated, was the possibility that the contamination was intentional. Sodium is one half of the molecule that makes up salt. Sodium-22 is a highly radioactive isotope, and in a laboratory setting, it is stored under heavily shielded conditions and handled with meticulous care. But it made sense that radioactive sodium might be found at a salt-dome test site. The animal tissues were not themselves appreciably radioactive; if this were discovered it could easily be explained away as a simple case of laboratory-equipment contamination. Many graduate students in the laboratory associated with antinuclear activist Lewis, who ignored Keiser's request to allow the laboratory to thoroughly confirm its findings. Finally, it made a case that everyone opposed to nuclear-waste repositories in the salt domes could support: salt domes could leak. The *Jackson Daily News* story that finally revealed the errors noted that it may have been a "college prank." Nonetheless, it frightened the people living near the Tatum Dome, and it undermined trust in scientific monitoring at the site. If it was a deliberate environmentalist action, the perpetrators ultimately saw their cause succeed, for in 1986 the Department of Energy removed the salt domes from consideration as waste depositories and instead concentrated on Yucca Mountain in Nevada.[19]

In a newspaper interview, Frank Tatum offered his opinion of the land he once again owned.

"We got lots of contamination down there," he said, pausing for a mock dramatic effect, "of salt. S-A-L-T. You know what that is? And that's it.

"Cattle have been grazing on it. Hunters have been hunting over it all the time. You can't keep fences up. Animals keep going in there to get that salt," he said. "If something was wrong, we'd have known by now."[20]

Tom Humphrey, a geologist working for the DOE, was also unconcerned by the radioactivity he encountered at the site. Noting that the highest tritium levels his team had discovered were about a quarter of the allowable maximum for drinking water, he offered a novel solution that he and his colleagues had developed for clearing out an accumulation of the isotope in their bodies: "People working at the test site occasionally get minor doses of the tritium and our treatment is to drink as much beer as possible—this simply flushes it out of the system."[21]

Yet another crisis developing around the test site was purely human. Despite assurances that the test site was safe, the government did admit that there was a certain amount of radioactive contamination at the surface and in the HT-5 injection well. Further studies revealed that tritium had indeed migrated into some of the subsurface water, but it all remained securely located at the test site. In the late 1970s and early 1980s, a group of plaintiffs who lived downwind of the Nevada Test Site (known as "downwinders") and military veterans who had taken part in atmospheric atomic maneuvers finally won their battle to get documents declassified. These documents supported their claims that the excessive amount of radiation to which they had been exposed had severely affected their health. During the period of atmospheric testing in the 1950s and 1960s, some downwinders had tried to take pictures of the mushroom clouds as they passed near their farms, only to have the intense radiation fog the film and render it nearly useless. Sheep, cattle, and deer died after nuclear tests, killed by unknown means. Previously healthy livestock miscarried or gave birth to hideously mutated stillborn young. And people living in the southwestern corner of Utah, who were repeatedly irradiated by fallout borne by the prevailing winds, developed skin burns, bleeding gums, gastrointestinal problems, and leukemia. They displayed clear symptoms of heavy radiation exposure, but the federal government denied them any compensation because the evidence of excessive fallout was classified for at least twenty-five years; in some cases it took repeated requests under the Freedom of Information Act to acquire the necessary documentation to file claims against the government.[22]

In the area around the Tatum Dome, people also got sick, although the cause was not as evident as it was in Nevada and Utah. Many wondered if their conditions were due to the tests conducted nearly two decades earlier. Repeated monitoring at the Dribble site showed that no contamination was moving off site and that tritium levels were rapidly falling due to natural decay. Still, the scare from the 1979 toad incident, and horror stories in the news of governmental abuse and denial of radiation injuries, caused many to wonder whether the same thing was occurring in the Piney Woods. Because radioactivity is intangible, except with measuring devices, explainable illnesses prompted fears that radiation was the culprit.[23]

More troubling was that the DOE was not forthcoming with information. The AEC had certainly been deceptive when dealing with the people living around NTS. The agency cloaked information with excuses that the issues concerning peoples' lives were matters of national security and could not be discussed. Periodic briefings and meetings would have allowed Tatum Dome area residents to address their concerns directly to the DOE, provided them updates on monitoring results, and given them the opportunity to speak personally to an official representative. Ironically, the AEC held such meetings before conducting tests. A grassroots demand for answers emerged in the Piney Woods, primarily as a result of the efforts of Hewie Gipson, a Lamar County resident who lived close to the test site. Gipson tirelessly agitated for government attention and collected whatever documentation he could about site remediation. According to him, "dozens" of his friends and neighbors who lived near the test site had developed cancer. In 1990 the DOE finally ordered further remediation studies to evaluate the site itself, as well as a cancer survey to determine whether there was a greater incidence of the disease—particularly leukemia—in the region. The initial survey showed no anomalous disease levels compared to the national average. Nor did the comprehensive analysis performed by the Mississippi Department of Environmental Quality's Division of Radiological Health. As noted in the 1995 Baseline Ecological Risk Assessment, BERA also found cancer rates in accordance with the national average.[24]

One might wonder why a rural area would have a cancer incidence approaching or surpassing the national average. Lamar County does have a Superfund site listed on the EPA National Priorities List, but it is not the Dribble site. The Davis Timber Company was a lumber mill and processing facility that operated from 1972 until it declared bankruptcy in the late 1980s. Located west of Hattiesburg, the factory used several chemicals that are known carcinogens in its processing facility. These included dioxin, furan compounds, and pentachlorophenol in discharged waste water, which had caused fish kills in a nearby lake as early as 1974. Granted, the Davis operation was at least twenty-five miles from the Tatum Dome, but it also was not the only source of industrial chemical pollutants. Historically, Lamar County depended on the timber and lumber industries. Chemicals released from processing plants, diesel fuel, pesticides, and oilfield contaminants such as heavy metals from drilling mud—all contributed to wider environmental pollution in the region.

Mercury releases have been recently reported in several instances in Lamar County, requiring hazardous-materials teams to respond and clean up the sites. The region around the Tatum Dome looks pristine but bears the invisible marks of industrial activity.[25]

In this respect, Lamar County and the Tatum Dome area tragically resemble the more agricultural regions of the South. Industrial chemicals and pesticides have been recorded there in hazardous quantities since the end of World War II, when the chemical industry manufactured substances to control the spread of agricultural pests. Left to the caprices of the wind and water, these chemicals, as insidious as radioactive fallout, spread beyond their intended areas of application, contaminating the environment. Like fallout, these chemicals, especially chlorinated hydrocarbons, remained deadly for a very long time. Affecting the liver, skin, and nervous system, they caused illness and death among those exposed to them. Poorly regulated, such chemicals found their way into household use in the form of domestic insecticides. In addition to these contaminants, the aforementioned industrial chemicals created a background "witches' brew" of exotic toxins, as difficult to ascertain in their effects as atomic radiation.[26]

The 1995 BERA of the site concluded that radioactive materials were still present, but their concentrations were low enough to present no immediate threat to the environment. Analyses conducted in several ecological "pathways" for contamination proved mostly inconclusive. The DOE and EPA sampled bodies of on-site water, including Half Moon Creek and Beaver Pond, for water and sedimentary contamination. Their biota were likewise sampled and analyzed. Benthic life, which includes sediments and organisms that live in creek and pond bottoms, appeared to be affected by something, but it was impossible to determine whether that was due to contaminants. In fact, the report noted that apart from elevated aluminum and manganese levels in the water, contaminants were absent. The tritium dosage absorbed by fish taken on site was far below levels that warranted concern. The tritium quantities were so low that they posed no threat to the great blue heron population, which subsists almost entirely on fish. Barium and manganese occurred in substantial levels in sediment samples but were not considered hazardous.[27]

On land, the situation was different. Three identifiable areas emitted substantial radiation: the clean burn pit not far from Station 1A to the northeast; an electrical substation at the western side of the test site; and the area around the HT-2 injection wells as a result of pumping contaminated waste water into the brine aquifer. The area around the substation also tested positive for high levels of copper. These areas were not considered to threaten human or animal life; they awaited more thorough investigation when the DOE was able to further disturb the land. That measure had to wait until the department bought the land from the Tatum and Bass families. The DOE initiated the purchase in 1994; by the time the 1995 BERA appeared, the government owned the land it had once leased from Frank Tatum.[28]

Not only did the DOE determine the Dribble site to be no threat to those living near it, but by 1999 it examined the potential hazards the low-level contaminants at the site might pose to those hiking, working, or perhaps even living there. Once the DOE owned the property over the salt dome, it engaged in cleanup activities of identified areas of further concern. Attention was diverted to the mud-storage pit close to surface ground zero. The DOE detected quantities of tritium and trichloroethane (TCE) below ground level, but excavations near the pit failed to show similar concentrations. This indicated that the mud pit was successfully containing the contaminants. Furthermore, despite the identification of several isotopes of lead, antimony, radium, and uranium, and the presence of arsenic on the site, concentrations of radioactive material were statistically low, and the arsenic, radium, and uranium were naturally occurring elements. The scenarios analyzed during the 1999 remedial investigation included potential cancer risks from radiological and chemical contaminants to park rangers working at the site, and to hikers and backpackers. Danger to residents was also analyzed, especially to young children, who might eat dirt and thus consume possibly carcinogenic materials. The report concluded that little risk existed.[29] In 1999, since water from on-site wells was considered the most likely vector for radioactive contamination, the DOE began installing a water system to service houses in the Tatum Dome area. It could be easily extended on site if future occupation looked likely and it thereby relieved any dependence on well water. Generally portrayed as a step to assuage the local population, the report pointed toward the Tatum Dome's future. EPA monitoring would continue for an indefinite period while the land reverted to its condition before the AEC had come to the Piney Woods—and even before the Tatum family had first cut a tree in its forests. By the turn of the millennium, it was expected that the former test site would soon serve as a working demonstration forest and wildlife refuge; it would eventually be returned to the state of Mississippi. In a little more than a hundred years of heavy human activity, the area over the Tatum Dome had almost come full circle.[30]

Conclusion: Costly Success

IN THE LATTER PART OF 2008, I VISITED THE FRONT GATE OF THE Dribble site. It was surrounded by tall fences and signs warning unauthorized personnel that they were being monitored. Faded, barely legible signs from the time of test activity still clung to posts near the front gate. A flatbed trailer, apparently abandoned, sat in the tall grass in an adjacent field. The road through the padlocked gate looked long unused, although the recent heavy rainfall and the reddish, gravelly soil made it hard to tell. Contrasting with the brownish grass on the civilian side, row after row of pine trees grew on the DOE's side of the fence, looking artificial. Ironically, the Cold War laboratory had so many trees one couldn't see much beyond the fence, while the surrounding area looked comparatively bare and practically despoiled. Then it became obvious: the trees looked unnatural because trees don't grow in rows, and the ones there looked young—perhaps planted in the late 1970s or 1980s. It is hard to tell the age of pine trees by simple observation because they grow very quickly.

The Dribble site is not a state park. It is unclear whether it ever will be one. Despite official reports to the contrary, local people still claim that cancer rates are high around the Tatum Dome. The fences will probably stay up until people forget why they are there and eventually take them down. Occasionally, newspaper and television reporters revisit the activity at the site. They are almost always wrong in failing to discern between "bomb" tests and "device" tests. No one tested bombs at the Dribble site; they tested seismometers and theories. And they tested the people who lived there and their collective patience.[1]

What were the results of the activities at the test site? Internationally, they were crucial. The Limited Test Ban Treaty was hampered without a scientific means to verify distant underground tests and their magnitude. The ability to detect possible cheating by using decoupling to mask seismic signals was a development that further reinforced this critical agreement between the superpowers. Subsequently, the Threshold Test Ban Treaty was inconceivable without teleseismic monitoring and the scientific accuracy that allowed such a treaty to be enforced with the trust of both major superpowers. Science, bolstering diplomacy, gave the superpowers a reason to trust each other. They negotiated, and, perhaps as a result, we did not enter into a thermonuclear war. This is the legacy of the Dribble tests.

The technology developed during the Vela Uniform program led to improved seismic-detection networks. Despite the cessation of the United States testing program in 1992, and the end of Soviet testing prior to the dissolution of the Soviet Union in 1991, other nations have since joined the "nuclear club" and tested their own devices. Pakistan conducted a five-detonation underground series on May 28, 1998, and a further test two days later, with yields ranging from "sub-kiloton" (likely a partial or unsuccessful reaction or "fizzle") to an estimated twelve kilotons. North Korea tested its first nuclear device on October 16, 2006, with a yield estimated at less than one kiloton. Seismic detection, coupled with air sampling, provided the conclusive evidence. This indicated that the North Koreans accidentally or intentionally released radioisotopes into the atmosphere during their test. America still has the ability to conduct atmospheric sampling, the original and preferable method of assessing foreign tests. It also shows a remarkable ability to detect and assess underground nuclear blasts with very low yields.[2]

Part of the story of nuclear-test detection is its civilian benefit. One way to ascertain whether a seismic event is an atomic test is to know where it has occurred and how large it is. The ability to quickly pinpoint the location, depth, and magnitude of an earthquake can save countless lives. Despite the high death toll of the "Christmas tsunami" on December 26, 2004, the seismological systems functioned perfectly; people died because of poor communications and lack of tsunami-warning systems that could have saved tens of thousands of lives. Monitoring personnel knew where the earthquake was and the likelihood of its generating a tsunami. They were finally able to communicate with embassy personnel in countries in East Africa and warn them of the impending danger, which did save lives.

What did Mississippi gain from the Dribble and Miracle Play tests? Initially, it benefited, and some local firms found work at the site. But most of the valuable contracts went to outside firms. The MCEC bid, held to be low on the list of bidders, was rejected with no explanation. It may not have been the most competitive bid, or there may have been backroom deals. It may have been a political decision, for the relationship between state and federal governments in the case of defense contracts was not equitable. The federal government controlled the purse strings and determined who would be awarded prime contracts.

Sadly, this extended to the particle-accelerator program. It appears that, despite Hattiesburg's eager presentation and its willingness to accede to the AEC's desire to conduct the atomic-test program, it did not attract the facility, nor did it seem to have ever stood a chance of bringing it to the Piney Woods. The evidence strongly suggests that the decision to award it to Texas A&M was made before the selection program began. Ultimately, the Dribble program achieved what the government wanted, but it failed the residents of Lamar and Forrest Counties.

Residents of the area were initially supportive of the program, and most appear to have tolerated it. A few expressed worry, but the test dates when locals were evacuated and went to the viewing areas had a festival atmosphere. Once the Salmon test was concluded and damage claims began rolling in to the Hattiesburg AEC office, the AEC became less forthcoming. It could have employed more local firms at the site, retaining at least a working relationship with some residents that would have resulted in a tangible benefit to the community. It failed to do this; instead small articles appeared in the *Hattiesburg American* about the number of damage claims. To be sure, the AEC felt it had to protect itself against unwarranted claims. It is impossible to imagine what liabilities such a test program would generate in today's litigious society, although in 1964 such opportunism was much less common.

By the time of the Sterling shot, the number of residents actively participating in the program through evacuation had dwindled considerably. By the time Miracle Play was announced, public resentment was openly evident. Local people were shut out of activities at the site; those conducting the gas detonations were outsiders. When news of the down-winders became public after 1980, it took the NRC and the DOE years to address the worries and fears expressed by those living in the area. These were people who had been roused from their beds in 1979, thanks to environmental activists and a panicked governor; it took the DOE twenty years to install a water system that removed the primary fear of contamination from residents' minds.

At the time of this writing, it has been a little more than forty-five years since the Salmon test. Most of the tritium has decayed into stable isotopes of hydrogen, and the dangerous materials are safely contained deep within the Tatum Salt Dome. The State of Mississippi acquired the land over the Tatum Salt Dome in December 2010. Except for the fences and signs at the gate, nothing hints at what occurred there. At surface ground zero there is a granite marker bearing two bronze plaques. The back side warns against drilling or excavating at the site without gov-ernment permission. The front bears a more descriptive plaque, outlin-ing in a brief, official fashion the events of six years of atomic and gas explosions twenty-seven hundred feet below. The marker is hidden by the trees.[3]

NOTES

INTRODUCTION

1. Peter Kuran, *Atomic Journeys: Welcome to Ground Zero*, VHS (Thousand Oaks, CA: Goldhill Video, 1999); Peter Kuran, *Trinity and Beyond: The Atomic Bomb Movie*, VHS (Thousand Oaks, CA: Goldhill Video, 1997).

2. Charles C. Bates, Thomas F. Gaskell, and Robert B. Rice, *Geophysics in the Affairs of Man: A Personalized History of Exploration Geophysics and Its Allied Sciences of Seismology and Oceanography* (New York: Pergamon Press, 1982), 204; Howard Ball, *Justice Downwind: America's Atomic Testing Program in the 1950s* (New York: Oxford University Press, 1986). Also see John G. Fuller, *The Day We Bombed Utah* (New York: New American Library, 1984). A census-data analysis shows that the collected population of the mentioned cities and towns within 150 miles of the Dribble test site in 1960 was 1,281,246 persons. This does not take into account adjacent towns as in the case of New Orleans which is abutted by Gretna, Metairie, Kenner, etc. In contrast, the population of Las Vegas was 139,216 persons. Data collected from www.census.gov/prod/www/abs/decennial/1960cenpopv1.html; www.censusscope.org/us/m4120/chart_popl.html (both accessed Sept. 12, 2011).

3. Dudley J. Hughes, *Oil in the Deep South: A History of the Oil Business in Mississippi, Alabama, and Florida, 1859–1945* (Jackson: University Press of Mississippi, 1993), 37–38.

4. Ibid., 49, 112–15.

5. Allan M. Winkler, *Life under a Cloud: American Anxiety about the Atom* (New York: Oxford University Press, 1993), 178–82; Harold Karan Jacobson and Eric Stein, *Diplomats, Scientists, and Politicians: The United States and the Nuclear Test Ban Negotiations* (Ann Arbor: University of Michigan Press, 1966), 178.

6. Bruce Joseph Schulman, "From Cotton Belt to Sunbelt: Federal Policy and Southern Economic Development, 1933–1980" (PhD diss., Stanford University, 1987), 333; Stephan D. Shaffer and Dale Krane in Dale Krane and Stephan D. Shaffer, *Mississippi Government and Politics: Modernizers Versus Traditionalists* (Lincoln: University of Nebraska Press, 1992), 39; Erle Johnston, *Mississippi's Defiant Years: 1953–1973: An Interpretive Documentary with Personal Experiences* (Forest, MS: Lake Harbor Publishers, 1990), 200. In 2009, the author telephoned the Mississippi Department of Archives and History to inquire about the location of Barnett's personal papers. Archivists had no knowledge of their status or location. It is likely that they are held by the Barnett family.

7. Schulman, "From Cotton Belt to Sunbelt," 228–42, 257, 332–33.

1. HUMBLE ORIGINS

1. Donald H. Kupfer, ed., "Mechanism of Intrusion of Gulf Coast Salt," *Symposium on the Geology and Technology of Gulf Coast Salt: Louisiana State University, 1967* (Baton Rouge: School of Geoscience, Louisiana State University, 1970), 25, 30.

2. Jack L. Walper, "Tectonic Evolution of the Gulf of Mexico," in Rex H. Pilger, ed., *The Origin of the Gulf of Mexico and the Early Opening of the Central North Atlantic Ocean: Proceedings of a Symposium at Louisiana State University . . . March 3–5, 1980* (Baton Rouge: School of Geoscience, Louisiana State University, 1980), 87.

3. Roger Sassen, "Organic Geochemistry of Salt Dome Cap Rocks, Gulf Coast Salt Basin," in Ian Lerche and J. J. O'Brien, eds., *Dynamical Geology of Salt and Related Structures* (Orlando, FL: Academic Press, 1987), 631–32.

4. Ibid., 638.

5. Douglas F. Williams and Ian Lerche, "Salt Domes, Organic-Rich Source Beds and Reservoirs in Intraslope Basins of the Gulf Coast Region," in Lerch and O'Brien, eds., *Dynamical Geology of Salt and Related Structures*, 751–52, 771.

6. Kupfer, "Mechanism of Intrusion of Gulf Coast Salt," 27.

7. Miguel Albornoz, *Hernando De Soto: Knight of the Americas, Translated from the Spanish by Bruce Boeglin* (New York: Franklin Watts, 1986), 321.

8. John H. Napier III, "Piney Woods Past: A Pastoral Elegy," in *Mississippi's Piney Woods: A Human Perspective*, ed. Noel Polk (Jackson: University Press of Mississippi, 1986), 12–13. *Coureurs de bois*, or "travelers in the woods," refers to European backwoodsmen, particularly fur trappers and traders in the northeast.

9. Gideon Lincecum, "Life of Apushimitaha," in *A Place Called Mississippi: Collected Narratives*, ed. Marion Barnwell (Jackson: University Press of Mississippi, 1997), 16; Napier "Piney Woods Past," in Polk, *Mississippi's Piney Woods*, 13–14. For fears and behavior regarding the endemic nature of malaria and yellow fever, see Joyce E. Chaplin, *An Anxious Pursuit: Agricultural Innovation and Modernity in the Lower South, 1730–1815* (Chapel Hill: University of North Carolina Press), 93–100.

10. J. F. H. Claiborne, "Rough Riding Down South," in Barnwell, *A Place Called Mississippi*, 86–87. "California fever" refers to the frantic rush westward to the gold strikes first reported in 1849 at Sutter's Mill in California.

11. Ibid.

12. Nollie W. Hickman, "Black Labor in Forest Industries of the Piney Woods, 1840–1933," in Polk, *Mississippi's Piney Woods*, 79–80.

13. Charles C. Bolton, *Poor Whites of the Antebellum South: Tenants and Laborers in Central North Carolina and Northeast Mississippi* (Durham: Duke University Press, 1994), 44, 107–108.

14. Napier, "Piney Woods Past," in Polk, *Mississippi's Piney Woods*, 20.

15. Hickman, "Black Labor in Forest Industries," in Polk, *Mississippi's Piney Woods*, 81–82.

16. Ibid., 82–83.

17. William Faulkner, "Mississippi," in Barnwell, *A Place Called Mississippi*, 103, 110.

18. Gilbert H. Hoffman, *Steam Whistles in the Piney Woods: A History of the Sawmills and Logging Railroads of Forrest and Lamar Counties, Mississippi*, vol. 5, *The Newman and Tatum*

Lumber Companies and the Mills at Lumberton (Hattiesburg, MS: Longleaf Press, 1998), 106–108, 116–22.

19. Hoffman, *Steam Whistles in the Piney Woods,* 108–109; Joe F. Tatum, *W. S. F. Tatum: This Is a Limited Biographical Sketch . . .* (paper presented at meeting of the Ciceronean Circle, Hattiesburg, May 29, 1991), Tatum Family Collection, McCain Archives, University of Southern Mississippi (hereafter referred to as MCAUSM).

2. TIMBER, OIL, AND ATOMS

1. Hoffman, *Steam Whistles in the Piney Woods,* 108–109.

2. Ibid., 114–16, 125.

3. Ibid., 109; Joe F. Tatum, *W. S. F. Tatum,* AM91–47, Tatum Family Collection, MCAUSM.

4. Hoffman, *Steam Whistles in the Piney Woods,* 108–11.

5. Ibid., 113–14.

6. Department of Commerce, Bureau of the Census, *Thirteenth Census of the United States Taken in the Year 1910, Volume II: Population 1910; Reports by States with Statistics for Counties, Cities and Other Civil Divisions, Alabama-Montana* (Washington, DC: Government Printing Office, 1913), 1031; Frank E. Smith and Audrey Warren, *Mississippians All* (New Orleans: Pelican Publishing House, 1968), 59–74.

7. Hoffman, *Steam Whistles in the Piney Woods,* 114–16, 125.

8. Ibid., 116–22.

9. Daniel Yergin, *The Prize: The Epic Quest for Oil, Money, and Power* (New York: Free Press, 1991), 82–85.

10. Hughes, *Oil in the Deep South,* 12, 23, 78, 103.

11. Ibid., 175.

12. Hoffman, *Steam Whistles in the Piney Woods,* 141.

13. Hughes, *Oil in the Deep South,* 93–95.

14. Ernest J. Hopkins, *Mississippi's BAWI Plan: Balance Agriculture with Industry: An Experiment in Industrial Subsidization* (Atlanta: Federal Reserve Bank of Atlanta, 1944), 1–4, 11, 34, 42–3.

15. Hughes, *Oil in the Deep South,* 144.

16. Gulf Oil emerged from a deal among Spindletop prospectors Guffey, Galey, and Lucas, backed by Pittsburgh bankers Andrew and Richard Mellon. In May 1901, Guffey secured funding from the Mellons through the sale of fifty thousand shares of stock, allowing him to buy out Galey and Lucas, creating the J. M. Guffey Company. Six years later, he merged his operation with the Gulf Refining Company, which later became the Gulf Oil Company. Shortly thereafter, Guffey was fired by the Mellons. See Neil McElwee, "Guffey and Galey— Some People Get Around." www.oil150.com/essays/2007/12/guffey-and-galey-some-people-get-around (accessed September 9, 2009); Hughes, *Oil in the Deep South,* 217–18.

17. U.S. Department of Commerce, Bureau of the Census, *Fifteenth Census of the United States: 1930. Population, vol. 3, part 1; Reports by States, Showing the Composition and Characteristics of the Population for Counties, Cities, and Townships or Other Minor Civil Divisions; Alabama-Missouri* (Washington, DC: Government Printing Office, 1932), 1301; U.S. Depart-

ment of Commerce, Bureau of the Census, *A Report of the Seventeenth Decennial Census of the United States. Census of Population: 1950, vol. 2, Characteristics of the Population; Number of Inhabitants, General and Detailed Characteristics of the Population, part 24: Mississippi* (Washington, DC: Government Printing Office, 1952), 24–27, 24–46.

18. Julius E. Thompson, *Lynchings in Mississippi: A History, 1865–2002* (Jefferson, NC: McFarland & Company, 2007), 12, 36, 49, 65, 84, 98, 120, 142, 158–60, 182–83, 185.

19. Johnston, *Mississippi's Defiant Years,* 28.

20. Ibid., 31; Stephan D. Shaffer, "Party and Electoral Politics in Mississippi," in *Mississippi Government and Politics: Modernizers versus Traditionalists,* ed. Dale Krane and Stephan D. Shaffer (Lincoln: University of Nebraska Press, 1992), 82–83.

21. Johnston, *Mississippi's Defiant Years,* 200; Stephan D. Shaffer and Dale Krane, "The Origins and Evolution of a Traditionalist Society," in Krane and Shaffer, *Mississippi Government and Politics,* 83.

22. *Hattiesburg American,* Feb. 3, 1961; Jan. 21, 1961.

23. Charles S. Bullock III and Janna Deitz, "Transforming the South: The Role of the Federal Government," in *The American South in the Twentieth Century* ed. Craig S. Pasoe, Karen Trahan Leathem, and Andy Ambrose (Athens: University of Georgia Press, 2005), 248; Bruce Joseph Schulman, "From Cotton Belt to Sunbelt: Federal Policy and Southern Economic Development, 1933–1980" (PhD diss., Stanford University, 1987), 228, 332, 360.

24. Tatum to Eastland, Stennis, and Colmer, Oct. 28, 1960, Subseries: Tatum Salt Dome T-2 1960–61, folder 27, series 12—Atomic Energy Commission, Box 1, Open-Partial, John C. Stennis Collection, Mississippi State University Congressional and Political Research Center, Mitchell Memorial Library, Mississippi State University (hereafter documents will be cited by document name, subseries file, Stennis Collection, MSUCPRC).

3. THE ROAD TO DRIBBLE

1. Explosive yields from nuclear weapons are expressed in terms of equivalent tonnage of TNT. The most common benchmark is the kiloton, or one thousand tons of TNT. Later devices reached the megaton range, which is one million tons of TNT or one thousand kilotons. All explosive yield data expressed in this work will be indicated by an Arabic numeral followed by the appropriate denotation kiloton (kt) or megaton (mt) where applicable.

2. Edward Teller, with Judith Shoolery. *Memoirs: A Twentieth-Century Journey in Science and Politics* (Cambridge: Perseus Publishing, 2001), 211. Teller recalled the upper figure was 40 kt; Richard Rhodes, *The Making of the Atomic Bomb* (New York: Simon & Schuster, 1986), 656.

3. Rhodes, *Making of the Atomic Bomb,* 656, 674, 677. Physicist I. I. Rabi won the bet; Rhodes notes that due to his being last to enter the pool, the only remaining slot was for eighteen kilotons—close to the actual yield; Charles A. Ziegler and David Jacobson, *Spying without Spies: Origins of America's Secret Nuclear Surveillance System* (Westport, CT: Praeger, 1995), 38.

4. Contrary to popular belief, neither the Hiroshima nor the Nagasaki mission was flown by single airplanes. They were accompanied by camera-carrying and instrumented B-29s charged with collecting data on the attacks.

5. Luis Alvarez, *Alvarez: Adventures of a Physicist* (New York: Basic Books, 1987), 139–41; Gregg Herken, *Brotherhood of the Bomb: The Tangled Lives and Loyalties of Robert Oppenheimer, Ernest Lawrence, and Edward Teller* (New York: Henry Holt, 2002), 139. Dropsondes or radiosondes collect information as they fall from an aircraft and transmit it telemetrically to a receiver. Many are specially outfitted to collect meteorological data such as temperature, humidity, barometric pressure, and wind speed. They are crucial tools in tropical-weather forecasting and research.

6. Ziegler and Jacobson, *Spying without Spies*, 38–39.

7. Ibid., 46. The Charlie test was cancelled due to the unexpected radiation from the Baker test; Charles Ziegler, "Waiting for Joe-1: Decisions Leading to the Detection of Russia's First Atomic Bomb Test," *Social Studies of Science* 18 (May 1988): 213.

8. Both acoustic and barometric means of monitoring nuclear tests are mentioned in reference to detection methods. The barometric methods utilized microbarographs and other sensitive equipment; the acoustic monitoring stations were literally a series of listening posts. Jonathan Weisgall, *Operation Crossroads: The Atomic Tests at Bikini Atoll* (Annapolis, MD: Naval Institute Press, 1994), 119; Ziegler and Jacobson, *Spying without Spies*, 45, 103.

9. Ziegler and Jacobson, *Spying without Spies*, 67, 102–103, 167.

10. Due to attempts to accommodate Western spelling and Pacific island languages, there are several ways to spell this name: Enewetak, Eniwetok, and Eniwetak.

11. Thomas B. Cochran, William M. Arkin, Robert S. Norris, and Milton M. Hoenig, *Nuclear Weapons Databook vol. 2, U.S. Nuclear Warhead Production* (Cambridge, MA: Ballinger, 1987), 151; Ziegler, "Waiting for Joe-1," 213, 215. Zeigler gives a detailed history of Tracerlab and its importance to radiological analysis of atomic testing debris; Richard Pfau, *No Sacrifice Too Great: The Life of Lewis L. Strauss* (Charlottesville: University Press of Virginia, 1984), 96.

12. Cochran et al., *Nuclear Weapons Databook*, 151; Ziegler and Jacobson, *Spying without Spies*, 133.

13. Richard Rhodes, *Dark Sun: The Making of the Hydrogen Bomb* (New York: Touchstone, 1995), 370–71.

14. Ziegler, "Waiting for Joe-1," 223–24.

15. Pavel Podvig, ed., *Russian Strategic Nuclear Forces* (Cambridge, MA: MIT Press, 2001), 485. These devices included the first Soviet thermonuclear bomb, with a yield of four hundred kilotons; Ball, *Justice Downwind*, 56–71; Cochran et al., *Nuclear Weapons Databook*, 152–54.

16. Rhodes, *Dark Sun*, 541–42. Castle Bravo was a weapon test that led to deliverable bombs.

17. It has been widely reported that Teller was a constant tinkerer and that those involved in the tests were relieved that he would not be present, but Teller claims that his involvement with the new Livermore Laboratory prevented his attendance despite the "kindly" invitation of Los Alamos Laboratory director Norris Bradbury to observe the test. Teller and Shoolery, *Memoirs*, 351–52.

18. Ibid., 433.

19. Thomas Ott, *The American Experience: Race for the Superbomb*, 51 Pegasi Pictures, 1999, videocassette; Podvig, ed., *Russian Strategic Nuclear Forces*, 443.

20. Robert Gilpin, *American Scientists and Nuclear Weapons Policy* (Princeton, NJ: Princeton University Press, 1962), 152.

21. Cochran et al., *Nuclear Weapons Databook* , 154–55; Podvig, ed., *Russian Strategic Nuclear Forces,* 486–87.

22. Edward Crankshaw and Strobe Talbott, trans. and ed., *Khrushchev Remembers* (Boston: Little, Brown, 1970), 342.

23. Gilpin, *American Scientists,* 144; Crankshaw and Talbott, *Khrushchev Remembers,* 400.

24. Gilpin, *American Scientists,* 162–63.

25. Cochran et al., *Nuclear Weapons Databook,* 157; U.S. Congress, Office of Technical Assessment, *The Containment of Underground Nuclear Explosions. OTA-ISC-414* (Washington, DC: Government Printing Office, 1989), 31.

26. The RAND (Research ANd Development) corporation is a think tank begun in 1946 by the air force. John McLucas, Kenneth J. Alnwick, and Lawrence R. Benson, *Reflections of a Technocrat: Managing Defense, Air, and Space Programs during the Cold War* (Maxwell Air Force Base, AL: Air University Press, 2006), 107.

27. George Kistiakowsky, *A Scientist at the White House: The Private Diary of President Eisenhower's Special Assistant for Science and Technology* (Cambridge, MA: Harvard University Press, 1976), 5–6; Gilpin, *American Scientists,* 102–103.

28. Ibid., 178.

29. Teller and Shoolery, *Memoirs,* 444.

30. Harold Karan Jacobson and Eric Stein, *Diplomats, Scientists, and Politicians: The United States and the Nuclear Test Ban Negotiations* (Ann Arbor: University of Michigan Press, 1966), 48, 73; Gilpin, *American Scientists,* 178–79.

31. Office of Technical Assessment, *Containment of Underground Nuclear Explosions,* 31–34.

32. Jacobson and Stein, *Diplomats, Scientists, and Politicians,* 74; Teller and Shoolery, *Memoirs,* 434.

33. Cochran et al., *Nuclear Weapons Databook,* 157–59.

34. Podvig, ed., *Russian Strategic Nuclear Forces,* 490–91; Jacobson and Stein, *Diplomats, Scientists, and Politicians,* 45–46.

35. Teller and Shoolery, *Memoirs,* 433; Jacobson and Stein, *Diplomats, Scientists, and Politicians,* 48, 53.

36. Jacobson and Stein, *Diplomats, Scientists, and Politicians,* 47, 49.

37. Ibid., 55.

38. U.S. Congress, Joint Committee on Atomic Energy, *Developments in the Field of Detection and Identification of Nuclear Explosions (Project Vela): Hearing before the Joint Committee on Atomic Energy,* 87th Cong., 1st sess. (Washington, DC: Government Printing Office, 1961), 6.

39. Herken, *Brotherhood of the Bomb,* 327.

40. Podvig, ed., *Russian Strategic Nuclear Forces,* 446–47.

41. Cochran et al., *Nuclear Weapons Databook,* 164.

42. U.S. Congress, Joint Committee on Atomic Energy, *Developments in the Field of Detection and Identification of Nuclear Explosions,* 3.

43. James C. Hagerty, press secretary, announcement of Project VELA, May 7, 1960. Attached to correspondence from Hollingsworth to Stennis, November 28, 1960, Subseries: Tatum Salt Dome T-2 1960–61, Stennis Collection, MSUCPRC. The Advanced Research Projects Agency (ARPA) would become known as the Defense Advanced Research Projects Agency (DARPA) in 1972.

4. COWBOY AND THE BIG HOLE THEORY

1. William E. Ogle, *An Account of the Return to Nuclear Weapons Testing by the United States after the Test Moratorium,1958–1961* (Las Vegas: U.S. Department of Energy, Nevada Operations Office, 1985), 151.

2. U.S. Department of Commerce, *Annual Report of the Director of the Coast and Geodetic Survey for the Fiscal Year Ended June 30, 1960* (Washington, DC: Government Printing Office, 1960), 37; Ogle, *Return to Testing*, 151; U.S. Congress, *Hearings before the Special Subcommittee on Radiation and the Subcommittee on Research and Development of the Joint Committee on Atomic Energy, Congress of the United States,* 86th Cong., 2nd sess. (Washington, DC: Government Printing Office, 1960), 129.

3. U.S. Congress, *Hearings before the Special Subcommittee on Radiation,* 125, 129.

4. Ibid., 129.

5. Ogle, *Return to Testing,* 151, 156.

6. Ibid., 95, 156.

7. Office of Technical Assessment, *Containment of Underground Nuclear Explosions,* 32–33.

8. Jacobson and Stein, *Diplomats, Scientists, and Politicians,* 35–36. For further information on Project Plowshare's nuclear earthmoving program, see Scott Kirsch, *Proving Grounds: Project Plowshare and the Unrealized Dream of Nuclear Earthmoving* (Princeton, NJ: Rutgers University Press, 2005).

9. Podvig, ed., *Russian Strategic Nuclear Forces,* 498; Gilpin, *American Scientists,* 253–56; Jacobson and Stein, *Diplomats, Scientists, and Politicians,* 280–82, 344.

10. D. S. Carder, W. K. Cloud, W. V. Mickey, J. N. Jordan, and D. W. Gordon, *U.S. Atomic Energy Commission Plowshare Program: Project GNOME Carlsbad, New Mexico December 10, 1961, Final Report; Seismic Waves from an Underground Explosion in a Salt Bed. PNE-150-F* (Washington DC: Coast and Geodetic Survey, 1962), 3, 7.

11. Carder et al., *Plowshare Program: Project GNOME,* 35–38; Cochran et al., *Nuclear Weapons Databook,* 159.

12. Carder et al., *Plowshare Program: Project GNOME,* 38.

13. Bruce Bolt, *Nuclear Explosions and Earthquakes: The Parted Veil* (San Francisco: W. H. Freeman, 1976), 231–33.

14. U.S. Congress, *Hearings before the Special Subcommittee on Radiation,* 155–57.

15. Cochran et al., *Nuclear Weapons Databook,* 160.

16. The nomenclature of the Dribble test series remained ambiguous even in government documents, where the program was occasionally referred to as Ripple. Project Dribble began as Ripple; it is likely that Cold War security habits led to the name change, although it was not a secret program. In this book, Dribble refers to the atomic-test program conducted in Mississippi as well as the test site itself. It does not refer to any particular test.

17. U.S. Atomic Energy Commission, *Re-Evaluation of Salt Domes for Project Dribble, Particularly the Hockley Dome* (Las Vegas: Nevada Operations Office, 1964), 9. NTA accession no. NV0338573.

18. *Hattiesburg American*, Mar. 4, 1961.

19. Tatum to Eastland, Stennis, and Colmer, Oct. 28, 1960, Subseries: Tatum Salt Dome T-2 1960–61, Stennis Collection, MSUCPRC.

20. *Hattiesburg American*, Sept. 12, 15, Oct. 7, 13, 1960.

21. Ibid., Sept. 12.

22. AEC Chairman Hollingsworth to Stennis, Nov. 28, 1960, Subseries: Tatum Salt Dome T-2 1960–61, Stennis Collection, MSUCPRC.

23. Tatum to Barnett, Oct. 31, 1960, Subseries: Tatum Salt Dome T-1 1960, Stennis Collection, MSUCPRC. Perhaps most noteworthy is the environmentalist argument, which predated Rachel Carson's *Silent Spring* by two years.

24. Alan Cockrell, *Drilling Ahead: The Quest for Oil in the Deep South, 1945–2005* (Jackson: University Press of Mississippi, 2005), 101–102, 273.

25. Mellen to Stennis, Nov. 22, 1960, Subseries: Tatum Salt Dome T-1 1960, Stennis Collection, MSUCPRC. Mellen's misidentification of the MITRC as the "Board" is not explained.

26. Memo from James Cannon, Office of Public Information, USAEC, to George Dennis, Office of Information, Albuquerque Operations Office, April. 25, 1961, Nuclear Testing Archive, United States Department of Energy (hereafter cited as NTA), accession number NV018673.

5. MITRC, MCEC, AND THE TATUM DECISION

1. *Hattiesburg American*, Jan. 19, 1960.

2. *Hattiesburg American*, Dec. 1, 1960; *Texas A&M News, University Information from Britt Martin VI 6–4919*, undated, Cushing Memorial Library and Archives, Texas A&M University, College Station, TX.

3. Pauling to Mellen, Dec. 20, 1960, Subseries: Tatum Salt Dome T-3 1961, Stennis Collection, MSUCPRC.

4. Tatum to Eastland, Stennis, and Colmer, Oct. 28, 1960, Subseries: Tatum Salt Dome T-2 1960, Stennis Collection, MSUCPRC.

5. Tatum to Eastland, Nov. 9, 1960, Subseries: Tatum Salt Dome T-1 1960, Stennis Collection, MSUCPRC. Emphasis in original.

6. Tatum to Barnett, Eastland, Stennis, Colmer, and Williams, June 27, 1961, Subseries: Tatum Salt Dome T-4 1961, Stennis Collection, MSUCPRC.

7. Tatum to Barnett, Stennis, Eastland, and Colmer, Nov. 23, 1960, Subseries: Tatum Salt Dome T-1 1960, Stennis Collection, MSUCPRC.

8. Jack N. Stuart to Marx Huff, Jan.3, 1961, Subseries: Tatum Salt Dome T-2 1960, Stennis Collection, MSUCPRC.

9. Mellen to Stennis, March 28, 1961, Subseries: Tatum Salt Dome T-3 1961, Stennis Collection, MSUCPRC.

10. Mellen to Stennis, Feb. 6, 1961, Subseries: Tatum Salt Dome T-3 1961, Stennis Collection, MSUCPRC.

11. William I. Marsalis to Stennis, April 11, 1961, Subseries: Tatum Salt Dome T-3 1961, Stennis Collection, MSUCPRC.

12. Mellen to Stennis, April 12, 1961, Subseries: Tatum Salt Dome T-4 1961, Stennis Collection, MSUCPRC.

13. Suttle to W. F. Libby, April 12, 1961, Subseries: Tatum Salt Dome T-4 1961, Stennis Collection, MSUCPRC.

14. Suttle to Stennis, April 14, 1961, Subseries: Tatum Salt Dome T-4 1961, Stennis Collection, MSUCPRC.

15. Frank Tatum stated in a letter to his representatives that the date was actually Feb. 18, 1961.

16. Tatum to Stennis and Eastland, May 26, 1961, Subseries: Tatum Salt Dome T-4 1961, Stennis Collection, MSUCPRC; Atomic Energy Commission, *Site Disposal Report Tatum Salt Dome Test Site,* 14, 16. NTA accession no. NV0338578; U.S. Congress, Joint Committee on Atomic Energy, *Developments in Technical Capabilities for Detecting and Identifying Nuclear Weapons Tests: Hearing before the Joint Committee on Atomic Energy,* 88th Cong., 1st sess., 1963, 501; *Hattiesburg American,* Feb. 8, 15, 1961.

17. *Hattiesburg American,* Feb. 8, 15, 1961.

18. *Hattiesburg American,* Mar. 4, 1961.

19. U.S. Congress, *Hearings before the Joint Committee on Atomic Energy,* 87th Cong., 1st sess., *On the Developments in the Field of Detection and Identification of Nuclear Explosions (Project Vela), July 25, 26, and 27, 1961* (Washington, DC: Government Printing Office, 1962) 130, 132–33.

20. Ibid., 130–33.

21. Podvig, ed., *Russian Strategic Nuclear Forces,* 493–99.

22. Cochran et al., *Nuclear Weapons Databook,* 159–63; Podvig, ed., *Russian Strategic Nuclear Forces,* 493–506.

23. "Significant Events in the Dribble Program," undated, NTA accession no. NV16661.

24. Tatum to Mellen, Mar. 31, 1961, Subseries: Tatum Salt Dome T-3 1961, Stennis Collection, MSUCPRC.

25. Tatum to Stennis, Dec. 2, 1960, Subseries: Tatum Salt Dome T-2 1960–61, Stennis Collection, MSUCPRC.

26. Tatum to Seaborg, undated, Subseries: Tatum Salt Dome T-7 1963, Stennis Collection, MSUCPRC.

27. *Hattiesburg American,* Jan. 21, Feb. 15, 1961.

28. Atomic Energy Commission, *Re-Evaluation of Salt Domes,* 7, NTA accession number NV0338573.

29. John S. Foster Jr., LRL, to Brig. Gen. A. W. Betts, AEC, Aug. 15, 1962, NTA accession no. NV00313001.

30. It is unclear what the exact role of the Corps of Engineers was in the condemnation decision, except that it was easier for the Corps to condemn property for government use than the AEC, which was technically a civilian entity. Alvin R. Luedecke to Stennis, September 26, 1962, Subseries: Tatum Salt Dome T-5 1962, Stennis Collection, MSUCPRC.

31. Tatum to Stennis, Eastland, Colmer, and Williams, September 26, 1962, Subseries: Tatum Salt Dome T-5 1962, Stennis Collection, MSUCPRC.

32. Ibid.

33. Press release HP-62-3, Nov. 15, 1962, NTA accession no. NVO326733.

34. Betts to Stennis, Dec. 14, 1962, Subseries: Tatum Salt Dome T-5 1962, Stennis Collection, MSUCPRC.

35. James Reeves to Stennis, Nov. 16, 1962; minutes from meeting between Mike Manatos and Stennis, Nov. 30, 1962, both in Subseries: Tatum Salt Dome T-6 1962, Stennis Collection, MSUCPRC.

36. "L. L." to "Eph," Dec. 12, 1962, Subseries: Tatum Salt Dome T-6 1962, Stennis Collection, MSUCPRC. There is no explanation of why the MCEC bid was "low on the list."

37. oilgas.ogm.utah.gov/Data_Center/LiveData_Search/view_pdf.php?file=4303710864 .pdf, 16; Frontier-Kemper Constructors, Inc. "Crosscut" Vol. 16, Issue 2, www.frontier-kemper .com/crosscut/ccyearend07.pdf (accessed Feb. 9, 2010).

38. Press release attached to Betts to Stennis, Dec. 14, 1962, Subseries: Tatum Salt Dome T-6 1962, Stennis Collection, MSUCPRC.

39. Oklahoma Energy Resources Board, "Oklahoma: Where Energy Reigns." www.oerb .com/Portals/0/docs/ForEducators/Oklahoma_Book_LR.pdf, p. 117 (accessed Feb. 9, 2010); Bulletin HA-63-5, U.S. Atomic Energy Commission, Hattiesburg Project Office, Hattiesburg, Mississippi, Jan. 18, 1963. NTA accession no. NVO326728.

40. Edgerton was also responsible for the development of ultra-high-speed photography. Slow-motion images of expanding atomic fireballs made within hundred-thousandths of a second, and fascinating movies of rifle bullets penetrating apples and cutting playing cards, were the result of his efforts.

41. Bulletin HA-63-10, U.S. Atomic Energy Commission, Hattiesburg Project Office, Hattiesburg, Mississippi, Mar. 9, 1963, NTA accession no. NVO326728.

42. Tatum to Eastland, Stennis, Colmer, and Williams, Dec. 18 and 31, 1962, Subseries: Tatum Salt Dome T-6 1962, Stennis Collection, MSUCPRC.

43. U.S. Atomic Energy Commission and U.S. Department of Defense, *Project Dribble* (Las Vegas: Nevada Operations Office, 1964), 10, NTA accession no. NVO0321724; Tatum to Eastland, Stennis, Colmer, and Williams, Mar. 6–Apr. 1, 1963, Subseries: Tatum Salt Dome T-7 1963, Stennis Collection, MSUCPRC; U.S. Atomic Energy Commission, Nevada Operations Office, *Site Disposal Report Tatum Salt Dome Test Site (Dribble/Hattiesburg) Lamar County, Mississippi NVO-88* (February 1971), 16, NTA accession no. NVO338578.

6. SALMON RUN

1. His name is recorded thus by the Hattiesburg city office. His wife, who also worked for the city, is recorded as "Mrs. C. B. Patterson."

2. The question regarding the suitability of the Hattiesburg airport was directly connected to weight, not length, for it was at least five thousand feet long; it is currently more than six thousand feet long.

3. Capt. S. E. McGrew, Deputy Commander AFTAC, to C. B. Patterson, Hattiesburg Public Works Commissioner, May 13, 14, June 13, 1963; Patterson to McGrew, May 21, 1963, folder 9, box 133: Commissioner C. B. Patterson: Atomic Energy Commission—Project Dribble (1963–64)—M208 Hattiesburg Municipal Records, Records of City Commissioners, McCain Archives, University of Southern Mississippi Manuscript Collections, MCAUSM (hereafter cited as M208 MCAUSM).

4. McGrew to Patterson, May 17, 1963, folder 9, box 133: Commissioner C. B. Patterson: U.S. Atomic Energy Commission—Project Dribble (1963–1964) M208 MCAUSM; Richard X. Donovan to Stennis, Mar. 21, 1963, Subseries: Tatum Salt Dome T-7 1963, Stennis Collection, MSUCPRC.

5. Bulletin HA-63-15, U.S. Atomic Energy Commission, Hattiesburg Project Office, Hattiesburg, Mississippi, May 15, 1963, NTA accession no. NV0326716.

6. Luedecke to Betts, "Project Dribble Progress Report," Apr. 5, 1963, NTA accession no. NV0075301.

7. Bulletin HA-63-22, U.S. Atomic Energy Commission, Hattiesburg Project Office, Hattiesburg, Mississippi, Nov. 18, 1963, NTA accession no. NV0326711; U.S. Atomic Energy Commission, *Project Manager's Report: Project Dribble (Salmon Event)*, NVO-24 (July 1966), 111, NTA accession no. NV0004351.

8. Bulletin HA-63-23, U.S. Atomic Energy Commission, Hattiesburg Project Office, Hattiesburg, Mississippi, Dec. 20, 1963, NTA accession no. NV0326710.

9. Schulman, "From Cotton Belt to Sunbelt," 358.

10. Dribble Public Safety Meeting, July13, 1964, 4, NTA accession no. NV0096095; U.S. Atomic Energy Commission, *Salmon Event of Project Dribble: Report to the General Manager by the Director of Military Application* (July 17, 1964), 30, 43, NTA accession no. NV0075308.

11. Atomic Energy Commission, *Salmon Event of Project Dribble*, 8, NTA accession no. NV0075308.

12. *Operation Order NV-OPO-5-64* (July 10, 1964), 7–8, 170, NTA accession no. NV0096218.

13. U.S. Atomic Energy Commission, *Re-Evaluation of Salt Domes*, 3, 4, 7, 13, 16, 18, 23, 25–27, NTA accession no. NV0338573.

14. *Pre-Shot and Standby Support for Residents Vicinity of Project Dribble—Salmon Event*, undated, NTA accession no. NV0096064.

15. *Operation Order NV-OPO-5-64*, 36–37, NTA accession no. NV0096218.

16. *Operation Order NV-OPO-5-64*, 17, 23–24, NTA accession no. NV0096218; U.S. Atomic Energy Commission. *Project Dribble* (Aug. 1, 1964), 18, NTA accession no. NVO0003295.

17. U.S. Atomic Energy Commission, *Appendices A, B, and C to AEC 1029/30—Salmon Event—Project Dribble* (July 20, 1964), 227, NTA accession no. NV0075315.

18. U.S. Atomic Energy Commission, *Project Dribble*, 18, NTA accession no. NV0003295.

19. *Transcript of Dribble Public Safety Meeting . . . August 6, 1964. . . Baxterville Mississippi*, NTA accession no. NV0017777.

20. U.S. Atomic Energy Commission. *Project Dribble*, 12–13, NTA accession no. NV0003295.

21. Spring Hill College (Mobile, AL), news release, obituary notice for Father Louis Eisele, S.J., died Oct. 3, 1988. Spring Hill College Archives, Faculty folder—Eisele, Father S.J.; New Orleans *Times-Picayune*, Oct. 31, 1976; Everett Larguier, S.J., ed., *Seismology at Spring Hill College* (Mobile, AL: Spring Hill College Press, 1990), 4–7. All in Spring Hill College Archives.

22. Press briefing statement, Aug. 7, 1964, Subseries: Tatum Salt Dome T-8 1963–67, Stennis Collection, MSUCPRC.

23. James E. Reeves to Claude F. Pittman and C. B. Patterson, Aug. 12, 1964, folder 9, box 133: Commissioner C. B. Patterson: Atomic Energy Commission—Project Dribble (1963–64). M208 MCAUSM.

24. Glenn Seaborg to Stennis, Aug. 28, 1964, Subseries: Tatum Salt Dome T-8 1963–67, Stennis Collection, MSUCPRC.

25. Winfred Moncrief Photograph Collection, PI/94.0005.0195, PI/94.0005.0199, PI/94.0005.0200, Mississippi Department of Archives and History, Jackson (hereafter cited as MDAH).

26. This most likely occurred on September 11 or 12, although no specific information on the transportation is available at present. A 1966 report on Salmon notes that device emplacement began on September 13. See U.S. Atomic Energy Commission. *Project Manager's Report, Project Dribble (Salmon Event)* (Las Vegas: Nevada Operations Office, July 1966), 33, NTA accession no. NV0004351.

27. Ogle, *Return to Testing,* 173; Chuck Hansen, *U.S. Nuclear Weapons: The Secret History* (Arlington, TX: Aerofax, 1988), 131–38.

28. U.S. Atomic Energy Commission, *NVO 24 Project Manager's Report, Project Dribble (Salmon Event)* (Las Vegas, Nevada Operations Office, 1966), 31, NTA accession number NV0018934.

29. U.S. Atomic Energy Commission, *Salmon Event—Project Dribble AEC 1029/30* (July 17, 1964), 2, NTA accession no. NV0075308; *Hattiesburg American,* Sept.11, 1964, from subject file Tatum Salt Dome, McCain Archives, University of Southern Mississippi (hereafter referred to as TSD-MCAUSM).

30. *Laurel (MS) Leader-Call,* Sept. 30–Oct. 5, 1964.

31. Ibid., Oct. 13–14, 1964; *Hattiesburg American,* Sept. 30, 1964, TSD-MCAUSM.

32. Hattiesburg American, Oct. 9, 1964, TSD-MCAUSM.

33. Public-information statement, Project Dribble Joint Office of Information, Oct. 20, 1964, NTA accession no. NV0326663.

34. *Hattiesburg American,* Oct. 9, 1964, TSD-MCAUSM; *Mississippi Press-Register,* Oct. 23, 1964; Bates, Gaskell, and Rice, *Geophysics in the Affairs of Man,* 203–204.

7. SHOOT THAT DAMN THING

1. *Hattiesburg American,* Oct. 1, 1964, TSD-MCAUSM.

2. *Hattiesburg American,* Oct. 8, 1964, TSD-MCAUSM.

3. *Hattiesburg American,* Oct. 13, 1964, TSD-MCAUSM.

4. Mrs. Clifford B. Jones to Mayor Paul Grady, September 23, 1964, folder 1, box 29: Mayor Paul Grady. This letter was damaged by a flood at the USM Archives, and though it was photocopied as quickly as possible, it was barely legible in most areas and completely illegible in others; Atomic Energy Commission (1962–72; undated), M208 MCAUSM.

5. U.S. Atomic Energy Commission. *NVO 24 Project Manager's Report, Project Dribble (Salmon Event)* (Las Vegas: Nevada Operations Office, 1966), 28, NTA accession no. NV0018934.

6. *Hattiesburg American,* Oct. 22, 1964, TSD-MCAUSM.

7. David E. Willis and Philip L. Jackson, *Collection and Analysis of Seismic Wave Propagation Data: Final Report* (Ann Arbor: University of Michigan, 1966), 47; *Hattiesburg American,* Oct. 22, 1964, TSD-MCAUSM.

8. *Hattiesburg American,* Oct. 22, 23, 1964, TSD-MCAUSM.

9. The difference between complaints and claims was that a complaint would typically be telephoned in for investigation as to whether the damage was preexisting or had been caused by the test. A claim involved paperwork and was considered for reimbursement.

10. *Hattiesburg American*, Oct. 26, Nov. 17, Dec. 1, 1964, TSD-MCAUSM; U.S Atomic Energy Commission. *NVO 24 Project Manager's Report, Project Dribble (Salmon Event)*, 54, 128, NTA accession no. NV0018934.

11. Lavern P. Smith to AEC, Oct. 22, 1962, NTA accession no. NV0016539; Frank L. Ingram to Lavern P. Smith, Oct. 28, 1964, NTA accession no. NV0016538.

12. *Hattiesburg American*, Oct. 22, 1964, TSD-MCAUSM.

13. U.S. Atomic Energy Commission, *NVO 24 Project Manager's Report, Project Dribble (Salmon Event)* (Las Vegas: Nevada Operations Office, 1966), 55–56, NTA accession no. NV0018934; James E. Reeves, *Work Authorization Number 1—Station 1A Re-entry, Project Dribble PPB: NLP-2062* (Jan. 3, 1966), NTA accession no. NV0096068.

14. U.S. Atomic Energy Commission, *NVO 24 Project Manager's Report, Project Dribble (Salmon Event)*, 35, NTA accession no. NV0018934; Donald H. Kupfer, ed., *Symposium on the Geology and Technology of Gulf Coast Salt* (Baton Rouge: School of Geoscience, Louisiana State University, 1970), 104; www.epa.gov/rpdweb00/understand/calculate.html (accessed September 15, 2009); handwritten memo: "Drillback to the Salmon Cavity, Project Dribble" (undated), 45–47, NTA accession no. NV0105416.

15. U.S. Atomic Energy Commission, *NVO 24 Project Manager's Report, Project Dribble (Salmon Event)*, 35, NTA accession no. NV0018934.

16. Handwritten memo: "Drillback to the Salmon Cavity, Project Dribble" (undated), 47–48, NTA accession no. NV0105416; U.S. Atomic Energy Commission, *NVO 24 Project Manager's Report, Project Dribble (Salmon Event)*, 35, 75–76, NTA accession no. NV0018934.

17. Handwritten memo: "Drillback to the Salmon Cavity, Project Dribble" (undated), 47–53, NTA accession no. NV0105416.

18. "Half-life" refers to the amount of time it takes for an isotope to lose half its radioactivity.

19. Undated lists, "State-by-State Applicants for AEC's Accelerator Laboratory," and "United States Atomic Energy Commission Proposals Identified by AEC for Further Consideration by NAS Committee." Also, "Enclosure I," document unknown, April 24, 1965, folder 1, box 29: Mayor Paul Grady: Atomic Energy Commission (1962–1972; undated) M208 MCAUSM; *Texas A&M University News*, VI 6–4919, undated, Cushing Memorial Library and Archives, Texas A&M University; Jon Sven Knudson, "Beam On: The Development of the Texas A&M Cyclotron Institute" (master's thesis, Texas A&M University, 1982), 27–33.

20. Opelika, Alabama, was on the list of prospective locations, as was New Orleans, despite its swampy terrain.

21. AEC bulletin H-94, *AEC-NAS Enter Agreement on Evaluating Sites for a Proposed New National Accelerator Laboratory* (Apr. 28, 1965), folder 1, box 29: Mayor Paul Grady: Atomic Energy Commission (1962–1972; undated), M208 MCAUSM.

22. "New Orleans Hurricane History," web.mit.edu/12.000/www/m2010/teams/new orleans1/hurricane%20history.htm (accessed Feb. 14, 2010).

23. *Hattiesburg American*, Sept. 15, 1965.

24. W. W. Allaire to AEC NVOO, March 11, 1965, NTA accession no. NV0096077.

25. Environmental Protection Agency, *Project Dribble Data,* April 21, 1971, NTA accession no. NV0037113. This file is a cumulative collection of air, water, and dairy sampling at the site. For further information on radionucleid health threats, see Winkler, *Life under a Cloud,* and Richard L. Miller, *Under the Cloud: The Decades of Nuclear Testing* (New York: The Free Press, 1986).

26. U.S. Atomic Energy Commission, *NVO 24 Project Manager's Report, Project Dribble (Salmon Event),* 95-96, NTA accession no. NV0018934.

27. *Hattiesburg American,* Oct. 22, 1965; Robert E. Miller to V. F. Denton, Oct. 12, 1965, NTA accession no. NV0096074; James E. Reeves, "Work Authorization Number 1—Station 1A Re-Entry, Project Dribble; PPB:NLP-2062" (Jan. 3, 1966), NTA accession no. NV0096068.

28. Cochran et al., *Nuclear Weapons Databook,* 166, 168-9; Dean W. Kolhoff, *Amchitka and the Bomb: Nuclear Testing in Alaska* (Seattle: University of Washington Press, 2002), 56-61, 105-106. Cannikin is notable for the environmental outrage it generated and for attempts by Sierra Club members to stop it by sailing the ship *Greenpeace* to the area; this action, motivated by the Milrow test and funded by an antitesting benefit rock concert, spawned the organization Greenpeace.

29. *Hattiesburg American,* Sept. 14-15, 1965; Hattiesburg Chamber of Commerce to Mayor Paul Grady, Nov. 24, 1965, folder 1, box 29: Mayor Paul Grady: Atomic Energy Commission (1962-1972; undated), M208 MCAUSM.

30. Dr. Spofford G. English to Mayor Paul Grady, Dec. 27, 1965; Mayor Paul Grady to Dr. Spofford G. English, Jan. 31, 1966, folder 1, box 29:Mayor Paul Grady: Atomic Energy Commission (1962-72; undated), M208 MCAUSM; *Hattiesburg American,* Dec. 1, Dec. 22, 1965; Schulman, "From Cotton Belt to Sunbelt," 272, 332, 353.

31. Knudson, *Beam On,* 33, 38, 67-71.

32. Ibid., 38.

8. A SILVER LINING AND A MIRACLE PLAY

1. Donald H. Kupfer, "Relationship of Internal to External Structure of Salt Domes," in *Diapirs and Diapirism: A Symposium . . . in New Orleans, Louisiana, April 26-29, 1965,* ed. Jules Braunstein and Gerald D. O'Brien (Tulsa, OK: American Association of Petroleum Geologists, 1968), 81.

2. "Unclassified Excerpt from Technical Concept, Project Sterling" (July 7, 1966), 6, NTA accession no. NV0096497.

3. Ibid.

4. Ibid., 10.

5. Dean Warner, "Project Payette" (Aug. 19, 1966), 4-6, U.S. Department of Energy, Department Office of Scientific and Technical Information (hereafter cited as OSTI), reference number 434320. Accessible via www.osti.gov.

6. Hansen, *U.S. Nuclear Weapons: The Secret History,* 107; James Norris Gibson, *The History of the U.S. Nuclear Arsenal* (Greenwich: Brompton Books, 1989), 79, 179, 187.

7. U.S. Public Health Service, "Vela Uniform Program, Sterling Event: Off-Site Surveillance," VUF-1036 (May 24, 1968), 6; John J. Burke to Stennis, Nov. 14, 1966, Subseries: Tatum Salt Dome T-8 1963-67, Stennis Collection, MSUCPRC.

8. United States Public Health Service, "Vela Uniform Program, Sterling Event: Off-Site Surveillance," VUF-1036 (May 24, 1968), 9–10, 14; *Mobile Press-Register*, Dec. 4, 1966.

9. "'Hill' Professor Does Something about Quakes," n.d., n.p., reference number 2006.002.4, Father Louis Eisele subject folder, Spring Hill College Archives; *Mobile Press-Register*, Dec. 4, 1966.

10. James E. Reeves to Governor Paul Johnston Jr., Jan. 10, 1967, box 48: Correspondence, Alphabetical A-Be, folder 6, Correspondence: Alphabetical: At-Ay, M191: Johnston Family Papers. MCAUSM.

11. U.S. Public Health Service, "Vela Uniform Program, Sterling Event: Off-Site Surveillance," VUF-1036 (May 24, 1968), 13–14. Accessed via the Defense Technical Information Center (DTIC), www.dtic.mil/cgi-bin/GetTRDoc?AD=ADA382680&Location=U2&doc=G etTRDoc.pdf (accessed September 30, 2009); *Mobile Press-Register*, Dec. 4, 1966.

12. D. Springer et al., "The Sterling Experiment: Decoupling of Seismic Waves by a Shot-Generated Cavity," *Journal of Geophysical Research* 73 (Sept. 15, 1968): 5995–96, 6000–6002, 6009–10.

13. "Unclassified Excerpt from Technical Concept, Project Sterling" (Jul. 7, 1966), 6, NTA accession no. NV0096497.

14. Tatum to Mellen, May 15, 1967, Subseries: Tatum Salt Dome T-8 1963–67, Stennis Collection, MSUCPRC.

15. Mellen to George Murphy, May 15, 1967, Subseries: Tatum Salt Dome T-8 1963–6, Stennis Collection, MSUCPRC.

16. Dean Warner, "Project Payette" (Aug. 19, 1966), 4, OSTI reference no. 434320.

17. Cochran et al., *Nuclear Weapons Databook*, 168.

18. O'Neill to Stennis, Nov. 25, 1968, Subseries: Tatum Salt Dome T-9 1968–70, Stennis Collection, MSUCPRC.

19. "Summary of Dec. 17, 1968, meeting at the Baxterville school," attached to Stradinger to Overby, Jan. 8, 1969, Subseries: Tatum Salt Dome T-9 1968–70, Stennis Collection, MSUCPRC.

20. "AEC Bulletin HA-68-9," Jan. 16, 1969; O'Neill to Stennis, Jan. 27, 1969; petition and letters from Talmadge S. Saucier to Stennis Dec. 23, 1968, AEC bulletins, Jan. 31, 1969, and Feb. 1, 1969, Subseries: Tatum Salt Dome T-9 1968–70, Stennis Collection, MSUCPRC.

21. AEC Bulletin HA-68–13, Feb. 2, 1969, Subseries: Tatum Salt Dome T-9 1968–70, Stennis Collection, MSUCPRC; Schulman, "From Cotton Belt to Sunbelt," 257.

22. AEC bulletin from O'Neill to Stennis, Apr. 22, 1970; O'Neill to Stennis, Jun. 23, 1970; both in Subseries: Tatum Salt Dome T-9 1968–70, Stennis Collection, MSUCPRC; Cochran et al., *Nuclear Weapons Databook*, 169.

23. U.S. Atomic Energy Commission *Site Disposal Report Tatum Salt Dome Test Site*, 1–2, 10, 40, NTA accession no. NV0338578.

24. Ibid., 25; U.S. Department of Energy, Nevada Operations Office. *Special Study Tatum Dome Test Site Lamar County, Mississippi Final Report*. NVO-200 (Washington, DC: Government Printing Office, 1978), 23–28.

25. U.S. Atomic Energy Commission, *Site Disposal Report Tatum Salt Dome Test Site*, 31, 36, 40, NTA accession no. NV0338578; Robert E. Miller to Mayor Paul Grady, Mar. 31,

1972, folder 1, box 29: Mayor Paul Grady: Atomic Energy Commission (1962–1972; undated), M208 MCAUSM.

26. Miller to Mayor Paul Grady, Mar. 31, 1972; Grady to Miller, Apr. 11, 1972, both in Records, folder 1, box 29: Mayor Paul Grady: Atomic Energy Commission (1962–1972; undated), M208 MCAUSM.

27. Cochran et al., *Nuclear Weapons Databook,* 169.

9. NUCLEAR WASTE

1. U.S. Department of Energy, Nevada Operations Office, *Special Study: Tatum Dome Test Site Lamar County, Mississippi Final Report,* NVO-200 (Washington, DC: Government Printing Office, 1978), 23–28.

2. Bruce W. Church, "Nevada Operations Overview," and Arden E. Bicker, "Site Decontamination," in *Environmental Decontamination: Proceedings of the Workshop December 4–5, 1979, Oak Ridge Tennessee,* ed. George A Cristy and Helen C. Jernigan (Oak Ridge: Oak Ridge National Laboratory, 1981), 62, 91–95, OSTI no. 6529387. Obtained through www.osti.gov (accessed Sept. 30, 2009).

3. This would have been liquids other than tritium-contaminated water.

4. Memo, Donald H. Edwards to William D. Smith Jr. re Disposal of Liquid Radioactive Waste, OSB:JRM-1829, Dec. 15, 1966, NTA accession no. NV0095861; memo, Otto H. Roehlk to W. W. Allaire re Contaminated Liquid—Project Dribble OSB:WRB-446, April 14, 1966, NTA accession no. NV0096184; U.S. Atomic Energy Commission, *Status and Alternative Plans for Cleanup Preparatory to Disposition of Tatum Salt Dome Test Site (Dribble/Hattiesburg), Report to the Assistant General Manager for Military Application by the Manager, Nevada Operations Office (NVOO),* undated (written after May 1970), NTA accession no. NV0095768; Church, "Nevada Operations Overview" and Bicker, "Site Decontamination," in Cristy and Jernigan, *Environmental Decontamination,* 62, 94, OSTI no. 6529387.

5. U.S. Department of Energy, *Salmon Site Remedial Investigation Report, vol.1—DOE/NV—494; vol. 1 /Rev.1* (Washington, DC: Government Printing Office, 1999), Sec. 1, pp. 10–12.

6. L. A. Glenn, "Comparing U.S. and Russian Experience with Cavity Decoupling in Salt," *Geophysical Research Letters,* 20 (May 1993), 919; Podvig, ed., *Russian Strategic Nuclear Forces,* 476–77, 512, 541.

7. Glenn, "Comparing U.S. and Russian Experience," 919, 921. Glenn cited an eight-kiloton yield, while Podvig lists the shot as being ten kilotons. As the comparative decoupling effects come from Glenn's article, his lower yield is used.

8. Podvig notes at least three Soviet tests listed in the range of "1,500–10,000" kilotons. They were conducted on Sept. 12, 1973, Oct. 27, 1973, and Nov. 27, 1974. All three were weapons-development tests conducted at the Novaya Zemlya range. Podvig, ed., *Russian Strategic Nuclear Forces,* 454, 522–25. The provision for combined-device tests was related to Plowshare and Peaceful Nuclear Explosions (PNE) where large excavation and earthmoving projects utilized several nuclear devices detonated in concert. The total yield could not exceed 1.5 megatons, which was the equivalent of ten devices at the TTBT limit of 150 kilotons.

9. Glenn, "Comparing U.S. and Russian Experience," 919, 921.

10. For the development of increasingly accurate ballistic missiles and MIRV technology, see Donald MacKenzie, *Inventing Accuracy: A Historical Sociology of Nuclear Missile Guidance* (Cambridge: MIT Press, 2001). Tables on pp. 428–29 show the comparative improvements in missile accuracy between the United States and Soviet land-based and submarine-launched missiles.

11. Stone and Webster Engineering Corporation, *Final Report on Decommissioning Boreholes and Wellsite Restoration, Gulf Coast Interior Salt Domes of Mississippi, Revision 0. Report Number DOE/CH/10285—T1* (1989), 6, OSTI no. 10122492.

12. Ibid. For a more thorough analysis of America's nuclear-waste storage, see J. Samuel Walker, *The Road to Yucca Mountain: The Development of Radioactive Waste Policy in the United States* (Berkeley: University of California Press, 2009).

13. *Jackson Clarion-Ledger*, Mar. 22, 1979; *Jackson Daily News*, Jun. 1, 1979, Subject File: Tatum Salt Dome, Mississippi Department of Archives and History (hereafter referred to as TSD-MDAH). For a full account of the Three Mile Island accident, and the loss of public confidence due to its handling by the Nuclear Regulatory Commission, see J. Samuel Walker, *Three Mile Island: A Nuclear Crisis in Historical Perspective* (Berkley: University of California Press, 2004).

14. *Jackson Clarion-Ledger*, Mar. 22, 1979; *Jackson Daily News*, Jun. 1, 1979, TSD-MDAH.

15. *Jackson Clarion-Ledger*, Mar. 22, May 26, 1979, TSD-MDAH.

16. *Jackson Clarion-Ledger*, Mar. 28, 1979, TSD-MDAH.

17. Many years later, at a reception at the National Atomic Testing Museum in Las Vegas, Wade told the author that the first indication that something was amiss with the radiation reports was when DOE personnel calculated that, to concentrate and emit the levels of radioactivity being given off by the toad-liver samples, the animal would have to have weighed more than four hundred pounds. Ibid., Mar. 22, 1979, TSD-MDAH.

18. *Jackson Daily News*, Jun. 1, 1979, TSD-MDAH.

19. Ibid., Stone and Webster Engineering Corporation; *Final Report on Decommissioning Boreholes and Wellsite Restoration*, 6, OSTI no. 10122492. Information on Sodium-22 radiation hazards and handling guidelines may be found at industry.ucsf.edu/ehs/12501-DSY/version/default/part/4/data/ (last accessed Aug. 30, 2011).

20. *Jackson Clarion-Ledger*, Jun. 18, 1979, TSD-MDAH.

21. Ibid., Aug. 15, 1979, TSD-MDAH.

22. For more information on the downwinders and their efforts to gain compensation from the government for radiation injuries, see Philip L. Fradkin, *Fallout: An American Tragedy* (Tucson: University of Arizona Press, 1989); Fuller, *The Day We Bombed Utah;* Thomas H. Saffer and Orville E. Kelley, *Countdown Zero* (New York: G. P. Putnam's Sons, 1982); and Ball, *Justice Downwind*.

23. *Hattiesburg American*, Nov. 2, 1990; *Jackson Clarion-Ledger*, Apr. 20, 1993, TSD-MDAH.

24. *Jackson Clarion-Ledger*, Apr. 20, 1993, TSD-MDAH; IT Corporation, *Baseline Ecological Risk Assessment: Salmon Site Lamar County, Mississippi DOE/NV—394 UC-700* (Las Vegas: Nevada Operations Office, 1995), 34, OSTI no. 64136.

25. Information on the Davis Timber Company and the mercury leaks comes from the EPA website www.epa.gov/region4/waste/npl/nplms/davtimms.htm (accessed Sept. 30, 2009).

26. Pete Daniel, *Toxic Drift: Pesticides and Health in the Post–World War II South* (Baton Rouge: Louisiana State University Press, 2005), 1, 3, 78, 130, 145–50, 169.

27. IT Corporation, *Baseline Ecological Risk Assessment,* 149–50, OSTI no. 64136.

28. Ibid.

29. Cancer risk, based upon complicated statistical analyses, is difficult to ascertain. Similarly, the cause of cancer is difficult to determine in many cases. The acceptable level for carcinogens at the Dribble site was low. Indeed, in the matter of some radionucleides, the allowable dose on site was less than was generally found elsewhere due to the fallout deposited during atmospheric testing. The microdoses of industrial chemicals were likewise extremely low. Still, they constituted a statistical risk.

30. U.S. Department of Energy, *Nevada Environmental Restoration Project,* 201–12, OSTI no. 14966.

CONCLUSION

1. WLOX-TV, a Biloxi television station, produced a two-part television report on the Dribble site in 2007. It is accessible at www.wlox.com/Global/story.asp?S=7836706 (accessed Feb. 21, 2010); in addition, several years ago a newspaper article appeared discussing the activities at the Dribble site. James W. Crawley, "The Day We Nuked Mississippi," Media General News Service, July 11, 2005, http://bridge.mgnetwork.com/index.cfm?S iteID=srl&PackageID=46&fuseaction=article.main&ArticleID=7294&GroupID=215. Last accessed Dec. 21, 2011.

2. This information comes from the Federation of American Scientists website, www.fas.org/nuke/guide/pakistan/nuke/index.html; www.fas.org/nuke/guide/dprk/nuke/index.html (accessed Oct. 2, 2009).

3. "Mississippi now owns nuclear testing grounds." www.wlox.com/Global/story.asp?S=13684766 (last accessed Dec. 21, 2011; "Salmon and Sterling Nuclear Detonation Test Site, Tatum Salt Dome, Baxterville, Mississippi, Mens et Manus.Net, 2006 October." www.mensetmanus.net/salmon-sterling-site/ (last accessed Feb. 21, 2010).

BIBLIOGRAPHY

PRIMARY SOURCES

Archival Sources

Mississippi Department of Archives and History
    Subject File, Tatum Salt Dome.
    Winfred Moncrief Photograph Collection.

Mississippi State University, Congressional and Political Research Center
    Collected papers of Sen. John C. Stennis.

Spring Hill College Archives and Special Collections
    Subject File, Father Louis Eisele, S.J.

U.S. Department of Energy, Nuclear Testing Archive

University of South Mississippi, McCain Archives Manuscript Collections
    Mayoral records: Mayor Paul Grady.
    Johnson family papers.
    Records of city commissioners: Commissioner C. B. Patterson.

Government Documents

U.S. Coast and Geodetic Survey. *Atomic Energy Commission. Plowshare Program: Project GNOME Carlsbad, New Mexico, December 10, 1961 Final Report; Seismic Waves from an Underground Explosion in a Salt Bed. PNE-150-F,* by D. S. Carder, W. K. Cloud, W. V. Mickey, J. N. Jordan, and D. W. Gordon. Washington, DC: Government Printing Office, 1962.

U.S. Congress. Joint Committee on Atomic Energy. *Developments in Technical Capabilities for Detecting and Identifying Nuclear Weapons Tests: Hearing before* the *Joint Committee on Atomic Energy*. 88th Cong., 1st sess. Washington, DC: Government Printing Office, 1963.

———. *Hearings before the Joint Committee on Atomic Energy Congress of the United States, on the Developments in the Field of Detection and Identification of Nuclear Explosions (Project Vela), July 25, 26, and 27, 1961*. 87th Cong., 1st sess. Washington, DC: Government Printing Office, 1962.

———. *Hearings before the Special Subcommittee on Radiation and the Subcommittee on Research and Development of the Joint Committee on Atomic Energy*, 86th Cong., 2nd sess. Washington, DC: Government Printing Office, 1960.

———. *Developments in the Field of Detection and Identification of Nuclear Explosions (Project Vela): Hearing before the Joint Committee on Atomic Energy*. 87th Cong., 1st sess. Washington, DC: Government Printing Office, 1961.

———. Office of Technical Assessment. *The Containment of Underground Nuclear Explosions*. OTA-ISC-414. Washington, DC: Government Printing Office, 1989.

U.S. Department of Commerce. Bureau of the Census. *Thirteenth Census of the United States Taken in the Year 1910, vol. 2: Population 1910; Reports by States with Statistics for Counties, Cities and Other Civil Divisions, Alabama-Montana*. Washington, DC: Government Printing Office, 1913.

———. *Fifteenth Census of the United States:1930. Population, vol. 3, part 1; Reports by States, Showing the Composition and Characteristics of the Population for Counties, Cities, and Townships or Other Minor Civil Divisions; Alabama-Missouri*. Washington, DC: Government Printing Office, 1932.

———. *A Report of the Seventeenth Decennial Census of the United States. Census of Population: 1950, vol. 2, Characteristics of the Population; Number of Inhabitants, General and Detailed Characteristics of the Population, part 24: Mississippi*. Washington, DC: Government Printing Office, 1952.

U.S. Department of Energy. *Salmon Site Remedial Investigation Report, vol. 1 DOE/NV—494-vol. 1/Rev.1*. Washington, DC: Government Printing Office, 1999.

SECONDARY SOURCES

Albornoz, Miguel. *Hernando De Soto: Knight of the Americas, Translated from the Spanish by Bruce Boeglin*. New York: Franklin Watts, 1986.

Alvarez, Luis. *Alvarez: Adventures of a Physicist*. New York: Basic Books, 1987.

Ball, Howard. *Justice Downwind: America's Atomic Testing Program in the 1950s*. New York: Oxford University Press, 1986.

Barnwell, Marion, ed. *A Place Called Mississippi: Collected Narratives*. Jackson: University Press of Mississippi, 1997.

Bates, Charles C., Thomas F. Gaskell, and Robert B. Rice. *Geophysics in the Affairs of Man: A Personalized History of Exploration Geophysics and Its Allied Sciences of Seismology and Oceanography*. New York: Pergamon Press, 1982.

Bolt, Bruce. *Nuclear Explosions and Earthquakes: The Parted Veil*. San Francisco: W. H. Freeman and Co., 1976.

Bolton, Charles C. *Poor Whites of the Antebellum South: Tenants and Laborers in Central North Carolina and Northeast Mississippi*. Durham, NC: Duke University Press, 1994.

Braunstein, Jules, and Gerald D. O'Brien, eds. *Diapirs and Diapirism: A Symposium, Including Papers Presented at the 50th Annual Meeting of the Association in New Orleans, Louisiana, April 26–29, 1965, and Some Others*. Tulsa, OK: American Association of Petroleum Geologists, 1968.

Chaplin, Joyce E. *An Anxious Pursuit: Agricultural Innovation and Modernity in the Lower South, 1730–1815*. Chapel Hill: University of North Carolina Press, 1993.

Cobb, James C. *Industrialization and Southern Society, 1877–1984*. Lexington: University Press of Kentucky, 1984.

———. *The Selling of the South: The Southern Crusade for Industrial Development, 1936–1990*. 2nd ed. Urbana: University of Illinois Press, 1993.

Cochran, Thomas B., William M. Arkin, Robert S. Norris, and Milton M. Hoenig. *Nuclear Weapons Databook, Vol. 2: U.S. Nuclear Warhead Production*. Cambridge, MA: Ballinger Publishing Co., 1987.

Cockrell, Alan. *Drilling Ahead: The Quest for Oil in the Deep South, 1945–2005*. Jackson: University Press of Mississippi, 2005.

Cristy, George A., and Helen C. Jernigan, eds. *Environmental Decontamination: Proceedings of the Workshop December 4–5, 1979, Oak Ridge, Tennessee*. Oak Ridge: Oak Ridge National Laboratory, 1981.

Daniel, Pete. *Toxic Drift: Pesticides and Health in the Post–World War II South*. Baton Rouge: Louisiana State University Press, 2005.

Fradkin, Philip L. *Fallout: An American Tragedy*. Tucson: University of Arizona Press, 1989.

Fuller, John G. *The Day We Bombed Utah: America's Most Lethal Secret*. New York: New American Library, 1984.

Gazit, Chana. *Meltdown at Three Mile Island*. Alexandria, VA: PBS Video, 1999. Videocassette (VHS).

Gibson, James Norris. *The History of the U.S. Nuclear Arsenal*. Greenwich, CT: Brompton Books, 1989.

Gilpin, Robert. *American Scientists and Nuclear Weapons Policy*. Princeton, NJ: Princeton University Press, 1962.

Glenn, L. A. "Comparing U.S. and Russian Experience with Cavity Decoupling in Salt." *Geophysical Research Letters*, 20, no. 10 (May 1993): 919–22.

Hansen, Chuck. *U.S. Nuclear Weapons: The Secret History.* Arlington, TX: Aerofax, 1988.

Herken, Gregg. *Brotherhood of the Bomb: The Tangled Lives and Loyalties of Robert Oppenheimer, Ernest Lawrence, and Edward Teller.* New York: Henry Holt and Co., 2002.

Hoffman, Gilbert H. *The Newman and Tatum Lumber Companies and the Mills at Lumberton.* Vol. 1 of *Steam Whistles in the Piney Woods: A History of the Sawmills and Logging Railroads of Forrest and Lamar Counties, Mississippi.* Hattiesburg, MS: Longleaf Press, 1998.

Hopkins, Ernest J. *Mississippi's BAWI Plan: Balance Agriculture with Industry, An Experiment in Industrial Subsidization.* Atlanta: Federal Reserve Bank of Atlanta, 1944.

Hughes, Dudley J. *Oil in the Deep South: A History of the Oil Business in Mississippi, Alabama, and Florida, 1859–1945.* Jackson: University Press of Mississippi, 1993.

Jacobson, Harold Karan, and Eric Stein. *Diplomats, Scientists, and Politicians: The United States and the Nuclear Test Ban Negotiations.* Ann Arbor: University of Michigan Press, 1966.

Johnston, Erle. *Mississippi's Defiant Years, 1953–1973: An Interpretive Documentary with Personal Experiences.* Forest, MS: Lake Harbor Publishers, 1990.

Khrushchev, Nikita. *Khrushchev Remembers.* Translated and edited by Edward Crankshaw and Strobe Talbott. Boston: Little, Brown and Co., 1970.

Kirsch, Scott. *Proving Grounds: Project Plowshare and the Unrealized Dream of Nuclear Earthmoving.* Princeton, NJ: Rutgers University Press, 2005.

Kistiakowsky, George. *A Scientist at the White House: The Private Diary of President Eisenhower's Special Assistant for Science and Technology.* Cambridge, MA: Harvard University Press, 1976.

Knudson, Jon Sven. "Beam On: The Development of the Texas A&M Cyclotron Institute." Master's thesis, Texas A&M University, 1982.

Kolhoff, Dean W. *Amchitka and the Bomb: Nuclear Testing in Alaska.* Seattle: University of Washington Press, 2002.

Krane, Dale, and Stephan D. Shaffer, eds. *Mississippi Government and Politics: Modernizers versus Traditionalists.* Lincoln: University of Nebraska Press, 1992.

Kupfer, Donald H., ed. *Symposium on the Geology and Technology of Gulf Coast Salt, Louisiana State University, 1967.* Baton Rouge: School of Geoscience, Louisiana State University, 1970.

Kuran, Peter. *Atomic Journeys: Welcome to Ground Zero.* Thousand Oaks, CA: Goldhill Video, 1999. Videocassette (VHS).

———. *Trinity and Beyond: The Atomic Bomb Movie.* Thousand Oaks, CA: Goldhill Video, 1997. Videocassette (VHS).

Kurlansky, Mark. *Salt: A World History*. New York: Walker and Co., 2002.

Larguier, Everett, S. J., ed. *Seismology at Spring Hill College*. Mobile, AL: Spring Hill College Press, 1990.

Lerche, Ian, and J. J. O'Brien, eds., *Dynamical Geology of Salt and Related Structures*. Orlando, FL: Academic Press, Inc., 1987.

MacKenzie, Donald. *Inventing Accuracy: A Historical Sociology of Nuclear Missile Guidance*. Cambridge, MA: MIT Press, 2001.

McLucas, John, Kenneth J. Alnwick, and Lawrence R. Benson. *Reflections of a Technocrat: Managing Defense, Air, and Space Programs during the Cold War*. Maxwell Air Force Base, AL: Air University Press, 2006.

Miller, Richard L. *Under the Cloud: The Decades of Nuclear Testing*. New York: The Free Press, 1986.

Ogle, William E. *An Account of the Return to Nuclear Weapons Testing by the United States after the Test Moratorium, 1958–1961*. Las Vegas: Nevada Operations Office, 1985.

Ott, Thomas. *The American Experience: Race for the Superbomb*. Boston: WGBH Educational Foundation, 1999. Videocassette (VHS).

Pasoe, Craig S., Karen Trahan Leathem, and Andy Ambrose, eds. *The American South in the Twentieth Century*. Athens: University of Georgia Press, 2005.

Pfau, Richard. *No Sacrifice Too Great: The Life of Lewis L. Strauss*. Charlottesville: University Press of Virginia, 1984.

Pilger, Rex H., ed. *The Origin of the Gulf of Mexico and the Early Opening of the Central North Atlantic Ocean: Proceedings of a Symposium at Louisiana State University, Baton Rouge, Louisiana, March 3–5, 1980*. Baton Rouge: School of Geoscience, Louisiana State University, 1980.

Podvig, Pavel, ed. *Russian Strategic Nuclear Forces*. Cambridge, MA: MIT Press, 2001.

Polk, Noel, ed. *Mississippi's Piney Woods: A Human Perspective*. Jackson: University Press of Mississippi, 1986.

Rhodes, Richard. *Dark Sun: The Making of the Hydrogen Bomb*. New York: Touchstone, 1995.

———. *The Making of the Atomic Bomb*. New York: Simon & Schuster, 1986.

Saffer, Thomas H., and Orville E. Kelley. *Countdown Zero*. New York: G. P. Putnam's Sons, 1982.

Schulman, Bruce Joseph. "From Cotton Belt to Sunbelt: Federal Policy and Southern Economic Development, 1933–1980." PhD diss., Stanford University, 1987.

Silver, James W. *Mississippi: The Closed Society*. New York: Harcourt, Brace & World, 1963.

Smith, Frank E., and Audrey Warren. *Mississippians All*. New Orleans: Pelican Publishing House, 1968.

Springer, D., M. Denny, J. Healy, and W. Mickey. "The Sterling Experiment: De-coupling of Seismic Waves by a Shot-Generated Cavity." *Journal of Geophysical Research* 73, no. 18 (September 1968): 5995–6011.

Teller, Edward. *Memoirs: A Twentieth-Century Journey in Science and Politics.* With Judith Shoolery. Cambridge: Perseus Publishing, 2001.

Thompson, Julius E. *Lynchings in Mississippi: A History, 1865–2002.* Jefferson, NC: McFarland & Company, 2007.

Twelve Southerners. *I'll Take My Stand: The South and the Agrarian Tradition.* Baton Rouge: Louisiana State University Press, 1977.

Walker, J. Samuel. *The Road to Yucca Mountain: The Development of Radioactive Waste Policy in the United States.* Berkeley: University of California Press, 2009.

———. *Three Mile Island: A Nuclear Crisis in Historical Perspective.* Berkeley: University of California Press, 2004.

Weisgall, Jonathan. *Operation Crossroads: The Atomic Tests at Bikini Atoll.* Annapolis, MD: Naval Institute Press, 1994.

Willis, David E., and Philip L. Jackson. *Collection and Analysis of Seismic Wave Propagation Data: Final Report.* Ann Arbor: University of Michigan, 1966.

Winkler, Allan M. *Life under a Cloud: American Anxiety about the Atom.* New York: Oxford University Press, 1993.

Wright, Gavin. *Old South, New South: Revolutions in the Southern Economy since the Civil War.* New York: Basic Books, 1986.

Yergin, Daniel. *The Prize: The Epic Quest for Oil, Money, and Power.* New York: Free Press, 1991.

Ziegler, Charles. "Waiting for Joe-1: Decisions Leading to the Detection of Russia's First Atomic Bomb Test." *Social Studies of Science,* 18, no. 2 (May 1988): 197–229.

Ziegler, Charles A., and David Jacobson. *Spying without Spies: Origins of America's Secret Nuclear Surveillance System.* Westport, CT: Praeger, 1995.

INDEX